ODD MAN OUT
THE STORY OF THE SINGAPORE TRAITOR

Also by Peter Elphick

Out of Norfolk: Seamen and Travellers
(1988)

ODD MAN OUT

THE STORY OF THE SINGAPORE TRAITOR

PETER ELPHICK AND MICHAEL SMITH

Hodder & Stoughton
LONDON SYDNEY AUCKLAND

British Library Cataloguing in Publication Data

Elphick, Peter
  Odd Man Out
  I. Title   II. Smith, Michael
  327.12092

ISBN 0-340-58762-8

Published by Hodder and Stoughton,
a division of Hodder and Stoughton Ltd,
Mill Road, Dunton Green, Sevenoaks, Kent TN13 2YA.
Editorial Office: 47 Bedford Square, London WC1B 3DP.

Photoset by Rowland Phototypesetting Ltd,
Bury St Edmunds, Suffolk

Printed in Great Britain by
Butler and Tanner Ltd, Frome and London

CONTENTS

LIST OF ILLUSTRATIONS

Acknowledgments

Acknowledgments and thanks for the illustrations are due to Sevenoaks
School; Cheltenham College; Major W. D. Pickett for those of the North-
West Frontier; Dr A. Nowell Peach for Alor Star; Guy Madoc for Mr and Mrs
Windsor; S/Ldr David Thomas for No. 62 Squadron and for the drawing of
Alor Star airfield; Mrs Elizabeth Leetham for Major James France; Jack Cayless
for Jack 'Bladder' Wells and Fred Cox; Rev. Donald Morrison Harper for the
Communion Set; Captain Philip Rivers for Kranji War Cemetery; *Daily
Telegraph* for the extract from 18 September 1946 edition.

AUTHORS' ACKNOWLEDGEMENTS

Our thanks are due to the following individuals for giving generous and always friendly help during the research for this book. The names are listed alphabetically:

Major P. R. Adams and Mrs Marguerite Adams; Richard J. Aldrich, University of Nottingham; Dr J. C. B. Anderson (Old Cheltonian); G. M. Bailey (100 Squadron Association); Dato H. F. Biles (Malaysia); Dr Peter Boyden and members of the staff of the National Army Museum, London; Mrs June Broughton (Local Archivist, Sutton Central Library, London); J. M. Bryce-Smith (Old Cheltonian); Dr T. C. Carter; Colonel J. L. H. Davis; Mrs J. Denholm (Far East Prisoners of War (FEPOW) Central Welfare Fund); G. T. A. Douglas; Peter G. Dunstan (who for nearly ten years has been conducting research into Far East Prisoners of War Graves Archives); Captain Alan Elliott; Mrs May Elson-Smith (Australia); Lieutenant-Colonel Patric Emerson (Indian Army Association); Stan Fielding (62 Squadron Association); Dr O. Elliot Fisher; S. G. Ford; Mrs Stella Forward; Dr A. W. Frankland; David Gibson; Basil A. Gotto (100 Squadron, RAF); Richard Gough; H. Gridley (Australia); Takeshi Hara (Military Historical Department, National Institute for Defence Studies, Tokyo); D. J. Hargreaves (ex-senior officer, Federated Malay States Police); Rev. Donald Morrison Harper; Vice-Admiral Sir John Hayes; the late T. A. Higson (Old Cheltonian); C. W. Holtham (Japanese Labour Camp Survivors' Association); Lieutenant-Colonel C. E. N. Hopkins-Husson; John Isherwood (Cheltenham College); Frank Jackson, Theresa Jeffery (*Daily Telegraph*); the late Brigadier J. D. King-Martin; J. E. Kelly (Ministry of Defence); Professor Edwin Lee (National University of Singapore); Mrs Elizabeth Leetham, daughter of Major James France, who kindly permitted the use of extracts from her father's memoirs to which she holds the copyright; Major S. T. A. Longley (New Zealand); Mrs Dorothy 'Tommy' Lucy; Lieutenant-Colonel K. McLeod (New Zealand); Guy Madoc (ex-senior officer, FMS Police); J. B. Masefield (ex-Senior Officer FMS Police); T. B. Mason (ex-Senior Officer FMS Police); Harry and Doreen Miller (Harry Miller was one-time Editor of the 'Straits Times'. He also edited the 'Changi Times', a PoW Camp magazine.); Captain D. M. Mills (16th Punjab Regiment Association); 'Sandy' Minns (ex-senior officer, Singapore Police. Sadly, Sandy died during 1992); Mike Minns (Australia), and Bill Minns (sons of Sandy Minns); George Money (FEPOW Association, West Essex); Captain R. B. Monteath; Nigel Morris (ex-Commissioner of Singapore Police); Roger Noyes (British Legion); F. D. G. O'Dwyer (Old Cheltonian); Dr A. Nowell Peach; Alan Pearce (Old Sennockian); Celia R. Pease (FEPOW Association, London); Bertie Perkins (FEPOW Association, East Dereham); Lieutenant-Commander Richard Pool; Julian Putkowski; Philip Reed (and other members of the Department of Documents at the Imperial War Museum, London); Captain P. J. Rivers (Malaysia); Emile M. Ryan (Singapore, ex-Singapore Police); Colonel Kikuji Sato (Intelligence Department, Japanese Defence Agency); Lieutenant-Colonel E. L. Sawyer; Brian Scragg (ex-Headmaster, Sevenoaks School); Jane B. Sealock (USA); Garry Sheffield (Lecturer in War Studies, RMA, Sandhurst); Squadron Leader J. A. Stephen; Major I. W. Stonor; R. G. Stride (ex-RCMP); Mr and Mrs Len Stubbs; Major Alisdair Ramsey Tainsh (Sweden); Sydney Tavender; Squadron Leader D. A. Thomas; Squadron Leader R. E. Wardrop; Douglas Weir; Jack 'Bladder' Wells, now known as Jack Cayless (a special thanks to Mrs Cayless for her kind hospitality); Major Ian Wethey; Duncan Wilson; Cecil Wright; Lieutenant-Colonel C. G. Wylie; M. J. J. M. Vissers (Royal Netherlands Embassy, London).

Grateful thanks are also due to those officers of the old Indian Army, and those ex-officers of the Malay States and Singapore Governments and Police Services, who have supplied invaluable information but who, for their own special reasons, wish to remain unidentified.

Thanks are also due to staff of the following organisations: India Office Library and Records (The British Library); Newspaper Library (The British Library); Kensington Central Library, London; Ministry of Defence, London; National Archives of New Zealand; Australian War Memorial, Canberra; Public Records Office (PRO), Kew; Registrar-General of New Zealand; Royal Artillery Association; Overseas Development Administration, Glasgow; National Library of New Zealand; Territorial, Auxiliary & Volunteer Reserve Association, East Anglia; University of Western Australia Press, Perth; Guildhall Library, London; Brecon Group (of which Steel Brothers Holdings is now part); Library of the School of Oriental & African Studies, University of London; Metropolitan Police Museum; City of London Police.

Documents under Crown Copyright in the Public Records Office, and in the Oriental and India Office Collections of the British Library, together with quotations from the Official History, *The War Against Japan*, appear by permission of HMSO.

Gratitude is expressed to the authors and publishers and trustees listed below for permission to make quotations from their books: Raymond Callahan and Associated University Press, New Jersey, for *The Worst Disaster*; Richard Pool and Leo Cooper Ltd, for *Course For Disaster*; E. J. and A. L. Howe, for *Singapore 1941–42 – The Japanese Version*; Duncan Wilson for *Survival Was For Me*; A. M. Heath and Harcourt Brace Jovanovich, for *Burmese Days* by George Orwell; Penguin Books Ltd, for *Bugles and a Tiger* by John Masters; Penguin Books Ltd and Guy Wint and John Pritchard, for *Total War*; George Chippington, for *Inexcusable Betrayal*; Random House, UK, for *The Jungle is Neutral* and *The Singapore Story*; Sir John Hayes and Pentland Press, for *Face the Music*; The Cheltonian Society, for *Then and Now*; Mrs A. D. Elson-Smith, for *Great was the Fall*.

Special acknowledgements for permission to quote from private documents (further details are given in the text and notes) are due to: Mrs J. H. S. Wild; Lieutenant-Colonel E. L. Sawyer;

Miss Susan Harrison; Lieutenant-Colonel C. G. Wylie; Basil Gotto; Mrs Elizabeth Leetham; Mrs Dorothy Lucy (née Hawkings); and Captain R. B. Monteath.

This list of acknowledgements would not be complete without recording the authors' indebtedness to the publishers' editor, John Bright-Holmes. He has given us expert advice and recommended many beneficial changes to the original manuscript.

AUTHORS' NOTE

Throughout this book the word 'Allied' has been used to describe the force which confronted the Japanese in Malaya. 'Commonwealth' might have been used instead, but would have been something of an anachronism. 'Empire' might have been misleading, for the Japanese had an empire as well as the British.

Large numbers of Indians, British, Australians, Malays and Chinese fought in Malaya; so did a few New Zealanders and South Africans. Dutch airmen fought there as well, and there were a handful of American pilots serving in the RAF.

After General Wavell was named as Supreme Commander, South-East Asia, American forces in the area came under his command. Taking all these factors into consideration, 'Allied' seems to be the best word to use.

In the case of Malay place names we have used the spellings current at the time. There are three ways to spell, for example, 'bharu' (new) as in Kota Bharu; we have used the more common one.

In the 1940s Thailand was still widely called Siam. Thailand was the word used in most British official documents dealing with South-east Asia. We have followed that precedent. Also in the style of dates and of regiments and battalions we have used those that were normally employed at the time.

INTRODUCTION

The fall of Singapore was a landmark in modern Asian history. In the years between the two world wars, there was a widespread belief that the very existence of the British Empire in the Indian and Pacific Oceans depended on the security of 'the Gibraltar of the East'.

When the Japanese captured what the British press unwisely dubbed 'the impregnable fortress' on Sunday 15th February 1942, Chinese New Year's Day, it was arguably the most significant of all their victories. For it showed to the world at large, and perhaps most importantly to the great imperial powers themselves, that the old colonial empires had outlived their useful existence, thus ensuring that, once the war was over, the nationalist aspirations which had been growing in the Far East for decades could no longer be contained or denied.

Things were never to be the same. One man who suffered more than three years of internment under the Japanese wrote: 'To be a loser, *and* white, in the Far East is not the best way to attract either sympathy or support'. The Asian world now knew that the European was no longer dominant, that he could be beaten, and well beaten, by an Asian army. He had lost 'face' which he would never regain. The days of European dominance were over for good.

This book is the story of a spy in the British forces whose treacherous activities played a significant part in that Japanese victory and perhaps, therefore, even in the end of the British Empire. There can be no doubt that the Japanese would have taken Malaya and Singapore without his assistance – their air forces were equipped with faster, more manoeuvrable aircraft and had better trained pilots while the preparation of their ground forces for jungle warfare was far superior to that of the British, Indian and Australian troops. But the information he provided certainly played a substantial part in the Allied defeat, and the Allied commanders, fearful of the effect on morale, imposed an official blackout on all news of the affair.

In normal circumstances, the records of courts-martial are kept secret for seventy-five years under the official British secrecy rules. If those rules were to remain the same – and since the excuse for such secrecy is to protect the families of the accused there seems no reason to suppose they would not – the file on the spy would only become open to public scrutiny in the year 2017.

But this case is unusual in that there are no longer any official British files on the affair. The Foreign and Commonwealth Office – which would have taken over any such file from the old Colonial Office – the Ministry of Defence and the India Office Library and Records have all stated categorically that they have no files, either open or closed, on the affair. The files that did exist appear to have been lost in those last terrible days before the fall of Singapore.[1]

The bulk of the information contained in this book has come of necessity therefore from interviewing survivors of the campaign, the youngest of whom is in his seventies. Other information has been gleaned from the written records of those present at the time, many of whom are long since dead. Although there appears to be no extant file on the affair, the existence of the Singapore traitor is confirmed in several documents preserved in files in the Public Records Office at Kew and in other documents in the Imperial War Museum.[2]

Uncovering the story was far from easy. Apart from the lack of any official files on the traitor, those who served with him felt bound by an unofficial code of silence. Others actually involved in the investigation had been sworn to secrecy and feared prosecution under the Official Secrets Act.

The unofficial cover-up was most prevalent among his fellow officers. This is not to suggest that any covert or orchestrated cover-up took place among these officers. There was no need for that. Old soldiers are proud men and justly so. One of their fellow officers had been a traitor, besmirching the honour of the regiment. So they simply avoided discussion of the affair, apart from occasionally, quietly, among themselves. It was certainly never mentioned to 'outsiders'.

Whenever they were questioned by historians or others who had heard rumours about the mysterious spy and wanted to know more, they denied all knowledge of the affair. Even when confronted with evidence naming the traitor, the initial reaction from most of the officers questioned was: 'we don't talk about him' or 'he was involved in a scandal which we would prefer to forget'.

This book is not the first to record what became known among those who served in Malaya as 'the officer traitor affair'. Several other published works have contained fleeting references to the spy, although only one, a collection of letters from a Royal Australian Air Force officer to his wife, mentioned him by name.[3]

The authors of the three most recent of these books believed him to be an officer in the Royal Air Force. This was common to the bulk of the rumours that circulated in Malaya and Singapore about the 'officer traitor' and was the result of popular assumption based on the information he gave away, which mainly concerned the activities of the Allied air forces.

In the second volume of their work *Total War*, Peter Calvocoressi and Guy Wint included the following brief note on the affair: 'An officer in the RAF, a citizen of southern Ireland, was pursuing his country's feud of twenty years back with the British government and was detected signalling to the Japanese. This affair was kept secret.'[4] So secret in fact that these two distinguished authors were wrong on at least two counts.

Raymond Callahan, in his book *The Worst Disaster* repeated the above quote, adding that the story had 'circulated widely' in Malaya at the time: 'There seems no doubt that, early in the campaign, an officer was arrested in northern Malaya and sent back to Singapore, charged with being in radio contact with the Japanese,' Callahan wrote. 'This incident is clearly the origin of the story which Calvocoressi and Wint printed.'[5] But perhaps the most accurate mention, by dint of its very ambiguity, came in Kenneth Attiwill's *The Singapore Story*. Attiwill quoted Ian Blelloch, the legal adviser to the north-western Malay state of Kedah, as saying that, while a refugee in Singapore, he had lost count of the number of times he was asked about the rumour of an officer arrested in the north-west.

The officer was variously described as being Irish, in the RAF or the British Army, or a member of the Australian Imperial Forces. He had either been shot, or court-martialled with varying consequences, or taken under escort to Singapore, or sent out of the country for trial or imprisonment.

'It was a vague story,' Blelloch said. 'Who he was and what exactly he was supposed to have done was never very clear. Whether there was any substance behind these rumours, and if so what it was, I never discovered. It was a fantastic time.' Blelloch told those who asked him that, as far as he knew, there was no truth in the story.[6] In fact there was at least some substance to much, although not all, of what he had heard.

This book attempts to tell the full story of 'the officer traitor affair' – what information he gave away and how, what effect his actions had on the course of the campaign, and the many complex reasons that led him to betray his country. It is the first time that the full story of his treachery has been told. Perhaps it will be the only time, for there seems little likelihood of much additional information coming from official sources in the future.

CHAPTER 1

PRELUDE TO WAR

The loss of Singapore, on 15th February 1942, within seventy days of Japanese troops landing in northern Malaya, was a devastating blow to the British war effort and indeed to the empire itself.

It was, said Winston Churchill, the Prime Minister, quite simply 'the worst disaster and largest capitulation in British history'. The island was to have been 'the impregnable fortress' that would stand firm to protect the British Empire against any war that might break out in the Far East.

In the years following the First World War, Britain and America had become increasingly worried by the threat posed by their former ally – Japan. A naval treaty signed at the 1921 Washington Conference had precluded both countries from building up naval bases close to Japan, including the British base in Hong Kong. But both Singapore and Pearl Harbor were excluded from this treaty and, as Japanese military might began to grow and its expansionist ambitions in China and other neighbouring states increased, the two bases were expanded to counter the potential threat.

The British poured £63 million into the construction of a vast naval base on the island of Singapore. The 'fortress' was given a series of fixed-gun emplacements. Five 15-inch guns, six 9.2-inch guns and eighteen 6-inch guns pointed out to sea, ensuring it was virtually unassailable from that direction. It is one of the myths of the Singapore debacle that none of these guns was capable of pointing towards the Malay peninsula; some were, but at the time when the base and its main defences were being built up, the threat of serious attacks from that direction was ruled out by the Chiefs of Staff Committee in March 1928. It was to prove a costly mistake. Even in 1942, when the Japanese were at the gates of the island fortress, there was not enough of the right type of ammunition for those guns that could traverse to engage them for any length of time.[1]

For some time Japan had believed that the only way the country could secure the necessary markets to keep its rapidly expanding population was by military conquest. Having already gained control over Formosa and the strategic Pescadore Islands, under the 1895 Treaty of Shimonoseki, and Korea, which it annexed in 1910, it turned its attentions to China.

Within weeks of the start of the First World War, Japan had joined in on the Allied side and began seizing the German possessions and interests in China's Shantung province. With Britain and the other European countries embroiled in fighting in the West, she saw the opportunity to play 'the thief at the fire', a policy which Emperor Hirohito was to advocate repeating a quarter of a century later, to extend her influence in China.

Early in 1915 Japan presented the Chinese government with the so-called 'Twenty-One Demands'. These included confir-mation of the transfer of the German treaty-ports to Japan, a demand that the Chinese employ Japanese military and political advisers, and an undertaking that China would purchase most of her war materials from Japan. Although the Chinese held out against some of the more extreme demands, they had little choice but to bow to others.

In 1931, the Japanese garrison in the northern Chinese prov-ince of Manchuria seized it from the local warlord to form the puppet state of Manchukuo. The so-called 'Manchuria Incident' provoked fury both abroad and in Japan itself, where the civilian government had been ignorant of what was going on. The Americans in particular, with strong missionary ties in China, were outraged by the bully-boy tactics of Japanese neo-colonialism.

Those wielding power in Japan were unrepentant. When a League of Nations commission, sent to China to investigate the annexation, condemned Japan as the aggressor, the Japanese quit the League in protest. By the end of 1934, having added Jehol to its northern Chinese territories, Japan abrogated the Washington treaties and, in 1935, withdrew from the Naval

Conference in London that would have renegotiated the treaties limiting its naval forces. From then on, Japan's ability to expand militarily was limited only by the country's resources.

In July 1937 Japan used a clash, just outside Peking, between Japanese members of the international embassy guard and Chinese government troops as an excuse to launch what was effectively an invasion of China. Within the space of six months, much of China, including the new capital of Nanking and its predecessor, Peking, had fallen under Japanese control. General Chiang Kai-shek, the leader of the Chinese government, withdrew to the interior.

The Japanese forces appeared to be out of control. During the six weeks of 'the Rape of Nanking' they massacred an estimated 200,000 Chinese civilians and prisoners-of-war in what remains one of the most appalling war crimes of modern times. They also risked war with the United States and Britain by attacking the USS *Panay* and the British gunboat HMS *Ladybird* which were patrolling the Yangtze river as part of an international flotilla. Only a rapid apology from Tokyo averted US military action although Britain's prime minister, Neville Chamberlain, with his mind on matters closer to home, failed to take a strong line over the attack on *Ladybird*.

Despite its confrontational approach towards Britain and America, Japan remained on the sidelines when war broke out in Europe. Incensed by the 1938 signing of the Molotov–Ribbentrop pact between Germany and its traditional enemy, the USSR, Japan ignored Hitler's offer of a military alliance. But this role of disinterested spectator was not to survive for long.

By the summer of 1940, Germany had overrun Norway, Denmark, Holland and France. Simultaneously a more aggressive government came to power in Japan with one of the most ardent proponents of the need for military expansion, General Hideki Tojo, as Minister of War. The Foreign Minister, Yosuke Matsuoka, was another strong supporter of the line held by Tojo, and most of his generals, that Japan should sign the military alliance proffered by the Germans. The two now argued

7

successfully that there was no way in which Germany could lose the war and, on 27 September 1940, Japan signed the Tripartite 'Axis' Pact with Germany and Mussolini's Italy.

Under the agreement, Japan would be allowed, after December 1941, to solve its needs for captive markets by setting itself up as leader of a 'Greater East Asia Co-Prosperity Sphere' which would extend from Burma in the west to the Marshall and Gilbert and Ellice Islands in the east and Timor in the south, taking in all the South-east Asian colonies of the European empires, including Malaya.

The Japanese government was now set on a course of continued confrontation with Britain and America, extracting an agreement from the Vichy French to allow it to use bases in French Indochina from which its aircraft could threaten not only Malaya, but also Burma, the Dutch East Indies and eventually even Australia.

In July 1941, in an attempt to appease Tokyo, the British government closed the Burma Road which was the main supply route for the beleaguered forces of Chiang Kai-shek. Pressure from the Americans, who were supplying much of the Chinese aid, forced the road's reopening while British diplomats around the world attempted to save face by claiming that its closure had been irrelevant since the monsoon would have made it unusable anyway.

The Japanese then cranked the screw one further turn. Tojo moved his troops into Indochina en masse, leaving the Vichy French government there no choice but to accept what was effectively a Japanese occupation and, in so doing, increasing the threat against Malaya, and the Dutch East Indies with whom negotiations on crucial oil supplies had broken down.

Western reaction to the occupation of French Indochina was swift and much as the Japanese had expected. Britain and America implemented an immediate economic blockade and froze all Japanese assets in their countries. A series of negotiations between the two sides failed to resolve the issue with Washington insisting that, if the blockade were to be lifted, Japan must withdraw its troops not just from Indochina but

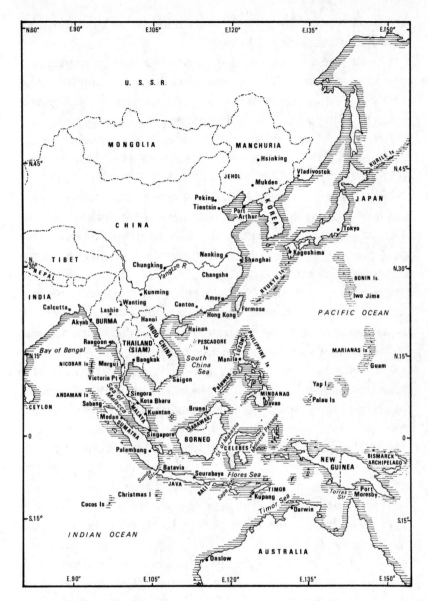

Malaya and its Far East context

also from China. Faced with either humiliating climbdown or war, the Japanese opted for war.

In fact, the Japanese armed forces had been preparing for war for some time and they now opted for a coordinated strike against Western interests in the region: two prongs going through Malaya and the Philippines and then on to capture the Dutch East Indies; an attack on Hong Kong from mainland China; and an air assault on the American naval base at Pearl Harbor.

Plans for the attack on Malaya had been under way since the summer of 1940. Early in 1941 Lieutenant-Colonel Masanobu Tsuji was placed in charge of the Taiwan Army Research Section, and given responsibility for planning the Japanese 25th Army's assault on Malaya.

Operational command of the 25th Army was given to Lieutenant-General Tomoyuki Yamashita. Yamashita had extensive experience of command but little of it in combat. Nevertheless, unlike his British counterpart, Lieutenant-General A. E. Percival, he was to learn fast and well. The Imperial Forces HQ believed that five Japanese divisions would be needed to capture Malaya. After examination of intelligence reports on the strengths, or rather weaknesses, of the Allied forces, this was reduced to four. But according to Colonel Tsuji, Yamashita was more confident than that. 'General Yamashita, after consideration of the fighting capacity of the British army at the beginning of the campaign, decided that three divisions were sufficient.'

Thus it was that three divisions – 5th and 18th Divisions plus the Imperial Guards and 3rd Tank Group, with 180 tanks, a total of 40,000 men – became the Japanese invasion force. They were supported by about 530 aircraft of the 3rd Army Air Group and the Japanese Navy. Most importantly, the Japanese aircraft were modern, fast, highly manoeuvrable and well-armed.

Colonel Tsuji was a good choice as the 25th Army's Chief of Operations and Planning Staff. He was to become an expert in jungle training, well aware of the particular problems that Malaya's mixture of mountains, swamp and jungle would present. 'The Malayan campaign could not be won by ortho-dox tactics,' he wrote later. 'In the rubber forest and the jungle, the authority of the naked sabre would be conclusive. For us the terrain provided ideal fighting conditions.'[2]

He oversaw a programme of research and training in amphibious landings and jungle warfare for the invasion force. The Taiwan Army Research Section produced 40,000 copies of a training manual entitled 'Read This Alone – And The War Can Be Won' – one for every man. It detailed what the Japanese troops could expect to encounter as they fought their way down the Malay peninsula.

In February 1941 Japanese troops carried out their first rehearsal for the invasion of Malaya, staging an amphibious assault against Kyushu in Japan across 1,000 miles of the East China Sea from Formosa. A second rehearsal involved an 'invasion' of Hainan island from mainland China by a spear-head battalion of infantry, plus supporting artillery and engineers to carry out more specialised training. Bridges were blown up and then repaired or replaced, and the troops gained experience of landings and operations under somewhat similar conditions to those they would experience in Malaya. The Jap-anese were highly prepared. To aid this training, intelligence from Japanese spies across northern Malaya was fed back via the Japanese embassy in Bangkok.

Despite the earlier decision by the Chiefs of Staff, the British were by now well aware that the main danger to Singapore came from the north. The defence of Singapore had been a favourite set-piece war-game at military academies in Britain and India for years, as indeed it had been in their Japanese counterparts, and most students had arrived at the same con-clusion – that an attacker would approach from the rear, down the Malay peninsula, rather than place himself at the mercy of the large guns that protected the island's seaward approaches.

A military intelligence unit, set up in 1936 by the then General Officer Commanding (Malaya), Major-General W. G. S. Dobbie, had even predicted that the Japanese strategy would be to land at Kota Bharu in northern Malaya, and at Singora

(Songkhla) and Patani in Thailand, where there were airfields from which Japanese aircraft could launch attacks on the British defences.

During 1940 the British Commander-in-Chief, Far East, Air Chief Marshal Sir Robert Brooke-Popham, devised a strategy for the defence of Singapore which was codenamed Operation Matador. A modified version of an earlier plan known as Operation Etonian, it involved an advance into Thailand to make the predicted attacks at Singora and Patani too dangerous to mount.

But the plan had a fatal flaw. Thailand was a neutral and ostensibly friendly country with whom Britain had recently signed a non-aggression pact. Operation Matador demanded that Britain should pre-empt a Japanese invasion of Thailand by invading it first. This would involve serious, and ultimately unacceptable, diplomatic repercussions. Churchill knew that American agreement would be needed to implement the plan and this was unlikely to be given unless the Japanese had already invaded, in which case it would be too late.

Brooke-Popham had been trying for some time to persuade London that he needed to be able to launch Matador on his own initiative and at a time of his own choice, but the response was always that political constraints were paramount and that war with Japan should be avoided at all cost. Brooke-Popham knew, however, that the timing of the operation was critical. It had been estimated that the Japanese would need a little over sixty hours from the time their ships left their bases in Indochina to reach the beaches at Singora, Patani and Kota Bharu and to establish bridgeheads there.

He was also aware that his own troops would require the same amount of time to cross the Thai border, move north, mopping up any Thai resistance along the way, and to establish their own defensive positions. They had been training extensively with this in mind. The railway stock and vehicles needed for the push north were ready and all the units involved knew exactly what they must do. But given that both sides needed approximately the same time to achieve their objectives, the timing of the order to implement Operation Matador was critical. Unless British and Indian forces were ordered across the border as soon as the Japanese were sighted leaving their bases in Indochina, the whole operation would be too late – strangled at birth by the need to observe a political code which the Japanese would happily ignore.

The attitude adopted by the government in London was all the more difficult to comprehend given that, by this time, they were receiving crucial information about Japanese intentions from American intelligence.

For some time, American intelligence analysts had been able to read the most secret Japanese diplomatic traffic. US codebreakers, working in tandem with their British counterparts at Bletchley who had broken the German Wehrmacht's Enigma ciphers, had cracked the Japanese diplomatic ciphers, generated by the 'Purple' machine.

The resultant intelligence material – classified 'TOP SECRET MAGIC' in the same way as the British codenamed material from Germany's Enigma codes and other Axis intercepts 'MOST SECRET ULTRA' – gave President Roosevelt and Churchill early warning that Japan was committed to a military offensive.[3]

As a result, Brooke-Popham received the following signal on Tuesday 2nd December 1941, nearly a week before the Japanese invasion:

FOLLOWING FROM MOST SECRET SOURCES.
ON 29 NOVEMBER BANGKOK INFORMED TOKYO THAT IN ORDER TO MAKE BRITAIN APPEAR AGGRESSIVE AGAINST THAILAND PRO-JAPANESE SECTION OF THAI CABINET SUGGESTS THAT JAP FORCES SHOULD LAND AT KOTA BHARU, THE BRITISH FORCES WOULD THEN ATTACK FROM PADANG BESAR AND THAILAND WILL DECLARE WAR ON BRITAIN.[4]

Brooke-Popham, believing that there was clearly little point in prevaricating, immediately sent a return signal asking once again for permission to implement Operation Matador.

PARA I IN THESE CIRCUMSTANCES NEED FOR
AVOIDING WAR WITH JAPAN WOULD NO LONGER
APPLY

PARA 2 JAP ATTACK ON KOTA BHARU COULD ONLY
BE A STAGE IN OPERATIONS AGAINST MALAYA AND
NOT REPEAT NOT AN END IN ITSELF. SEIZURE OF
SINGORA AREA MIGHT BE NEXT STEP THOUGH I
THINK IT MORE LIKELY THAT BOTH WOULD BE
TRIED AT ONCE.

PARA 3 IF, HOWEVER, THEY GO ONLY TO KOTA
BHARU THE MILITARY ARGUMENT IN FAVOUR OF
DOING MATADOR STILL HOLDS GOOD.

PARA 4 MOST UNLIKELY THAT POLITICAL AIMS OF
SETTING THAILAND AGAINST US WOULD INFLUENCE
JAP STRATEGY TO EXTENT OF ALLOWING US SUCH A
GOOD OPPORTUNITY OF OCCUPYING SINGORA AREA.

PARA 5 I REQUEST AUTHORITY TO ORDER MATA-
DOR IN CIRCUMSTANCES OF 55260 SHOULD BE CON-
SIDERED NOW.[4]

The War Office finally agreed. Brooke-Popham was given permission to implement Matador 'should the Japanese violate any part of Thailand, or if there is good information that a Japanese expedition is advancing with the apparent intention of landing'.

But Churchill still had serious doubts about the military viability of the plan, which would be hindered by the quality and quantity of the ground and air units that made up Malaya Command. He and his advisers believed it was probably beyond the strengths and capabilities of the troops based in Malaya. On paper, there were thirty battalions of British, Indian and Australian troops on the Malay mainland and in Singapore, plus two battalions of Malay troops and five battalions of Indian State Forces, the latter being units raised and paid for by Indian princes. There were also many units of support troops (see Appendix I). Although there were some famous regimental names among the British and Indian battalions in Malaya, with few exceptions they included many virtually untrained men.

The loss of large numbers of experienced officers to new units being formed to fight the war in Europe had left many of the British Army units in Malaya stretched to breaking point. In addition, the experienced men they had lost had been replaced by newly conscripted junior officers.

The Indian Army units had also lost many of their British and Indian officers in the same way. Their replacements were often unable to speak Urdu, the language which lay at the heart of the Indian Army's command structure, and there was a general lack of confidence between the new officers and their men. The six battalions of Australian troops which constituted the 22nd and 27th Brigades were also mostly raw troops with many inexperienced officers. Major-General Gordon Bennett, their commanding officer, described some of them as having been 'recruited on a Friday and sent to Malaya on a Monday'.

In addition, there were serious concerns about the dislocation of the Allied ground forces. A 1938 decision to give the RAF control over the defence of Malay and Singapore meant that the army was not consulted over the location of new airfields. These were subsequently built without consideration being given as to how the ground forces might defend them, leaving troops impossibly dispersed.

So the total force of around 87,000 men in Malaya on the eve of the war was not nearly as powerful as it appeared on paper. It was also extremely short of equipment – there was not a single tank in Malaya until the Japanese brought them in. The other theatres of war were being given higher priority by the British, a fact which perturbed the Australian and New Zealand governments although, until the Japanese attack, they officially endorsed the policy that the European front remain paramount.

If this was not enough, in direct contrast to the Japanese forces there had been a gross failure to give Allied troops a proper grounding in jungle training. There were notable exceptions to this, the outstanding one being the 2nd Battalion of the Argyll & Sutherland Highlanders commanded by Lieutenant-Colonel Ian Stewart. Stewart had his men training in the jungle for months, but, until the war started, he was considered to be a bit of a maverick.

The lack of provision for jungle training came as a surprise to many experts. When Brigadier W. St J. Carpendale of the 28th Indian Brigade arrived in Malaya in August 1941, he asked if men from his units could be sent to the jungle warfare school. 'I was informed that such a school did not exist and that it was not proposed to start one.'[5]

If the Army was ill-equipped for war, the Allied air forces were in an even worse position. Of the twenty-four airfields in Malaya, only seven had metalled runways. There were four other airfields on Singapore itself and a total of 158 operationally serviceable aircraft – 60 Brewster Buffaloes, 47 Blenheim bombers, a number of which had been modified as night-fighters, 24 Vildebeeste torpedo bombers, 24 Hudson Mk II bombers, and three Catalina flying-boats. In addition, there were a further 88 reserve first-line aircraft – a total of 246, well below Malaya Command's own estimated requirement of nearly 600 aircraft, not to say the 336 promised by the Chiefs of Staff 'by the end of 1941'. Perhaps more importantly there were 534 first-line aircraft available to the Japanese.[6]

The majority of the British aircraft were obsolete or obsolescent. The Brewster Buffalo fighter, dubbed 'the Peanut Special', had long since been retired by the US Army Air Force while the open-cockpit Vildebeeste torpedo-bomber – 'the Flying Coffin' – was barely capable of speeds faster than 100 mph. Nearly all the Vildebeeste pilots and observers were to die during the campaign.

But although Brooke-Popham had made it clear that his greatest worry was fighter aircraft, he had to accept that the European front had precedence and claimed to be satisfied with the Brewster Buffalo. 'We can get on alright with Buffaloes out here, but they haven't got the speed for England,' he said. 'Let England have the super-Spitfires and hyper-Tornadoes. Buffaloes are quite good enough for Malaya.'

According to the British official history, by Major-General S. W. Kirby, the Vice-Chief of the Naval Staff had advocated the despatch of Hurricane fighters to Malaya during a meeting of the Chiefs of Staff on 25th April 1941. But the RAF was not prepared to be told its business by a 'matelot' – in this case the Vice-Chief himself. The Vice-Chief of the Air Staff immediately replied that Buffalo fighters would be more than a match for the Japanese aircraft which were 'not of the latest type'.

A month later, a Japanese Zero fighter was shot down in China. Details of the armament and performance of the aircraft, showing that it could outmatch the Buffaloes in virtually every respect – it had a top speed of 325 mph – were forwarded to the Air Ministry and the HQ Air Command, Far East, at the end of September. But, again according to the official history, 'faulty organisation resulted in this valuable report remaining unsifted from the general mass of intelligence information and in no action being taken'.

Unsatisfied with the operational viability of Matador, Churchill initiated his own plan for the defence of Singapore. A naval task force, to be known as Force Z, was to be sent to the region. It was to be led by the brand new battleship HMS *Prince of Wales* and the battle-cruiser HMS *Repulse*. They were to be supported by the aircraft-carrier HMS *Indomitable* and four destroyers – HMS *Electra*, HMS *Express*, HMAS *Vampire* and HMS *Tenedos*. But *Indomitable* ran aground in the West Indies, leaving the force without any integral air support. Limits on the operational range of the Malaya-based Buffaloes meant that Force Z would have to spend at least some of the time on patrol without air cover of any sort.

The task force arrived in Singapore on Tuesday 2nd December 1941 amid a blaze of publicity. This was the deterrent force that would save the island from the Japanese. But its lack of air cover meant that it posed little threat to the Japanese. To make matters worse, the two different plans, Matador and Force Z, each with their own inherent defects, were to be controlled by two separate commands with little or no coordination between the two. Force Z was commanded by Admiral Sir Tom Phillips, C-in-C Far Eastern Fleet. He and Brooke-Popham were given joint responsibility for Far East strategy. But Phillips knew

Brooke-Popham was to be replaced by General Sir Henry Pownall early in December 1941 and saw no reason to get along or cooperate closely with someone who was on the way out. Then Pownall's arrival in Singapore was delayed, leaving Brooke-Popham in charge but with little or no control over the British naval units.

The signal giving him permission to implement Operation Matador had effectively made him responsible for the invasion of a friendly country. This created a new dilemma for him and his staff. How was he to be absolutely sure that an invasion was about to take place until Japanese troop transport vessels were actually in position and in the process of making the assault?

Late on the morning of Saturday 6th December, the heavy monsoon rains that had closed down the airfield at Kota Bharu for forty-eight hours previously eased sufficiently to allow three Hudson reconnaissance aircraft of the Royal Australian Air Force based there to trundle down the rain-soaked runway and take off in search of the Japanese invasion force.

Shortly after midday Flight Lieutenant Jack Ramshaw, the pilot of one of the Hudson reconnaissance aircraft, spotted three Japanese vessels through a break in the clouds. Ramshaw, who was to be killed in a sortie the following day, was about 180 miles north-east of Kota Bharu, at the very edge of his aircraft's range. Fifteen minutes later he saw a much larger group of ships. Seeking cover in the towering cumulus clouds, he radioed a warning back to base. Not long afterwards the sighting of a large invasion force was confirmed by another Hudson. In all, there were nearly forty ships – one heavy cruiser, five cruisers, seven destroyers and 25 merchant ships. The aircraft lost visual contact with the Japanese task force among the low monsoon clouds and fierce squalls, but US intelligence sources in Indochina confirmed that a large naval force had slipped out of Camranh Bay and Saigon and were heading south-west.

For months Brooke-Popham had been pleading for permission to launch Operation Matador on his own initiative, but now, with the onus fully on him to decide if war was inevitable, he hesitated. The reports from the RAF reconnaissance patrols reached him at about 1400 hours, but it was not clear in which direction the force was heading. Were they on their way to Thailand as predicted? It might be a manoeuvre to test the Allies' nerve or trick them into making the first move and sending troops into Thailand, something the Japanese were known to be keen to do.

Explaining his indecision, Brooke-Popham later wrote: 'Bearing in mind the policy of avoiding war with Japan if possible and the situation in the United States with talks still going on in Washington, I decided that I would not be justified in ordering Matador on this information.'[7] Instead, he ordered the RAF to find the Japanese convoys and shadow them and the troops to be brought to a first degree of readiness.[8] They moved into position in driving monsoon rain and awaited the order to implement Operation Matador. But the weather had closed in and there were no more sightings reported. Overnight, two Royal Air Force Catalina flying-boats out on patrol failed to return. At least one made contact with the enemy and was shot down – the first casualty of the Pacific War, although this was not to be known until after VJ Day in 1945.

Early next day, Brooke-Popham's reluctance to implement Matador was reinforced by a panicky telegram from Sir Josiah Crosby, the British Minister in Bangkok. 'For God's sake,' it read, 'do not allow British forces to occupy one inch of Thai territory unless and until Japan has struck the first blow at Thailand.'[9]

That morning there was a further sighting of Japanese ships, now said to be heading for the Thai-Malaysian border area where the landings were expected to take place. Then, at 1545 hours, a Hudson spotted a Japanese merchant vessel, its decks crowded with soldiers and heading south. As dusk closed in, four more large ships were spotted apparently making for Patani. Quite extraordinarily, none of this information reached Brooke-Popham until 2100 hours that night.

At around 2300 hours, Brooke-Popham had a crisis meeting with Admiral Phillips and General Percival, GOC Malaya.

Percival told them that, if the Japanese ships were part of an invasion force, a fact which no longer seemed in much doubt, there was no point in implementing Operation Matador anyway. It was already too late.

CHAPTER 2

THE BATTLE FOR MALAYA

It was just after one o'clock in the morning of Monday 8th December 1941 when Japanese troops began their assault on Kota Bharu beach on the east coast of Malaya. Shortly afterwards, Japanese troops began landing in much larger numbers across the border in Thailand to secure the airfields at Singora and Patani. From there they could strike at Allied positions in northern Malaya, and their ground forces could advance south towards the main ground defences at Jitra, on the west coast of Malaya.

The landings at Kota Bharu were the first part of a carefully coordinated series of attacks which signalled the start of the Pacific War. Shortly afterwards, the Japanese launched their raids on Clark Air Base in the Philippines, on Hong Kong, and most important of all, on Pearl Harbor.

The history books record that the attack on the US Pacific Fleet took place on 7th December, Roosevelt's 'Day of Infamy'. But in fact it came one hour and ten minutes after the invasion of Malaya. The misleading difference in dates is due to the fact that Hawaii lies on the other side of the International Dateline, and seventeen hours behind Malayan local time. Nevertheless, the timing of the attack on Kota Bharu was determined by the fact that it was Sunday 7th December in Hawaii. Sunday was the day when most of the US Fleet would be expected to be inside its Pearl Harbor base, a sitting target for Japanese aircraft.

In northern Malaya, the men of III Indian Corps, under Lieutenant-General Sir Lewis Heath, had been in position for Operation Matador and on stand-by for more than twenty-four hours, many of them exposed to the full force of monsoon rains. They had been on alert for even longer. Tiredness was beginning to sap at their morale, a problem not helped by the apparent indecision of their commanders over what to do next.

Despite fierce resistance from the men defending the beaches at Kota Bharu, a series of air attacks from Allied bombers, and a north-east monsoon wind that was whipping up high seas as they came ashore, the Japanese succeeded in securing a bridgehead.

Throughout the early hours of Monday morning, Royal Australian Air Force bombers stationed at Kota Bharu flew sortie after sortie against Japanese troopships. One of the three troop transports was left burning in shallow water and the other two were heavily damaged. The Japanese casualties amounted to nearly 900 dead and wounded. It was their heaviest casualty toll of the campaign.

The men of the 3/17th Dogras, part of the 8th Indian Brigade, were defending the broken stretch of beach to the north of Kota Bharu. Shells rained down on them from Japanese warships anchored off the coast and there was heavy hand-to-hand fighting, during which a third of the first wave of Japanese soldiers were killed.

'The Japanese landed under a blanket of naval shelling,' says Captain R. B. Monteath, one of the Dogra officers on the beach. 'The shells were throwing up sand which the monsoon blew through the slits in the pill-boxes, and they also filled with the smoke from our own Bren guns as the fighting became more intense. It may have been the sand and fumes that stung our eyes and faces or it may have been a kind of tear gas. Whatever it was we had to fight in our gas masks.' Lieutenant-Colonel O. B. M. North, M C, who was a young officer and second-in-command of a company on the beach that night, was always convinced that the Japanese had used some form of tear gas during those initial landings.

The terrain and the lack of any proper roads added to the defenders' difficulties. 'If you visualise a stretch of beach fourteen miles long and think of defending it with 800 men, then add to that the lack of any proper all-weather roads, you will begin to get the picture,' Captain Monteath says. 'We had two World War One 18-pounders but the southern one did not engage the enemy because it could not even see the battle.'[1]

His battalion's companies were isolated from each other and based in separate hutted camps. One was at Bandung Beach, more than seventeen miles from Battalion HQ. The road between was so bad in the monsoon that only one of the unit's vehicles and one civilian lorry a day were allowed to use it in the hope of keeping it passable. The Dogra's bren-gun carriers tried to use the road during the battle but never got through. The regiment lost many of its men defending the pill-boxes along the beach, but put up a good fight before being ordered to withdraw.

The turning-point in the battle for Kota Bharu came at around four o'clock in the afternoon. A rumour spread that the Japanese were at the perimeter of the airfield. Orders were given to evacuate and there was a mad panic among the airmen manning the station. The airfield denial system scheme was only partially implemented. Airmen fled for the railhead in any available vehicle, leaving runways intact, the stocks of bombs and petrol alongside them ready for the Japanese to use. Within hours the Japanese had taken Kota Bharu airfield, from where their aircraft were soon able to strike at the retreating Allied forces.

Shortly after the Japanese invasion began, the population of Singapore received their first taste of war when seventeen Japanese navy bombers flying from southern Indochina launched a raid on the city. Despite the fact that the radar defences gave more than thirty minutes' warning of the attack, no air-raid warnings were given and the city's lights guided the bombers in.

To make matters worse the night-fighters, which were supposed to protect the city, did not take off since it was believed that the inexperienced gunners manning the air defences might shoot them down, a fear that seems unfounded given that none of the Japanese bombers was brought down. Despite the advantages the limited air-raid defences afforded them, the Japanese aircraft caused little damage to their intended targets at Tengah and Seletar airfields. But some bombs fell on the heavily populated centre of the city, causing some two hundred casualties among the Asian population.

For three days the Indian troops on the east coast tried unsuc-
cessfully to halt the Japanese advance, but after the remaining
two airfields in the north-east, at Gong Kedah and Machang,
fell, it became futile for the remnants of the 8th Indian Brigade
to remain at the end of a long and vulnerable line of communication. They began a fighting retreat down the 120 miles of
winding railway to Kuala Lipis in central Malaya, blowing up
the bridges as they passed them, sometimes only just ahead of
the pursuing Japanese.

There was no direct road link from Kota Bharu to the west
coast, so the bulk of the Japanese invasion force was landed at
Singora and Patani in Thailand with the intention of pushing
down the road links which led to the main towns and cities of
west and central Malaya. The British commanders were aware
that the main body of their troops, concentrated around Jitra,
was highly vulnerable to an enemy flanking attack down the
Patani–Kroh road. To pre-empt any such advance, they had
drawn up a contingency plan for a column codenamed 'Krohcol'
to advance into Thailand to secure 'The Ledge', a piece of high
ground inside Thailand which dominated the road and was
thought to offer the best defensive position against a Japanese
advance.

But, yet again, Brooke-Popham hesitated. Because of difficulties with communications, he had not received confirmation
of the Japanese landings at Singora and Patani until around
1000 hours that morning. Already the enemy had gained a
significant advantage in time. But still Brooke-Popham waited,
finally cancelling Matador but ordering Krohcol forward early
in the afternoon.

'It is possible that he did not fully realise the importance of
speed,' says the official history in a less than convincing attempt
to excuse the procrastination. 'The need for a quick decision
was not apparently realised at Headquarters, Malaya Command
. . . The enemy was thus given a start of some ten hours over
III Corps; this was to prove disastrous.'

Krohcol, a depleted force compared to the one originally
planned, now comprising 3/16th Punjabis plus an Australian

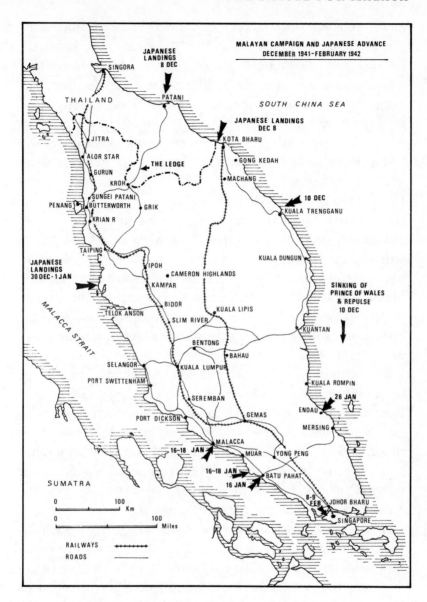

MALAYAN CAMPAIGN AND JAPANESE ADVANCE
DECEMBER 1941–FEBRUARY 1942

The arrows indicate the times and places of the major Japanese landings.

motor transport unit – and only later to be reinforced by 5/14th Punjabis – crossed the Thai border at 1330 hours. Its advance was delayed by 'unexpected' resistance from Thai police who barricaded the road, and it never reached 'The Ledge'. A mechanised unit of the Japanese 42nd Infantry Regiment got there first. The column made contact with the Japanese on the morning of Wednesday 10th December, when it was still about six miles short of its objective, and was forced to withdraw. By Saturday 13th December, the defeated remnants of Krohcol were back inside Malaya.

The morale of the troops further over on the west coast had not been helped by the fact that the need to hold the northern airfields, and the deployments required to implement Matador, were incompatible. When the order eventually came to drop Matador and to deploy to defensive positions around Jitra to protect the airfield at Alor Star, the psychological effect of the move from an offensive to a defensive stance took another heavy toll on morale.

Poor communications meant it was an additional four hours before the order reached the troops of 11th Indian Division at Jitra who now, with the demise of Matador, had to move to mainly half-finished defensive positions around the town. For two days they had been 'standing to' in driving monsoon rains. Now, already demoralised, they returned to finish building the defences only to find them inundated by the rain. They had little more than a day to repair the damage.

A few hours before dawn on Wednesday 10th December, Japanese forward units which had raced down the Singora–Jitra road, crossed the Malayan border, their immediate objective being the 11th Indian Division, still struggling to repair its positions along the so-called 'Jitra Line'. The Japanese first made contact with forward outposts manned by 1/14th Punjabis. The Punjabis slowly withdrew under pressure, and that evening the 2/1st Gurkha Rifles Battalion was sent up to occupy the outpost position at Asun some two miles in front of the main Jitra positions. On the morning of 11th December the Punjabis again came under attack and followed orders to 'withdraw in accordance with enemy pressure'. In the late after-noon, at a position to the north of the Gurkhas at Asun, the Punjabis were overrun by Japanese infantry supported by tanks. The tanks caused 'utter consternation' among the Indians, most of whom had never even seen one before.

Meanwhile 2/1st Gurkhas had been hastily digging defences and laying wire at Asun after reconnoitring the position with the help of Captain Mohan Singh of 1/14th Punjabis, who was captured shortly afterwards and went on to become leader of the Japanese-sponsored Indian National Army.

According to the unpublished war diary of Captain (later Lieutenant-Colonel) C. G. Wylie of 2/1st Gurkha Rifles, the Japanese began to attack outlying Gurkha positions at 1815 hours. With one of only two anti-tank rifles issued to the bat-talion only days before, the Gurkhas disabled three tanks. Half an hour later, Wylie records, 'Japs. came close, flourishing swords and shouting war cries', but were beaten off. Ten minutes later they were back. 'Japs. again attacked frontally and received the fire of many Bren guns. After a few minutes, 7 Jap medium tanks came down the road. 2 drove past the position and did not stop. 5 others stopped head to tail opposite the posn. and began firing . . . Many trucks and lorries were set on fire. Small-arms fire proved ineffective against the tanks. Molotov cocktails could not be lit as the action was fought in tropical rain . . . in view of the fact that there were no effective anti-tank weapons, the C.O. decided to evacuate the position'.

Wylie's words graphically illustrate one of the basic problems faced by Indian and other troops throughout the campaign. Not only had they never even seen tanks before; they had few anti-tank weapons, and those they did have were largely in-effective.[2]

Major-General D. M. Murray-Lyon, commander of the 11th Division, asked early on for permission to withdraw to a more tenable position thirty miles south, but the request was refused by General Percival because 'it would be bad for morale'. But what was to ensue as the Japanese launched themselves at the main Jitra defence positions, was to have a far, far worse effect

on morale. Despite stiff resistance from 11th Division, two battalions of Japanese infantry, supported by a company of tanks,
gradually forced the Indian and British troops back, until
Murray-Lyon finally obtained permission to withdraw south.
This disengagement and withdrawal took place during the night
of 12th/13th December. In the 36-hour battle and subsequent
withdrawal, the 11th Division had suffered severe casualties
and lost much equipment. It was a major disaster.

The problem of poor communications, which had delayed
11th Division's preparations at Jitra, was to bedevil the campaign. Few of the army units based in Malaya had been supplied
with radios. Those that did have them often found them un-
reliable due to atmospheric conditions that made reception
poor. So most communications had to be carried out over signal
wire and by telephone.

The official history says that the troops defending northern
Malaya had 'no proper signal organisation. They had to rely
almost entirely on civilian communications.' The 2nd Battalion,
East Surrey Regiment, at Jitra, for example, had only one
'No. 19' wireless set. This linked them to 15th Brigade HQ, but
all other communications were made by line or runner.

The battalion's position at the time of the battle was in
paddyfields, and the monsoon rain was almost continuous. Laying signal wire in such conditions, or through tropical jungle
and rubber plantations, was difficult even when there was sufficient cable available, which frequently there was not. So the
public telephone system was used for much of the army's communications. Up until the Japanese landed, and sometimes after
it, the army was given little in the way of priority by the civilian
operators.

The system was impossibly overloaded. Shortly before the
Japanese invasion, the signals section at HQ Singapore complained that many of the cables laid on the island were 'completely full. This state has been caused mainly by the expansion
of HQ and demands for additional RAF circuits, and re-routing
now becomes practically impossible,' the section said.[3]

One signals officer reported, perhaps jokingly, that even

carrier pigeons were being overloaded. He wrote in his log on Monday 1st December 1941, that 'owing to pressure of work, pigeons are being overloaded. This has resulted in false launchings in which bird has failed to take off and damaged crown of head.'[4]

One military operator recalls that even after the invasion there was a built-in delay of forty-five minutes in getting calls through the civilian telephone exchanges. 'We were putting calls through as fast as we could. Obviously many calls were to HQ Far East at Singapore. We had to use our own judgement as to which calls to give priority to and who to keep waiting and we were the most unpopular section in the organisation at the time.'

There were a number of complaints at how slow the operators were being so they decided on their own order of priority, he says. 'First, General Percival, then the scrambler phone to HQ Far East, followed by Deputy Director Medical Services. Then whoever was polite and grateful and lastly anyone who put in a complaint.'[5]

A story circulated at the time that, on one occasion when Brooke-Popham was talking to General Percival on a trunk call, the operator interrupted with the words, 'Your three minutes are up, sir.' Like many such stories, it was probably apocryphal but amply illustrates the problems both of priority and, more important, security. All the lines were open and could be easily tapped into. Although, since the operators were mainly local civilians, some of whom had more sympathy for the Japanese than for the British, this was scarcely necessary.

The more important calls between Percival and his divisional commanders were scrambled. But all others were open lines and few officers were aware of the need for communications security. Former Bletchley Park codebreakers say that the keys to many of the great SIGINT (Signals Intelligence) coups of the war, on both sides, were provided by officers who found it impossible to understand that their conversations were being monitored.

Even professional signallers were not totally comfortable with the use of the scrambler. On one occasion, a signaller about to go off shift found himself handing over to a colleague at the same time as General Percival was making a call on a scrambler phone. The new man pulled the plug on Percival with the words, 'Bloody Chinese, they are talking on that line.' Fortunately for the signaller concerned, civilian operators ended up with the blame.[6]

In their opening thrusts of the war the early establishment of air superiority was a major objective for the Japanese. Their aircraft struck hard at Malayan air bases which would then be overrun and used for further raids deeper into Allied territory.

The Malayan campaign was a textbook example of this strategy. One of the principal early objectives of the Japanese was to take the airfields in northern Malaya and destroy the Allied air force. The Japanese attacked the airfields time and time again, firstly with aircraft fitted with long-range fuel tanks and flying from bases in Indochina, and later from captured airfields in Thailand. The onslaught was accurate and decisive.

The Japanese aircraft used light bombs in order to reduce damage to the airfields which they planned to use later themselves. They struck hard at aircraft and ground installations, wherever possible leaving the runways intact, and within the first few hours had all but achieved their objectives. Their air intelligence was remarkable. Aircraft were frequently destroyed on the ground and there were reports that the Japanese appeared to know the coded recognition signals, allowing them to attack with impunity.

At the start of the campaign, there was a total of 86 British aircraft based at airfields in northern Malaya. By the evening of the first day that number had been cut to around half. By the next evening, thirty-six hours after the first Japanese attack, the combined British bomber and fighter force in the north amounted to just 10 aircraft, and a day later even these had been withdrawn south to protect the naval base at Singapore.

'The intensity of the Japanese air attacks against forward airfields in northern Malaya throughout the 8th December had disastrous consequences,' the official history records. 'As a means of defence and as support for land operations in the forward areas, the British air effort had almost ceased to exist within twenty-four hours of the opening of hostilities.' The loss of any effective air cover was a devastating blow, not just to the ground forces as they retreated down the Malay peninsula, but also to the Royal Navy.

At dusk on Monday 8th December, the *Prince of Wales*, the *Repulse*, and the other ships of Force Z had slipped out of Singapore naval base bound for Singora and Patani with the intention of launching a surprise attack on the Japanese and stopping them on the beaches.

Admiral Sir Tom Phillips, C-in-C Far Eastern Fleet, who was commanding Force Z, believed that with fighter support and an element of surprise, he would be able to smash the Japanese task force. He was warned before sailing that the air support he needed might not be possible and that the enemy had large numbers of torpedo-bombers at its bases in Indochina, but he still went ahead. Anything appeared better than futile and dangerous inactivity in Singapore, where his ships were also vulnerable to air attack.

He requested air reconnaissance for 100 miles ahead of his fleet together with fighter cover for the actual attack, which was planned for Wednesday 10th December. Air Vice-Marshal C. W. H. Pulford, Air Officer Commanding, could only promise the former. Fighter cover was doubtful because of the battering being taken by the airfields in the north-east, where Kota Bharu was already in enemy hands, and the restricted range of the fighter aircraft he had available.

The next day, Phillips received a signal from Rear-Admiral A. F. E. Palliser, Chief of Staff, Far Eastern Fleet, telling him: 'Fighter protection on Wednesday 10th [the date Force Z was expected to make contact with the Japanese] will not, repeat not, be possible.' But Phillips' ships had the cover of the weather, which had closed in around them, and he continued on course for Singora.

Around 1700 hours on Tuesday 9th December, the weather having cleared, Japanese aircraft were spotted and, with his force now deprived of the only advantage it had left, that of surprise, Phillips called off the mission. In fact, the British ships had already been spotted, three hours earlier, by the Japanese submarine *I–65*, but this was not known until after the war.

On Wednesday 10th, following up a false report that the Japanese were landing troops at the east coast port of Kuantan, Force Z changed course to investigate. They found nothing and moved away from the coast. But the deviation led to their being spotted by Japanese aircraft based in Indochina. The Japanese 22nd Air Flotilla, with 33 high-altitude bombers and 52 torpedo-bombers, was ordered to attack.

By early afternoon both capital ships of Force Z had been sunk. It was a devastating blow to morale not just in Malaya but also at home. The realisation that Britain's great navy could no longer rule the waves hit hard at the heart of the maritime nation.

Churchill was lying in bed, going through his despatch boxes, when he heard the news. The bedside telephone rang. The First Sea Lord, Sir Dudley Pound, was on the other end of the line, and his voice sounded so odd that at first Churchill could not understand what he was saying. Then the awful news registered. He wrote later that he was thankful to be alone. 'In all the war, I never received a more direct shock. As I turned over and twisted in bed, the full horror of the news sank into me. There were no British or American capital ships in the Indian Ocean or the Pacific except the American survivors of Pearl Harbor, who were hastening back to California. Over all this vast expanse of waters Japan was supreme and we everywhere were weak and naked.'[7]

Heavily exposed by their lack of air support, the British and Indian forces in western Malaya withdrew from Jitra during the night of 12/13th to positions at Gurun, some thirty miles to the south – the 'better' positions that Murray-Lyon had wanted to occupy earlier. The Gurun defile lies between Kedah Peak to the east and the jungle around Bukit Kuang in the west, and was one of the strongest natural defensive positions in Malaya. It also had strategic importance as the point where the main road south and the railway converged. But no great effort had been made to fortify it, and now there was little time left. The British and Indian troops were on the run while the Japanese were steadily building up momentum.

On Sunday 14th December, Murray-Lyon informed his immediate superior, General Heath, that the 11th Division's losses were already of the order of fifty-five per cent. As the Japanese forces, on anything from tanks to bicycles, poured south towards the symbolically important island of Penang – Britain's earliest possession in the Far East – the decision was made to withdraw to the Muda river, twenty miles further south, in an effort to defend the island's vital port facilities and communications centre. But the island had been under air attack since 11th December and the British commanders knew it was indefensible.

The military authorities ordered the evacuation of all European women and children from the island on the night of Monday 13th December, leaving all Asian women and children to an uncertain fate. It was one of the most discreditable acts of the whole campaign.

Many of the Europeans themselves protested the decision, which later caused an international furore, especially in the United States, and led to a number of questions being asked in the House of Commons. More importantly, it had a devastating effect on the morale of the Asian population of Malaya who now knew precisely what help they could expect from the British authorities.

The Governor of the Straits Settlements, Sir Shenton Thomas, told the Settlements' mixed-race Legislative Assembly the next day that there would be no discrimination during evacuations. 'In any withdrawal or movement of population, there will be no distinction of race,' he said. 'No European male or female will be ordered by the civil authorities to withdraw. We stand by the people of this country, with whom we live and work, in this ordeal.'

A week later, Sir Shenton met senior members of the Asian community in Singapore in an attempt to reassure them that the Penang evacuation was not a precedent for the future. 'Such grave forebodings about Penang that I had to meet representative Asiatics this afternoon,' he wrote in his diary for 20th December. 'Had to tell them I knew nothing of the evacuation until it had been carried out, that I had instructed there was to be no racial discrimination. It was the most difficult speech I have had to make.'

Quite how difficult has not until now been entirely clear. It was one of the great myths of the Malayan campaign that Sir Shenton knew nothing of the terms of the evacuation until after it had taken place, a myth continued by his biographer and other writers.[8] But his persistent denials that he was not informed of what was to occur can now be shown to be outright lies. There is no doubt that he had gone on record as being against racial discrimination, but even if he did not agree with the evacuation himself, a document that has until now lain undiscovered in a file in the India Office Library clearly shows that both Sir Shenton and the British government did know about it at least six hours before it took place.[9] In the following secret message to the Secretary of State for the Colonies, Lord Moyne, timed at 1609 hours on 13th December, Sir Shenton warned him it was about to happen:

NO. 627 GOVERNMENT HOUSE

NOT FOR PUBLICATION

PENANG HAS BEEN RAIDED SEVERAL TIMES BY DAYLIGHT AND DAMAGE TO ASIATIC QUARTERS HAS BEEN EXTENSIVE. SO FAR IT IS KNOWN FATAL CASUALTIES 200 WOUNDED ABOUT 1,000 ALL ASIATIC. OWING TO DESTRUCTION OF AERODROMES IN THE NORTH AIR DEFENCE HAS BEEN IMPOSSIBLE AND ASIATIC MORALE IN CONSEQUENCE BAD. MILITARY AUTHORITIES IN COLLABORATION WITH THE RESIDENT COUNCILLOR ARE ARRANGING TO CONTROL THE TOWN. EUROPEAN WOMEN AND CHILDREN WILL BE EVACUATED AS SOON AS POSSIBLE.[9]

Harold Macmillan, then Under-Secretary of State for the Colonies, later told Parliament that no 'discrimination of any kind was made in connection with opportunities for evacuation', and Duncan Sandys, Financial Secretary to the War Ministry, even went so far as to claim in Parliament that there had been 'no desire on the part of the Asiatic population to leave the island'.

By 17th December Penang had been evacuated by the remaining British forces and there was now no need for the Muda line to be held. In addition, British and Indian troops ran the risk of being outflanked by the Japanese troops pouring down the Patani–Kroh road following the forced withdrawal of the Krohcol column. So once again they began to fall back – thoroughly demoralised, shattered and hungry.

Even the Gurkhas, one of the world's most feared fighting forces, were affected by the general malaise, as one of their officers described in his personal war diary. 'In four and a half days, the battalion had fought an action, dug three positions, marched 64 miles; and not had a single regular ration meal and only one other meal (36 hours previously), and had had only a few hours' spasmodic sleep,' wrote Captain C. G. Wylie. 'In this last march, nearly everyone was marching asleep, automatically. After a halt it was the greatest difficulty to wake everybody up and get on the move again.'[10] Morale was particularly low among the Indian troops, many of whom were cajoled and coerced after capture by the Japanese into joining the ranks of the Indian National Army, the pro-independence, anti-British force created by the Japanese.

Mistake followed mistake. The failure of the garrison of Penang to carry out a proper denial system left the Japanese with still more valuable equipment, including twenty-four motor launches and a number of other craft which they were able to put to good use later. The denial system, a less extreme version of the 'scorched earth' policy practised by the Russians on the eastern front, did not work well. As they retreated the British and Indian forces were supposed to destroy anything that might be of assistance to the Japanese. But large amounts of equipment fell into enemy hands, so much so that the Japanese described them as 'Churchill Supplies'. Food, fuel, vehicles, weapons, were all left behind and used by the Japanese. At Penang, it was not just the boats in the harbour that were left intact. Very shortly after capturing the island, the Japanese were able to use the wireless station to broadcast the news of their latest success across South-east Asia, with further damaging effects on the morale of Allied troops and Asians alike.

As the western railroad became crowded with troops and equipment moving south, large numbers of railway vans were shunted into sidings at Kuala Lumpur to relieve congestion. One of these was loaded with British Army maps of Singapore, which Malaya Command had had printed in Kuala Lumpur. But as the British withdrew, it was left behind and fell into enemy hands. So the Japanese had large numbers of up-to-date maps of the city, while the British were forced to make do with what they had.

Even the systematic destruction of the bridges by the retreating forces was ineffective in slowing the Japanese advance. Japanese engineers were able to repair the bridges using stocks of timber stacked there earlier, possibly by Public Works Department engineers, possibly by fifth-columnists helping the Japanese. For example, at Alor Star, which lies on the Kedah river, an officer of the 1st Leicesters watching a bridge being blown up noticed a stockpile of timber lying nearby. 'I wondered afterwards,' he wrote, 'if their location was deliberate, placed there by some thoughtful person to facilitate repairs should the bridge be destroyed.'[11]

Major Freddie Spencer Chapman, who was attached to the Special Operations Executive and was operating behind enemy lines, said he and his men found that the retreating British forces were dismantling the bridges but were leaving the timbers close by. 'All the plank bridges on this side had been removed to stop the Japs using it,' he said. 'But when we replaced them, we found it just passable.'[12]

The Allied troops now withdrew to the Krian river where it

was hoped the swampy river basin would provide a natural anti-tank barrier, giving the exhausted soldiers time to rest and regroup behind it. But many units found it impossible to dig in as the river was tidal and their positions prone to flooding at every high tide. So the Krian river fell the way of all the other supposedly good natural defensive positions that had preceded it, and by Saturday 20th December, the troops were in retreat again.

The threat of a flanking movement by the Japanese heading down the road from Kroh on his right was causing General Heath considerable concern, and he obtained permission to withdraw to the Perak river. The task of delaying the Japanese advance down the Kroh road fell to the Argylls of 12th Brigade, while to their west it was the task of the 28th Brigade. The two forces took it in turn to withdraw, each covering the flank of the other.

The Perak river runs north/south, parallel to the line of the Japanese advance, so by no stretch of the imagination was it a good line of defence. It did give some of the defenders a brief respite in which to rest and regroup, but all the while Yamashita's army was being reinforced by more men and tanks.

The Japanese captured the important town of Ipoh on Saturday 27th December, and on the same day Brooke-Popham was finally relieved of his command, his reputation among his fellow commanders in tatters and a whispering campaign against him in full swing. The known disagreements among the Allied senior commanders cannot have helped the progress of the Malayan campaign. The Australian Major-General Gordon Bennett, an experienced soldier but not one noted for either modesty or tact, seems to have got on with no-one. There were also signs of strain in the relationship between Percival and Heath. Perci-val, who was fifty-three, tall and lean, had a fine record dating from World War One, and had served on the General Staff. He was a pleasant man and intelligent, but he lacked that special drive and brilliance that is so necessary for field leadership. Heath was probably the most able of the generals in Malaya.

He had arrived there after taking a brilliant part in the campaign for Eritrea. He was affectionately known by his men as 'Piggy' Heath.

The next major position the British and Indians tried to hold was the Slim river with its strategic bridges. They had only forty-eight hours to dig themselves in. Under the all but incessant Japanese air-raids the exhausted and demoralised men were forced to work at night, with little opportunity to sleep. 'The battalion was dead tired,' Colonel Deakin of 5/2nd Punjab Regiment wrote. 'The battalion had withdrawn 176 miles in three weeks and had had only three days' rest. It had suffered 250 casualties of which a high proportion had been killed. The spirit of the men was low and the battalion had lost fifty per cent of its fighting efficiency.

'During 5th January, I found a most lethargic lot of men who seemed to want to do nothing but sit in slit trenches,' Deakin continued. 'The deadly ground silence emphasised by the blanketing effect of the jungle was getting on men's nerves . . . The jungle gave the men a blind feeling.'

The jungle provided immense difficulties for all the Allied troops. Maintaining morale in any retreating force presents great problems. Doing so in an unfriendly environment is close to impossible. The difficulty of cutting a path through the dense undergrowth, the disorientating effect of not being able to see a clear way ahead and the discomfort created by monsoon rain, high humidity and mosquitoes, all had a severely debilitating effect on morale.

The Slim river battle began on the night of Tuesday 6th January. The Japanese pushed forward with tanks 'nose-to-tail', their crews yelling and firing and their engines racing. Infantry units were close behind firing mortars. The British tried to knock out the tanks with their few anti-tank guns and with Molotov cocktails. Throughout the night and into the following morning, all along the line, the battle degenerated into a mass of small, bitterly fought fights. 'The din defied description,' said one British officer. By the end of that day, 11th Indian Division had been virtually destroyed and many more Indian captives were soon bolstering the burgeoning ranks of the Indian National Army.

The Slim river battle was a 'major disaster', says the official history. 'It resulted in the early abandonment of central Malaya and gravely prejudiced the chances of holding northern Johore long enough to enable the reinforcing formations, then on their way to Singapore, to arm and prepare for battle. For some time to come the 11th Division ceased to be an effective fighting force.'

The speed at which the Japanese were pushing forward was phenomenal. On Friday 2nd January, Major Spencer Chapman, who was in the process of planning an operation behind enemy lines, went to see Brigadier A. C. M. Paris, who had earlier taken over command of 11th Division from Murray-Lyon. 'I asked him how long he thought I had before the Japs reached Tanjong Malim,' Spencer Chapman recalled later. Paris replied: 'I will make no real promises, but you can safely rely on at least a fortnight.' The town fell just six days later.[12]

Kuantan on the east coast was evacuated on Saturday 3rd January. Kuala Lumpur, the federal capital of Malaya on Sunday 11th, leaving the Japanese with vast new stocks of 'Churchill Supplies' and yet another still usable airfield. The Japanese were soon into Johore State and within grasp of their main objective. But their rapid push forward had left their lines of communication and supply stretched almost to breaking point, and without the supplies they had captured they would have been in great difficulties. In addition they now had the Australians to deal with.

Several units of the Australian forces had been in the fight from the very beginning. Major Kiernan's 2/3 Motor Transport Company was one of these. This unit, made up of veterans from World War One, had been in support of Krohcol. During that mission and several times later they had bravely extricated Indian Army units from some very difficult situations. (They 'rescued' the 5/14th Punjabis several times. They had served with that battalion's commanding officer, Lieutenant-Colonel Stokes, in Mesopotamia in the First World War, and there was 'no way they were going to let their old mate down'.) But the

bulk of the Australians had been held back to guard the vulnerable south-east coast of Malaya around Mersing in Johore.
Now, on the orders of General Sir Archibald Wavell, who had
taken over the Supreme Command in Java on 3rd January with
Pownall as his Chief of Staff – and who was impressed with
the self-confidence shown by General Bennett – certain new unit
dispositions, and some changes in the command structure, were
made. A number of British and Indian units were placed under
Bennett's command.

The key to north-west Johore was the area between the inland
town of Gemas, and Malacca and Muar on the coast. Bennett
sent his best troops, the 27th Australian Brigade, to positions
astride the main trunk road at Gemas. The 9th Indian Division
was placed behind them and other Australian and Indian troops
were in flank positions. The newly arrived 45th Indian Brigade,
made up of largely untrained troops, guarded the Muar area.

A great believer in the value of ambushes, Bennett decided
the best place to spring one was on the trunk road west of
Gemas, and the 2/30th Australian battalion had been rehearsing
this for some time. The trap was set on the trunk road where
a bridge crossed a small river. The bridge was wired up for
demolition and a battery of field artillery positioned to fire on
the area west of the bridge where the Japanese were expected to
collect after the bridge was blown up. A company of Australian
infantry concealed itself in thick jungle along the road east of the
bridge. The trap was sprung on the afternoon of 14th January.

A Japanese column of cyclists riding six abreast, unaware of
what lay in store for them, crossed the bridge. The Australians
let about two companies pass, and then as more were seen
approaching the far side of the bridge, which was itself full of
Japanese soldiers, it was blown up. At the same time, murder-
ous crossfire cut down those who had already crossed. Many
Japanese were killed. But it would have been far worse for them
had not one of their infiltrating patrols found and cut the signal
wire leading to the Australian artillery position. The gunners
could hear the battle but were unable to join in without orders
and knowledge of the situation.

Even though the ambush had cost the Japanese dear, it had no long-term effect on their advance. On the following day, after what was, even by their own standards, a remarkably swift repair job on the bridge, the Japanese had tanks and more infantry across the river. The Australians made some initially successful counter-attacks but, as pressure grew, the 2/30th were forced to withdraw.

Over to the west, the inexperienced 45th Indian Brigade lost Muar on 16th January, exposing Bennett's left flank. He ordered forward his reserve battalion, the Australian 2/29th, to support the Indians. The Australian troops took up positions at Bakri, south of Muar, and were soon confronted by a squadron of Japanese tanks advancing without infantry support. They knocked out eight of them, but continued Japanese pressure all along the line, and a landing from the sea by a Japanese battalion at Batu Pahat in the rear of the Allied lines, caused the Australians and Indians to fall back. At Bakri, the 2/29th found themselves cut off by the Japanese 4th Guards. Two Australian companies were destroyed, and it was only through the brave leadership of an Australian officer, Lieutenant-Colonel Charles Anderson, who won one of the campaign's four VCs, that 900 Indian and Australian survivors managed to fight their way back to their lines. From then on, despite the occasional small success, the Allied forces scarcely stopped retreating until they crossed into Singapore Island.

As the Allied troops fell back on Singapore, the depleted RAF was at last able to provide some very limited air cover from the only bases available to them, on Singapore Island itself. As a result, these airfields became a prime target for the Japanese aircraft which attacked them with increasing intensity. Some of the British bombers were withdrawn to Sumatra for safety. A number of Dutch fighters stationed in Singapore were also withdrawn to protect the Dutch East Indies. Fortress Singapore was becoming an increasingly uncomfortable place to be in as the Japanese moved ever closer.

Early on the morning of Saturday 31st January 1942 the last organised units of British troops crossed the causeway from

Johore to Singapore. The last unit of all was the 2nd Battalion of the Argyll & Sutherland Highlanders, or what was left of it, piped across by the battalion's two remaining pipers. The causeway was then blown up behind them and with it the pipeline bringing fresh water to the island's reservoirs, thereby ensuring that the city would not be able to hold out for long.

After fifty-five days of brilliant campaigning, the Japanese had arrived at the back-gate of Singapore. In the process, they had virtually destroyed two Indian Army divisions, eliminated the Royal Air Force and sunk two capital ships, including one of the most modern and powerful battleships in the world. Just two weeks later, on Sunday February 15th, Singapore itself capitulated.

In the majority of accounts of the campaign, the most commonly used expression is 'passed through' as each unit took its turn in rearguard action before leapfrogging yet another series of temporary defensive positions set up by the unit behind them. The British, Indian and Australian forces had no tanks and few anti-tank weapons. They were largely untrained in jungle warfare and from the second day onwards had no effective air cover. They did achieve a number of minor successes but not one major victory that would have helped to restore their badly battered pride.

'Most of our troops except those of the permanent garrison were inexperienced and semi-trained,' General Percival reported later. 'Even the regular units had been so diluted as to lose some at least, and in some cases a great deal, of their pre-war efficiency. No units had had any training in bush warfare before reaching Malaya. Successful fighting in jungle training is largely a question of confidence and self-reliance of the individual. These cannot be acquired without a reasonable period of training in such conditions,' Percival added. What he failed to explain was why so many 'long-stay' units stationed in Malaya and under his command had not been given jungle training.

He was also disparaging of the quality of some of the late reinforcements. The 7,000 Indian troops who arrived on 22nd January were 'raw and untrained', he said. They included very few non-commissioned officers 'or even potential leaders'. The 2,000 Australian reinforcements who arrived on 24th January had only had a few weeks' training and had not been in the army long enough to learn 'true discipline'.

The behaviour of some of these Australian reinforcement troops overshadowed the bravery shown by their compatriots at Gemas and, after the final capitulation, General Wavell, the Supreme Commander, ABDA (American, British, Dutch and Australian) Command, compiled a report, backed up by about fifty statements by eyewitnesses, effectively blaming the Australians for the defeat.

In one of the statements appended to the Wavell report an officer described how mass desertion by Australian troops allowed the Japanese to advance on to Singapore Island itself. Citing 'the behaviour of the Australian Imperial Forces' as an example of what he called 'the lack of discipline in Malaya', Captain L. G. Young of the 2/9th Gurkha Rifles, said:

The Australian division was entrusted with the defence of the NW and W coast of Singapore Island. The area was half-mangrove swamp. No attempt was made to patrol this swamp – Dalforce [a volunteer force of Chinese led by Colonel John Dalley] did it for them. No attempt was made to recce the far side of the bank. At last they were 'induced' to, on the night of 8th February (and discovered all preparations for a move across the Straits by a large force), and on the night of 9/10th February, the Australians, without orders, left their area. The unit occupying the area next to the Causeway handed a scrawled note to a 2/2 GR [Gurkha Rifles] Havildar which merely said, 'Position so and so Bde now 13 m.s. (3 miles back)'. And that night, the Japs landed on the west coast.

On the 10th morning, an effort was made to drive the Japs back into the sea. Three battalions were to advance in line. But there was a battalion missing and the Japs walked through the gap. The missing battalion was an Australian battalion. It reappeared in Singapore town, preferring drink and rape to doing its duty.

The mass of statements collected from eyewitnesses, and other letters from escapees intercepted by the censors, provided a damning indictment of the Australians who had fought so bravely earlier in the campaign. Many took care to balance their reports with praise for that earlier courage, but all were highly critical. One letter said that 'the one and only reason for the sudden collapse of the Singapore defences was the Australian troops. That Singapore might have fallen in any event after a long struggle may be true but if Monday night–Tuesday morning, the soldiers who were allotted the task of holding the Bukit Tinnah [sic] road had not just thrown down their arms and run into Singapore it may have been a different story.'

A British official in Ceylon, who was handling evacuees from Singapore, spoke of numerous reports that 'on many occasions Australian troops refused to fight in contrast to the magnificent behaviour of the British and Indian troops'.

Another letter said it was 'the universal opinion that the Aussies let us down. Their conduct pre-Japanese invasion in Malaya made them scorned. Scrounge was their password, women and wine their one aim. The Tommies held the Japs in the centre and the Aussies let them infiltrate in the flanks.' The attitude towards the Australians was summed up by one British major who said that they seemed to regard the scorched earth policy ordered by Churchill, in an attempt to prevent the Japanese getting their hands on anything that might help their war effort, as 'simply an excuse for looting'. He concluded: 'The Australians were known as daffodils – beautiful to look at but yellow all through.'

Wavell personally endorsed some of the statements as 'fair and accurate' and they were recycled by Churchill's government in a response to an Australian request for evidence to back up the allegations that Australian troops had performed badly in Malaya.

The War Office compiled a report on the Australians' behaviour which was sent to an Australian military representative in London. But it was considered so sensitive that it contained the remarkable caveat that the High Commissioner could see it only if he promised not to pass the information back to Canberra.

Nor were the statements the only mention of Australian failures. One memo to Churchill, on a call for the death penalty to be introduced for cowardice, said the behaviour of the Australian troops provided 'powerful justification, but we daren't divulge these facts'.[13] (This passage ended with the words, 'we cannot legislate for the Australians anyway'.)

There are several possible reasons for the bad behaviour of the Australian troops. The 2,000 raw reinforcements rushed to Malaya in late January were spread among the more experienced Australian troops and any breaking of ranks would have had a knock-on effect. The renowned fighting qualities of the Australian soldier are based on his individualistic approach to life, which can be a valuable asset in a soldier on the offensive. But a major retreat requires different virtues, the main one being discipline, a quality that even the Australians would not attribute to themselves in great measure. In addition, following the debacle in Crete in April and May of 1941, the Australians had been promised that they would never again have to fight with inadequate air cover, which, of course, was exactly what they were required to do in Malaya.

The Japanese by contrast had no such problems. They were highly mobile, imaginatively led and supported by tanks and extremely professional engineer units. Their tactics were unorthodox but effective. They advanced through the 'impenetrable' jungle with comparative ease, infiltrating behind the defending forces wherever they were held up. They pressed forward at speed, ignoring fatigue and continuing through the night. They used their air power and their tanks to drive the Allied troops away from the roads and into the jungle where the Allies' inexperience and lack of training could be exposed.

According to the official history, the Commonwealth dead and wounded from the Malaya Campaign amounted to some 8,700 as opposed to the Japanese 9,824. But the Allies also lost more than 130,000 men as prisoners of war, many of whom were to die in the camps. The Americans held a number of inquiries into Pearl Harbor, but despite Churchill's expressed desire for 'a formal pronouncement by a competent court on the worst disaster and largest capitulation in British history', there was never a similar British inquiry into the fall of Singapore.

In a memorandum to the then US Secretary of the Navy,

Franklyn Knox, dated 2nd May 1942, the US Navy's Admiral Harold R. Stock said Churchill had told him that the British government would not set up a commission to investigate the fall of Singapore because this would contribute nothing to the war effort and might indeed even damage it. He did believe however that, in justice to the men who fought in Malaya, there should be an inquiry as soon as the war was over. But it never took place, much to the chagrin of many of those who had returned home after years spent in Japanese prisoner-of-war camps and who saw the lack of any investigation into the affair as part of a vast cover-up of the incompetence, errors of judgement, and dilatoriness on the part of many of those involved, not least Churchill himself.

The Allied forces were ill-prepared, ill-equipped and, for the most part, poorly generalled. There had been political and military neglect pre-war, and political and military mismanagement after hostilities began. But the killer blow was the loss of air cover. As has been shown on numerous occasions since, modern warfare is won or lost by air power.

For the Allied forces in Malaya the lack of air superiority was to lead inevitably to defeat. There were, of course, many other causes but no other was so crucial. 'How desperately was felt the need of an air arm throughout the campaign,' lamented General Heath later.[14] If the Royal Air Force and its Australian counterpart, the RAAF, had managed to keep up the devastating performance of the RAAF in the first hours of the Kota Bharu landings, then the campaign might well have had a different ending. If the Japanese had been delayed in northern Malaya, perhaps additional British reinforcements might have been sent and certainly those that did arrive late in the campaign would have had the opportunity to receive some jungle training and to become acclimatised before being plunged into battle.

The lack of air cover was due in part to complacency among the Chiefs of Staff who, as the official history records, foolishly believed the lightweight Buffalo fighter aircraft available to the RAF would be 'more than a match' for the Japanese Zero. But perhaps the most damaging role was played by one man – a Japanese spy in a secret British air intelligence unit.

Many of those in Malaya at the time believed there must be a spy in the British ranks. 'We were sure that someone was passing on information on our every move,' said Major-General Murray-Lyon, after ordering the spy's arrest. 'It has always been my contention that our extremely inadequate air defences were also subverted by a spy or we would have put up a better show,' says one Squadron Leader who was then stationed in northern Malaya.[15]

There was indeed a spy. Thanks to information provided by him, the Japanese knew the complete state of defences of the northern airfields, enabling their pilots to intercept Allied aircraft as they were taking off or landing and therefore when most vulnerable to attack.

The spy who betrayed these vital secrets and many more was a man with a grudge against authority and the British establishment, a man whose crucial role in the fall of Singapore has until now remained covered in a web of secrecy.

CHAPTER 3

THE PLANTER TURNED NAVAL OFFICER

More than one member of the British forces in Malaya was suspected of helping the Japanese. An officer in the Royal Artillery, said to be of Italian extraction, was taken to Singapore and shot during the first days of the conflict after refusing to order his gun crews to fire on Japanese aircraft.[1] One British veteran officer remembers hearing that two 'officer spies' had been detained in northern Malaya. And on 20th December 1941, a naval lieutenant was arrested in the wake of the sinking of the *Prince of Wales* and *Repulse*, accused of creating a diversion to draw them towards the coast near Kuantan, a small seaport on the east coast of Malaya, and leave them sitting targets for the Japanese aircraft.

The Kuantan incident, as it came to be known, involved a false report that the Japanese were landing troops just north of the town. The two British capital ships and three of their escort vessels in Force Z changed course to investigate. Had they not done so they might have escaped detection by the Japanese bombers. But the background to those reports has never been fully explained and to this day it remains shrouded in mystery.

At the centre of this mystery is a man who might have stepped out of a novel by Joseph Conrad and who was to make the perfect scapegoat when the British cast around for someone to blame for the humiliating loss of two of their most prestigious warships.

C.J. Windsor was a tough English planter who made his living running jelutong, a resin used for medical and industrial purposes, up and down the coast of Malaya. Approaching fifty, he was short and stocky with piercing blue eyes and short blond hair. He knew the south-east of the peninsula and every river along its coast intimately, and he spoke Malay like a native, ruling the local crew of the *Kelana* – the small, but modern, diesel-powered trading ship he used to ferry the resin up and down the coast – with a rod of iron.

'C.J.' had a factory at Kuantan, where he built the *Kelana*, naming her after the Malay word for wanderer, and a sister ship. He was a man of some standing in the local community, serving as a member of the Kuantan Sanitary Board, the Malayan equivalent of a town council, and, as a permanent European resident, giving it a rare continuity of service. He was also a chemist and an engineer, having developed the process by which the American company Wrigley's used jelutong in the manufacture of their chewing gum and a remote control system that enabled an auxiliary yacht's engines to be controlled from the deck.[2]

When the Second World War broke out in September 1939, Windsor took a commission in the Malay Royal Navy Volunteer Reserve (MRNVR), mounting a three-pounder gun on the *Kelana*'s fore-deck and roving the east coast in the role of 'security intelligence'. And with those sorts of credential he might well have been completely safe from accusations of treachery. But for one thing. He had been the subject of a pre-war Intelligence report. A police file, compiled by a senior policeman called Basil O'Connel, said that he was a 'naturalised German' who had changed his name to Windsor from Winckle.

In truth he was nothing of the sort. His grandfather, from whom he no doubt inherited his Teutonic looks, had emigrated to England from Germany in the mid-nineteenth century, living in Sheffield where he worked in the steel industry. But 'C.J.' was British, born in Hereford on 12th July 1893 and christened Cyril Joseph Winckle. His father was a railway clerk.

'C.J.' arrived in Malaya some time before the First World War, working on a rubber plantation at Kapar, Selangor. When that war broke out, like many other Britons of German descent, he did indeed change his name, taking his mother's maiden name, Windsor, as his own.[3] By the time the Second World War came along, he had developed into a minor legend, in the style of a Conradian seafaring adventurer. He probably knew more about the east coast of Malaya and its rivers south of Kuantan than any other European, and had a vast store of 'secret' sources for the jelutong and the rare, and highly profitable, hardwood timbers he purchased from the natives.

Ex-Malayan Police Superintendent J. B. 'Jack' Masefield, who helped to compile the police file on Windsor, says that 'one of the main reasons for suspecting Windsor was that he had constructed a trace – a jungle road – running inland from Kuala Rompin which is on the coast south of Kuantan. It ran for seventy or eighty miles to Bahau in Negri Sembilan and it was capable of taking wheeled traffic. Windsor was known to speak fluent German, and it was reported in 1940 that German agents had made contact with him. He had a huge jungle empire centred on Kuantan. He also spoke Sakai, one of the native dialects, as well as Malay.'[4]

But the trace was far from secret. Guy Madoc, another senior police officer who went on to become General Gerald Templer's Director of Intelligence during the Malaya Emergency of 1954–57, says it was even used by the Argyll & Sutherland Highlanders during their jungle training.[5]

In what appears to have been seen as another crucial piece of evidence against Windsor, he was widely believed to own an old abandoned rubber plantation along the coast. Just a mile north of Kuantan lay a stretch of beach called Chempedak which, before the war, was popular with the town's European residents as a venue for beach parties. A quarter of a mile further on was a very much smaller beach, which was difficult to reach because of a jumble of rocks. On the hillside above that beach was the old rubber estate supposedly owned by Windsor.

Unfortunately, this was the general area where the Japanese were reported to be landing on the night of 9th December 1941. So when *Prince of Wales* and *Repulse* went down, and people began to question if there had ever been a landing at all, the authorities came looking for 'C.J.', 'the naturalised German', suspecting him of causing a diversion to lure the two ships towards the shore and leave them 'sitting ducks' for the Japanese aircraft.

Windsor was arrested for a short period, but he was eventually released and spent the rest of the war in South Africa.[6] He returned to Malaya after the war, died in 1970, and is buried in Telok Sisek Christian Cemetery in Kuantan. Despite his best efforts to clear his name, the allegations against him still remain. But a re-examination of the available evidence throws considerable doubt on whether he was ever involved in the incident at all, at least in the way the authorities thought.

On the evening of Monday 8th December, the day the Japanese invaded Malaya, Force Z had left Singapore Naval Base and headed towards the Japanese beachheads at Singora and Patani hoping to catch the enemy landing ships unawares. But on the following evening, 9th December, it became clear that they had been spotted by a Japanese aircraft. Admiral Sir Tom Phillips, handicapped by his lack of fighter cover, decided to call off the attack and ordered his ships to alter course back towards Singapore.

What happened next sealed Force Z's fate by ensuring it was again detected by the Japanese whose 22nd Air Flotilla, based in Indochina, was waiting for news of the ships. To this day what followed remains unexplained. It has been described by Vice-Admiral Sir John Hayes, now the most senior survivor of Force Z, as the 'Kuantan Enigma'.[7]

The mystery begins just before Phillips gave the order to turn back, when the pilot of a Hudson reconnaissance aircraft reported to base that he had sighted what looked like a troop transport vessel and a group of barges moving towards the port of Kuantan, about 150 miles south of Kota Bharu where the Japanese had landed. Soon after darkness fell that night, Indian troops stationed in beach positions at Besarah, just north of Kuantan, thought they detected a number of small boats approaching the coast and opened fire. The relevant war diary of HQ Singapore gives the following sequence of reports:

2025 hrs. Large merchant v/l reported Kuantan

2210 hrs. Info from 22 Brigade that landing believed taking place at Sungei Karang near Besarah. The Brigadier considers a substantial attempt at landing to take place at Kuantan. He asks for RAF and Naval help.

2350 hrs.   BGS [Brigadier, General Staff] phoned that 3 Corps confirmed that enemy are feeling for weak places at various points along beaches at Kuantan.[8]

There was general acceptance of the reports among the senior military officers. General Heath, commanding III Corps, phoned the BGS, Brigadier K. A. Torrance, at 2235 hours to tell him that 'we should accept the landing as true bill'. More importantly, Torrance had already told Rear Admiral Palliser, Phillips' Chief of Staff in Singapore, that he believed the source of the report to be reliable.

At 2300 hours, the RAF reported that it had lost all contact with its observation post near Kuantan 'two hours ago'. Communications were not re-established until 0400 hours the following morning, a break of seven hours without explanation.

Palliser meanwhile had radioed Phillips aboard *Prince of Wales* to tell him of the reported landing. Keen to salvage something from his abortive mission, Phillips ordered Force Z to alter course for Kuantan at 0052 hours on what was to be the momentous day of Wednesday 10th December 1941. Maintaining absolute radio silence, he did not inform Singapore of his decision.

Around 0230 hours, the ships were spotted by the Japanese submarine *I-58* which signalled the news back to Saigon and the waiting aircraft of 22nd Air Flotilla. At 0310 hours, III Corps reported that all was quiet, except for some slight shelling from seaward. By 0430 hours RAF Vildebeeste torpedo-bombers from 36 Squadron, RAF, had been sent in, and reported that they had fired torpedoes at three craft, each sixty or seventy feet in length and rectangular in shape, one mile south of Batu Balok and near to Kuantan. They were unable to say what damage, if any, they had inflicted and reported no activity from the beach.[9]

In an entry timed at 0810 hours, the Singapore HQ war diary recorded that the enemy at Kuantan, 'made a number of attempts to land in small numbers at Sungei Karang just north of Besarah at 2200 hours. Presumably to test defences, and small pockets are believed to be still in northern sectors. At 0520 situation reported quiet with occasional shelling from two ships close in. Otherwise no change.'[10]

But from then on, it gradually became apparent that, whatever else had happened, it was not a major Japanese landing. As day broke and Force Z closed the coast, it spotted a tug towing some barges a good distance away which, after a cursory investigation, it ignored. Nearer the coast, Phillips catapulted off a reconnaissance aircraft which reported no sign of the enemy at Kuantan. The destroyer *Express* was sent ahead to have a closer look but she also reported all quiet.

Phillips, disappointed, altered course away from the coast and towards the tug and barges they had spotted earlier. It was then that things began to go badly wrong. At around 1000 hours the destroyer *Tenedos* to the south, which had been detached earlier because it was short of fuel, radioed that she was under attack from enemy bombers. (How the *Tenedos* after only a day and a half at sea could have been short of fuel is itself a mystery which has never been satisfactorily explained.) Her message was received by Phillips aboard his flagship but not by Singapore. Phillips altered course, increased speed and ordered his anti-aircraft gun crews to 'action stations'.

A short while later, with tension mounting on board all the ships in the fleet, the radar on *Repulse* picked up approaching aircraft from the south. At 1100 hours, eight Japanese Nell bombers came in sight at around 10,000 feet. Phillips altered course yet again and increased his speed to 25 knots. Everyone was now at 'action stations' as Force Z sped through the sea with the three escorting destroyers forming the head of an arrow formation. 'You could almost feel the electricity,' reported one of the men on board.*

---

* Japanese aircraft were allocated codenames by the Allies. Bombers were all given girls' names. The Japanese gave their military aircraft numerical designations corresponding to the last two digits of the year in which they were introduced into service. The Western year 1940 corresponded to the Showa year 2600, which is why the famous Japanese fighter introduced in 1940 was called the Zero.

The eight Japanese aircraft, armed with 250-kg bombs, came in high above the ships in line abreast and, at 1115, the British guns opened fire. All eight Nells were hit but that did not stop them pressing forward the attack against *Repulse*. The aircraft released their bombs simultaneously. The men watching from on board the destroyer *Electra* saw the battle-cruiser disappear behind a wall of water sent up by the cascade of bomb bursts. As it reappeared virtually unscathed, a loud and relieved cheer went up from the *Electra*'s company.

A quarter of an hour later, at 1130, two squadrons of Japanese torpedo-bombers arrived and, surprised to discover no sign of British fighter cover, took their time to form up for the attack. At 1150, nine of them began their long approach dive towards the port side of *Prince of Wales*. Under heavy fire, they split into three groups to attack from different angles. In a manoeuvre known as combing – the tracks of several torpedoes are like the teeth of a comb, and the vessel under attack attempts to place itself between them – Captain J. C. Leach turned his battleship towards the attackers to present as small a target as possible and allow the torpedoes to pass harmlessly by. But at least one, possibly two simultaneously, hit the ship where it was most vulnerable – on the quarter – and there was a tremendous explosion. The ship's rudder was destroyed and the port propeller shafts were jammed.

The warship's speed was halved, she was listing heavily to port, and she had lost her steering gear. In addition, she had no power to a number of her guns and her radar and radio were no longer working. In an incredibly short space of time, and with the minimum of difficulty, the Japanese had left the world's finest battleship crippled in the water.

There had been some initial hesitation on the part of the leader of the second squadron of torpedo-bombers – he had believed *Repulse* was the Japanese battleship *Kongo* which was, in fact, somewhere off the coast of Indochina – but now he ordered his aircraft in towards her port side.

Waiting until the last possible moment, and with his guns throwing up a hail of fire, Capt. W. G. Tennant turned his ship as if it was a destroyer and combed the tracks of the torpedoes, successfully avoiding them all.

But there was to be no respite for Captain Tennant and his crew. Another squadron of eight bombers came in using the same line-abreast tactic as its sister squadron had earlier. Handling his ship with consummate skill, Tennant again avoided all the torpedoes. His reward was a further attack from eight more torpedo-bombers flying in from the east, but once more *Repulse* avoided being hit and managed to shoot down one of the attackers in the process.

Less than an hour had passed since the first sighting of enemy aircraft, but for most of the men on board the ships, it had seemed like a lifetime.

During the ensuing lull, Tennant signalled Phillips aboard the flagship, using both Aldis lamp and radio. But he received no response. Checking with his signal staff, he discovered that Phillips had not radioed Singapore, so he did so himself. The signal reached HQ Far Eastern Fleet at 1204 hours and within minutes eleven Buffalo fighters were in the air and heading north. They were to arrive too late.

At 1220, a squadron of nine Japanese Betty bombers carrying torpedoes appeared just above the horizon on the starboard bow of *Repulse*. They split into two sections, one keeping on towards the battle-cruiser, the other feinting as if to attack the flagship. Tennant was heading his ship to comb the torpedoes of the first section when the second section suddenly swung to port coming straight at his ship.

The scissors movement left him trapped. With torpedoes criss-crossing his position, combing the torpedoes of the first section had left him broadside on to those of the second. If he attempted to turn back, he risked placing his ship in the path of the earlier torpedoes.

One torpedo from the second section struck the *Repulse* amidships, but it seemed to cause little damage and she was still under control. The *Prince of Wales* was not so lucky. Another squadron of nine Japanese aircraft roared in on her and three torpedoes struck home, causing further damage to her stern.

The flagship could now make only eight knots and she was showing signs of settling by the stern.

At 1225, the last torpedo-carrying squadron of Bettys arrived. They used a different technique this time, coming in like wolves at their prey from both sides. Aboard *Repulse* Tennant did his level best and one of his gunners shot down another Japanese aircraft, but first one torpedo and then three more slammed into the ship. She began to list heavily to port and Tennant knew at once that his ship was sinking. A little before 1230, he ordered 'abandon ship' and ten minutes later, the ship slid stern first under the waves, taking with her 513 officers and men. In the words of one of those plucked from the sea, her bow swung 'straight up in the air like a church steeple'.

Even as the destroyers *Vampire* and *Electra* began rescuing survivors from the sea, the last Japanese squadron to take part in the attack arrived on the scene. They were Nells equipped with 500-kg bombs which they dropped from a height of 10,000 feet on the *Prince of Wales*. One hit amidships on the port side. Thick clouds of rolling, black smoke were billowing from the ship which was struggling now to make six knots.

As she settled lower and lower in the water, the destroyer *Express* came alongside to take off the wounded and everyone else not essential to working the ship, for Phillips and Leach were still not ready to admit that the pride of the Royal Navy was already lost. But the ship kept on settling and at 1310 hours Leach finally ordered his men to abandon ship. Those who could save themselves did so, but within ten minutes the mighty battleship had joined her consort at the bottom of the sea with the loss of 327 officers and men, including both the admiral and the captain.

'The loss of the two great ships cast a gloom over the whole English-speaking world,' says the official history. 'The catastrophe led to a belief in the invincibility of Japanese air power, a belief which was given strength by the ease with which the enemy outmatched the obsolescent Allied aircraft. It created a myth of Japanese superiority in all three services, which took a long time to die.' It was the first time that capital ships had been sunk *at sea* by air power alone. The battle had created a precedent for future air attacks, changing the nature of naval warfare forever.[11,12]

Five days later a Royal Navy launch was despatched from Singapore to arrest Windsor, probably at the instigation of the military authorities themselves. On Monday 15th December, HQ Singapore received a signal from Commander Frampton, RN, which informed them that the Navy was sending the armed launch *Hungjao* to Kuantan to arrest Windsor. This decision was apparently taken without the knowledge of, or at least without the consent of, Windsor's senior officer, Rear Admiral E. J. Spooner at Singapore, who was in charge of all coastal defences.

The signal said that the *Hungjao* would arrive at Kuantan on the 17th. On Tuesday 16th, HQ 9th Indian Division had been informed that a naturalised German called Windsor, an estate owner at Kuantan, was suspected by the Navy of being a German agent. He was under investigation and if he was arrested he would be handed over to the Army.

The next day, the 17th, at 1300 hours, the Divisional HQ was informed by 22nd Indian Brigade that Windsor had left Kuantan with his wife for the inland town of Raub on the previous evening without notifying the military authorities, the implication being that he went without permission. His servant told the Army that he was expected back around noon on the 17th. At 1700 hours it was reported that Windsor had returned to Kuantan. The *Hungjao* meanwhile had been delayed, but on Saturday 20th December she reported that Windsor was under arrest on board and requested permission to proceed to base.

Early on Saturday morning, Windsor's arrest was discussed extensively in a telephone conversation between Major Angus Rose, an officer of the Argylls attached to HQ General Staff, and Captain Brasher of III Corps. Brasher, interested to hear that Windsor had been arrested, asked if permission could be obtained to arrest another suspect called Penseler who was a gold miner at Raub and whom the police and III Corps agreed was 'in the same game as Windsor'. Mrs Windsor had stayed with the Penselers after leaving Kuantan. Major Rose agreed to look into the matter.

Later that same night a HQ liaison officer reported that a launch, believed to be the *Hungjao*, had arrived off Kuantan, and that Lt Windsor, RNVR, who went off to pilot her in, had been arrested the minute he stepped aboard. The launch then put to sea with Windsor detained on board. The liaison officer also reported that Windsor's launch, the *Kelana*, was still at Kuantan and put forward the suggestion that the Navy take her over and man her completely. Another staff officer reported that Windsor was engaged in fifth-column work for the Japanese.

In his book *Face the Music*, Vice-Admiral Sir John Hayes recounts the recollections of a former Malayan customs officer.[13]

'The whole basis of my hypothesis is conjecture but in my view fierce conjecture,' the customs officer says. 'I am very happy that you should use it for I feel it should be projected. Thirty miles upstream on the Endau river was a Japanese-owned bauxite mine. The ore was loaded onto barges (possibly including those sighted by Force Z) once every ten days before being transferred to a Japanese freighter. To assist me in my inspection, there were patrol boats, some armed and some not, commanded by Reserve officers and equipped for coded communication with the Naval base on the Johore Strait. Among these [was] the *Hungjao* under Lieutenant Bill Mellor, RNZVR (a great guy).

'Then there was the *Klana* [sic]. This was a smallish trading vessel owned by a jelutong planter, Windsor, at Kuantan. He had been there since the mid-thirties and traded jelutong up and down the coast ... By early 1939, he had got himself commissioned in the RNVR ... So his boat became a patrol vessel of which we were very short. He was thus allowed code books. I met him often on patrol, a strange fellow: short, fair-haired, pale blue hard eyes, taciturn, almost secretive in a way. He spoke fluent Malay and dominated his Malay crew.

'December 8th 1941. The Japs landed at Kota Bharu. I am

at Mersing/Endau now openly an Intelligence Officer on staff of 22nd Australian Brigade.

'Morning December 10th. Force Z closes the coast to offshore Kuantan and to disaster. Where is *Klana*?

'Night of December 11th. I am at Endau wharf. In comes Bill Mellor with his *Hungjao*. We had a drink as the rain teemed and the wind blew. "Michael," he said, "you'll never guess where we are going. Up to Kuantan. I've orders to arrest Windsor."

'"Bloody . . . why?"

'"The bastard's been shooting off his three-pounder. There is no bloody landing at Kuantan and you know about Force Z. I have to take him back to naval HQ for interrogation."

'Some time in 1943, Bill Mellor and I fetched up in the same Japanese PoW camp. I asked him what had happened to Windsor.

'"He was cleared," said Bill. "Got away to Colombo, South Africa, I don't know."

'But by 1946, Windsor was back in Kuantan, trading jelutong once more up and down the coast where I again met him on my station. I never asked him about December 10th 1941. Maybe I should have; but sleeping dogs are at times best left asleep. You see, Windsor was a naturalised German. His original name I think was Mueller. So what is the truth? We shall never know. Your guess is as good as mine.'

The implications of the customs officer's account are clear and appear to reflect accurately the beliefs of those who sent Mellor to arrest Windsor. One: that he was a naturalised German, and therefore a prime suspect as an enemy agent. Two: that since he was in possession of naval code books, he was in a position to know where Force Z was and what it was doing. And three: that he had deliberately fired off the *Kelana*'s gun, thereby sparking off the reports of Japanese landings, in a deliberate attempt to lure Force Z into a position where it would be vulnerable to Japanese attack.

None of these holds water. The first is clearly based on prejudice alone. Windsor was not a naturalised German, but a Briton of fairly distant Prussian ancestry who, like many other Britons, including the Royal Family whose name he now shared, had changed their names when Britain went to war with Germany in 1914.

The second is also a nonsense. Even if Windsor had been involved in anything subversive, the code books would have been no help to him at all in locating Force Z. Even Admiral Palliser, the Chief of Staff in Singapore, had no idea where Force Z was because of the radio silence maintained by Admiral Phillips, so Windsor certainly could not have known.

Nor is the third suggestion any more plausible. It is of course possible that the *Kelana* did take part in the shelling reported by the coastal defences early on that night of the 9th/10th December. Presumably, as the Navy appears to have been certain that she did so, she was logged as being in the area and some of her three-pounder shells must have been used up. But since Windsor could not have known where Force Z was, it is difficult to see how this might have been part of some attempted diversion. The *Kelana* was after all a legitimate patrol boat and if she spotted something suspicious would have been justified in taking some form of offensive action.

Even the goldminer, Penseler, who was allegedly 'in the same game as Windsor' appears to have been innocent. He was Dr Wulfram Penseler, General Manager of the Australian Gold Mining Company at Raub, an Australian citizen who died in Changi jail during the occupation. He was among the more than forty inmates of Changi who died as a result of torture, beatings and deprivation by the *Kempetai*, the Japanese secret police, in retaliation for 'Operation Jaywick', a British/Australian raid in which thousands of tons of Japanese shipping were blown up in Singapore harbour. In April 1944 Penseler was among a group of prisoners taken to Singapore for further interrogation by the *Kempetai*. He was returned to Changi on 24th October 'in poor condition' and died nine days later. It was hardly the way the Japanese would have treated one of their agents, or indeed, a German agent.

Furthermore, Windsor's 'unauthorised' trip to Raub on the

16th December which raised further suspicions against him, could have been quite innocent. Maybe he decided to get his wife Edna away to a safer place, and so took her to Penseler who was both a friend and a business acquaintance. Windsor had shares in Penseler's mine which before the war paid excellent dividends.

Whatever did happen that night off Kuantan, Windsor was certainly not responsible for sending the original signal informing Singapore that landings were taking place and, if he did fire off his gun, he was not alone. The shore defences opened up, and the RAF Vildebeestes fired their torpedoes at something. But at what? And why?

There is of course always the possibility that the initial report was based on nothing more than the nerves of trigger-happy Indian Army sentries posted along the beach. The 'shelling' of their positions could have been stray animals, or even the tide, setting off mines. The war diary of HQ 22nd Brigade reported only a week later that high tides had exploded shrapnel mines along the sea shore.

But the most likely explanations are suggested by the recorded comments of the two senior Army officers most involved.

Brigadier G. W. A. Painter, the Commanding Officer of 22nd Brigade based in the Kuantan area, reported to III Corps at 1630 on Wednesday 10th December, only a few hours after the Japanese attack on Force Z, that he was 'not satisfied as to the accuracy of certain front-line reports received last night of enemy landings. Unidentified craft were undoubtedly seen off the beaches but he was doubtful whether a landing did in fact take place,' records the Brigade's war diary.[14]

Perhaps Painter's 'unidentified craft' were merely Malay fishing boats breaking the curfew. Maybe they were the tug and barges spotted early on Wednesday 10th December by Force Z, and looked over so cursorily. There was a major Japanese mine at Endau, a port one hundred miles to the south of Kuantan, where Japanese ships were loaded with the aid of tugs and barges. With Operations 'Collar' and 'Trousers', the rounding up of all Japanese nationals in Malaya, in full swing, the tug and barges spotted by Force Z were probably fleeing from the Japanese mine at Endau and proceeding north to get closer to their advancing army.

The barges could have formed the basis for 22nd Brigade's reports of boats approaching the coast. They would also fit the 'rectangular' description of the craft attacked by the RAF Vildebeestes. If the fire from the shore, the attacks of the Vildebeestes and, if she did indeed take part in the shelling, fire from the *Kelana*, were to some effect, then maybe some of those aboard the tug and barges took to whatever small boats they had and made for the shore, leaving enough men on board to work the tug. This may explain the discovery, four days later, on the beaches south of Kuantan, of several small boats, riddled with bullets and containing Japanese weapons and equipment. It is known that many of the Japanese 'civilians' in Malaya were in fact military people. Force Z's 'inspection' of the tug and barges was made at a distance, so even if they had been damaged by shell fire the previous night, the damage would not have been noted by the British ships.

General Heath, on the other hand, remained convinced that some form of attempted landing, 'a reconnaissance that failed', had taken place.[15] He cited the discovery of the bullet-riddled boats with their Japanese weapons and equipment as evidence. There was some justification for his view. Based on the prevailing winds and currents at that time, local Malay fishermen believed they had probably drifted south after having been abandoned near the mouth of the Sungei Balok river, precisely the area where the landings were reported to have taken place.

But if Heath was right, who was landing and where did they go? The answer may lie with eleven armed Japanese men dressed in civilian clothes arrested two days later, on Friday 12th December, by a patrol from the Kuantan based 2/18th Royal Garhwal Rifles. 'These men were in a military area carrying arms and could have been shot on sight,' the III Corps report of the incident stated. The prisoners were taken to Kuala Lumpur for interrogation by the Criminal Intelligence Bureau and military intelligence. 'After interrogation, Corps request disposal orders,' the report continued ominously. 'Corps do NOT want to hand these men over to the civil authorities for civil trial.'

That same day, HQ 22nd Brigade reported that 'armed Japanese civilians taking over civil administration down coast Trengganu including Dungun'.[16] Before the war, there were about 1,000 Japanese living in Dungun, a small port some sixty miles north of Kuantan. Most of them worked for yet another Japanese mining company based at Bukit Besi, a few miles inland and connected to Dungun by a private railway which brought the iron ore down to the port. Many of these Japanese had left just prior to the war but some seventy remained behind. They were detained when Operation 'Trousers' was implemented early on the morning of 8th December, but were almost immediately released by a pro-Japanese Malay police officer. 'Returning to the area, [they] caused us considerable trouble,' the war diary of the 5/11th Sikhs reported. Unfortunately no further details were given.[17]

The eleven armed Japanese arrested by the Garhwalis could have been among those released by the Malay policeman or they could have come ashore in those bullet-riddled boats, possibly from the tug and barges that may have come under fire from the British defences at Kuantan, or possibly as part of a special forces operation aimed at sowing insurgency. General Heath's views certainly provide a better match to the sequence of reports logged by HQ Singapore's war diary, which had a number of small boats approaching the shore late on Tuesday 9th December, some hours before the Vildebeestes attacked the barges.[18]

Whatever happened, there appears to have been a determined attempt to make Windsor take the blame and he was far from happy to do so. After the war, he approached Guy Madoc, a very senior and highly respected officer in the Malayan Police Service whom he had known since before the war and asked him if he would mount an investigation to clear his name. 'Windsor asked me to investigate him and I consented to do so,' says Madoc, who at the time was Deputy Director of the Malayan Security Service.

Windsor told Madoc that 'the admiral at Singapore had protested in very strong terms and that he was released at once'. However, this claim was no longer directly verifiable. The admiral in charge of Malayan coastal defences, including *Kelana*, was Rear Admiral Spooner who died in an attempt to flee Singapore in February 1942. Commander Frampton, who sent the *Hungjao* to arrest Windsor, died in the same escape attempt, so his account could not be checked either.

There were also contradictions between Windsor's account and that logged by the Royal Navy. Windsor told Madoc that he had been arrested by Basil O'Connel, the policeman who compiled the file on him, and not by a naval officer. He also said the arrest occurred at Endau, not at Kuantan. And although there is evidence that the Royal Navy was still using the *Kelana* in January 1942, Windsor said it was moved to a more open anchorage where it was sunk by Japanese aircraft.

Most of these apparent contradictions can be sorted out. The officer behind the arrest, although not present at it, was indeed Basil O'Connel, and Madoc was able to verify that Admiral Spooner had threatened A. H. Dickinson, Inspector-General of the Straits Settlements Police, that he would have O'Connel arrested by the military unless he laid off Windsor. The *Kelana* was at some stage sunk by the Japanese, only to be salvaged later by them and used as a patrol boat, the *Sukei No. 22*. Lastly, Madoc was able to retrieve part of a file on Windsor (which had escaped wartime destruction) and he came to the conclusion that the allegations in it which had been used to justify Windsor's arrest did not stand up to close scrutiny. Indeed, some details in the file were petty and ludicrous.

But the customs officer who wrote to Admiral Hayes remains convinced that Windsor was involved in the Kuantan incident. 'After the war, I was stationed at Raub, Pahang, when one day Windsor breezed into my office. I refused to shake hands with him, don't ask me why. I just couldn't. He was an odd bod with an odd crew. I can prove nothing but I have no doubt in

my own mind that he and his *Klana* [sic] did create the disturb-
ance at Kuantan on 9th December 1941 which brought the
Prince of Wales and the *Repulse* too close in and you know the
result. I have no doubt that Windsor was a Jap sympathiser,
nay more than that. He must have hoodwinked the boys at the
Naval Base.'[19]

Guy Madoc meanwhile is equally adamant that Windsor was
not guilty. 'There was nothing in O'Connel's report to prove
that Windsor was a traitor,' he says. Despite having seen the
reports that have come to light since he first investigated the
case in 1946, including the customs officer's testimony, he has
not changed his mind. 'I am sure Windsor was innocent,' he
maintains.[20]

Wading in to support Guy Madoc's stand is Dato H. F. Biles,
a longtime and well-respected resident in Malaya. ('Dato' is an
honorific conferred by a Malay sultan.) He met Windsor after
the war, and learned a great deal about the affair from Windsor
and others. Dato Biles says that Windsor 'was a man of strong
principles, disliked inefficiency and corruption and was critical
of some government servants (European). Many of their wives
were jealous of him as he was a financial success while their
husbands had to live on moderate salaries.'

But if the available evidence points away from Windsor, it is
still far from clear what precisely happened at Kuantan.

The effects of the report of the false landing had such terrible
consequences for the British war effort that a deliberate cover-
up cannot be ruled out. Force Z was very much Churchill's
baby, his own plan to save Singapore taken against the advice
of the Sea Lords and even of Admiral Phillips, who had been
Vice-Chief of the Naval Staff in London when the matter was
first raised. Senior commanders would have been anxious to
mollify Churchill's anger by producing someone who could be
blamed for the loss of Force Z, and Windsor, with a 'damning'
report hanging over him as a suspected German sympathiser,
would have made a perfect scapegoat.

There is one further mystery. The unit stationed on those
beaches north of Kuantan, the unit which gave the false report,

if that is what it was, was the 2/18th Royal Garhwal Rifles. It is understandable, in the debacle that was the Malayan campaign, that the war diaries of units serving in that war – documents that are required to be kept by Army Regulations – end well before the fall of Singapore, in December 1941 and January 1942 mostly. The Royal Garhwalis war diary is unique in that it fails to cover the Malayan campaign at all, for it ends in October 1941. This prevents any examination of the regiment's own record of the affair and increases the impression that what really occurred was the subject of a cover-up.

If the Windsor affair was the result of a cover-up, it was not the only one. Many of the true facts of the fall of Singapore have been kept hidden, partly by the lack of an official inquiry, partly by the loss of files during the chaos of the city's last days, and partly by the obsessive secrecy of successive British governments.

But perhaps the most crucial of the Singapore secrets was the existence of the man who helped rip the heart out of the Allied air defences in the very first days of the war and left the British, Indian and Australian troops with little option but to retreat.

CHAPTER 4

HUMBLE ORIGINS

The spy who was to play such an instrumental part in that Japanese victory was born on Friday 29th July 1910, in the middle of a southern winter, in a small New Zealand mining town called Reefton. His name was registered simply as Patrick Vaughan Stanley, the last being his mother's surname. There was no mention of his father at all. For Patrick was born illegitimate, a bastard in the true sense of the word, and while this might have been unremarkable in a frontier mining town like Reefton, in later life it was to be a damaging stigma that he would go to great lengths to cover up.

His mother, who called herself Annie on Patrick's birth certificate, was born Ann Stanley on 8th December 1882 at Stratford, Taranaki, on New Zealand's North Island. Her parents were both from England. Robert Stanley, an ironmoulder from Liverpool and Ellen Stanley, née Hunt, originally from Nottingham, had emigrated to New Zealand shortly after marrying at Oldham on 7th October 1877. What took the twenty-eight-year-old Annie Stanley to Reefton, we can only guess. Perhaps she had found work in one of the settlement's lodging houses or bars. Perhaps she was looking for a husband from among the itinerant male workers who frequented the town.

Reefton lay at the foot of hills to the west of the northern end of the Southern Alps, a chain of mountains which runs like an offset spine down the length of the South Island. It was protected from the north by the Lyell mountain range. The town was a rough, dreary and unkempt place – what the Americans might call a one-horse town. Apart from being a small rail terminus – the railway's main purpose being to transport coal to the port of Greymouth on the coast – it had only one claim to fame. In 1888 it became the first settlement in the southern hemisphere to have a hydro-electric plant.

Except for the rail link with Greymouth, a journey of forty-six miles that took a full three hours, Reefton was an extremely difficult place to get into and out of. It was serviced by stage-coaches drawn by five-horse teams and run by firms with names like Newmans, and Cobb & Company. The roads leading to the town through the surrounding mountains had been metalled but not rolled and were very narrow in places. Some sections were notoriously dangerous in bad weather, especially those stretches high up in the mountains where visibility was often impaired by low level cloud and mist. The roads into Reefton twisted and turned, clinging to the mountainside as they fol-lowed the paths of the gorges and rivers that had carved their way through the mountains. Passengers on the stagecoaches frequently found themselves forced to walk over particularly difficult stretches of road in order to spare the horses.

Streams were crossed by either rickety bridges or rocky fords; wider rivers by ferries which were simply punt-rafts guided by overhead cables. Around the time of Patrick's birth, the rivers would have been relatively quiet. But in the spring, when the ice and snow began to melt, they would turn into raging tor-rents, making travelling even more difficult.

The boom time for Reefton had been back in the 1870s when the prospectors who flooded there looking for gold had dubbed it Quartzopolis after the gold-bearing quartz conglomerate beds, or reefs, that had been found in the area. There were also large deposits of coal – to this day mining remains an important industry in Reefton. The town is home to the New Zealand School of Mining and a mining museum.

But in 1910, the year Patrick was born, Reefton was much the same as it had been in those early days. It still looked like a typical Wild West frontier town, made up of wooden shacks and lodging houses straddling the main street. There was a handful of stores, a coach way-station, a blacksmith's shop and a coal and timber depot. For entertainment there were a few hotels, disreputable places catering for the needs of the thirsty miners who came into the town for the night looking for alcohol and their share of the limited female company available. Reefton, as one tourist made clear when hurriedly recording her impressions of the town, was no place for a lady.

'Reefton is prettily situated at the foot of densely wooded hills, but being only a little mining town planned strictly for use and not for ornament, it has nothing to recommend it to the artistic eye,' wrote Alys Lowth in *Emerald Hours in New Zealand*. 'When we arrived there, by horse-drawn coach, at four o'clock, we drove straight through to the railway station, where we caught a Greymouth train.'[1]

By 1910 the more easily accessible gold around Reefton had been mainly worked out, but the area still played host to the many men who had come there over the years to seek their fortunes. Most now worked the coal and, as in the other mining areas of New Zealand, a significant proportion of these were of Irish extraction and ardent supporters of the Republican cause.[2]

They included one George Charles John Heenan. He was born on 13th September 1855 in the northern Indian city of Bhagalpur, the son of an Irish civil engineer named Robert Heenan and his wife Kate Mary. George Heenan attended Cheltenham College from 1869 to 1871 when his records show an address for an uncle, apparently his guardian, in Mullingar in County Westmeath, in the middle of Ireland.

At some point, George Heenan and Annie Stanley met up, and eventually they travelled to Burma as man and wife. It is not clear whether George Heenan was the young Patrick's natural father. But apart from the absence of his name on the birth certificate, there is another curious piece of evidence which suggests he was not. Patrick, now with the surname Heenan, was baptised at the St John Catholic Military Church in Rangoon on 21st April 1912 when he was twenty-one months old. On the baptism certificate, George Heenan dropped the name John, substituting it with Vaughan, the second name given to Patrick by his mother, to become George Charles Vaughan Heenan. It was a strange thing to do; possibly it was a device to make it look as if Patrick was his son.

It appears to have been the only gesture George Heenan made in this direction, since there is no record of him having married

Annie Stanley either in New Zealand or in Burma. She was certainly still single, but he may have been already married and, as a Catholic, unable to divorce. Whatever the circumstances, the young Patrick had acquired an Irish name and perhaps with it a loyalty to Irish traditions.[3]

But another factor, one that was to prove far more important to the young man, was the colour of his skin. Several of his contemporaries are on record as saying that his skin was slightly dark. This may have been just the result of a childhood spent in Burma. It may have come from his real father, if that was not George Heenan. Indeed, if George was his natural father, he himself had been born and brought up in India and might well have had some trace of native blood in his veins, a common occurrence at the time and one that most of the people concerned attempted to disguise.

The baptism certificate also recorded that the order of the young Patrick's names had changed. Possibly to match the order of Heenan senior's names, he had become Patrick Stanley Vaughan Heenan.

George Heenan gave his profession on the baptism certificate as 'mining expert'. This matches up with the Old Cheltonian records, which have him listed as a 'geologist' but that is an ambiguous description and seems designed to make his job sound more impressive than it actually was. He certainly had no university education during which to study geology and there is other evidence to suggest that his job in Burma was of fairly low status.

He did not appear in either of the two annual almanacs listing Europeans working in Burma at the time.[4] This was something of a status symbol and omission would have been an indication of being in a relatively unimportant job, although it is possible he had not been in Burma for long enough. Another piece of evidence which gives a clue to George Heenan's status comes from Patrick Heenan's baptism certificate, which lists a Millie Gomez as his godmother. The name suggests she might have been Eurasian. Such were the mores of the time that any Briton of standing would have used Europeans as stand-in godparents.

Within six months of the baptism ceremony, tragedy struck the Heenan family. George died on 24th October 1912 in Pauk, a small town with a population of around 2,000, which was situated at the junction of the Kyaw and Yaw rivers some forty miles west of the main district town of Pakakku in Upper Burma. Why the Heenans were in Pauk is not clear, but the town had sandstone and laterite quarries and there were also oil wells nearby as well as some poor-quality jade mines.[5] There is no record of how George died, but by 1912 he was fifty-seven years old, an age when most Europeans in British India would have long since gone home to retire.

What then did a thirty-year-old woman, with a young son to support, do if she found herself 'widowed' in a remote corner of the British Empire in the early part of the twentieth century? Annie Heenan, as one would expect of someone who had lived in a frontier mining town like Reefton, appears to have been a tough character. Certainly she survived, staying in Burma until young Patrick Heenan was twelve years old. Possibly she worked as a governess or nanny for other people's children. There would have been very few other avenues open to a woman in her circumstances. It is impossible to be certain what she did to keep herself and her young son fed and clothed, but at some point between George Heenan's death and her departure with Patrick for England, she met a young man called Bernard Carroll.

Carroll was a junior accountant with a firm called Mower, Cotterall & Co. and, unlike George Heenan, was important enough to appear in the almanacs of European residents. He was only twenty-two when he married a Lena Simpson, eight years his senior, on 9th November 1911, at the same St John Catholic Military church where Patrick was baptised eight months later. Carroll soon got a better job with the British Burma Petroleum Company and the couple had two children, a boy and a girl, both of whom were baptised at the same small garrison Catholic church.

It may be that Annie Heenan became governess to the Carroll children, or possibly to a family who knew the Carrolls.

Whatever the link, it was clearly close. By 1927, when Lena Carroll died, both the Heenans and the Carrolls were living in England and two years later, in April 1929, in south London, Annie Heenan and Bernard Carroll were married.

The period of Patrick's boyhood in Burma remains something of a mystery. In all probability he was educated at a mission school and the majority of these, particularly in places like Burma, were not noted for their academic excellence. They were often small, sometimes with only one teacher, and standards were generally low. Certainly, on returning to England, he struggled to keep up with his classmates, creating an early feeling that somehow he did not fit in.

If young Patrick was at all influenced by the anti-British sentiments of the father he barely knew, then the Burma in which he was brought up would have done nothing to change them. British exploitation of the Burmese was already leading to the formation of a sizeable nationalist movement. The British considered the country to be part of India. The Burmese, not unnaturally, disagreed. They not only disliked the way the British exploited them commercially, they hated their racialist attitudes.

Burma had become economically prosperous. She was the world's leading rice exporter and also sold substantial amounts of oil, hardwood, cotton, pulses, sugar cane and jute. Rising world commodity prices for rice, oil and timber had created a balance of trade ostensibly in favour of Burma, but the Burmese themselves saw little of this new-found wealth. As far as they were concerned, it was an imaginary benefit, for control over most businesses lay in the hands of the non-Burmese.

The oil and timber industries were each virtually monopolised by one British company – in the case of oil, this was the British Burma Petroleum Company, for which Bernard Carroll worked. The rice market was controlled by a handful of British firms who kept the price paid to native rice producers artificially low. The mining industry was also dominated by British firms, the largest being Burma Mines Ltd with interests in lead, silver, zinc and copper.

The major utilities were also in the hands of British companies. The railways were British, but more importantly, so was the Irrawaddy Flotilla & Burmese Steam Navigation Company which owned the vast river fleet that serviced the backbone of the country's transport system, the Irrawaddy river. The Irrawaddy was navigable for nine hundred miles into the interior in all seasons, and a further one hundred miles in the dry season when there were no rapids. The other main river, the Chindwin, was navigable for four hundred miles above its confluence with the Irrawaddy and was also serviced by the Irrawaddy Flotilla. The company, set up in 1865, must have been a double affront to any Burmese with nationalist views. Firstly, it had been created on the basis of a contract to carry British troops along the river during the Anglo–Burmese war of that year. Secondly, its shallow-draft steamers towed strings of cargo-carrying flats and barges behind them, driving out of business many of the native boatmen who had plied their trade up and down the rivers since time immemorial.

But perhaps the worst aspect of the economic exploitation of Burma was the lack of control over foreign exchange remittances. There were no records of any sort and the Burmese, used for centuries to bartering for goods, were unable to prevent British, Indian and Chinese firms and businessmen taking as much money out of the country as they liked. The country had acquired great wealth, but the Burmese themselves saw little if anything of it. In the words of one commentator, 'the Burmese found themselves, instead of being a poor people in a poor country, a poor people in a rich one, which is a very different thing'.[6]

But if the commercial exploitation of the Burmese were not enough, the British treated the Burmese in a crudely racialist fashion. George Orwell, who under his real name of Eric Blair served with the Indian Imperial Police in Burma between 1921 and 1927, resigned from his post in protest at such bigotry, going on to base his first novel *Burmese Days* on the indignation that had grown in him there, an indignation perhaps best illustrated by a quotation from his book: 'After all, natives were natives – interesting, no doubt, but finally only a subject people, an inferior people with black faces.'[7]

Hemmed in by the mountains on three sides and by the ocean on the fourth, the Burmese had always been a relatively insular people. Despite many Indian influences and a close affinity with other adjacent cultures of South-east Asia, their culture had remained distinctive. When Buddhism arrived there in the eleventh century, it had been embraced wholeheartedly, but in a way that had blended it in harmoniously with the existing folk culture. The Buddhist doctrine of social equality had no difficulty in subsisting alongside the existing Burmese tradition that men and women were born equal. But this tradition was shattered by the British who, having made the country a province of India on 1st January 1886, began importing Indians into most of the government posts not filled by Britons and treating the Burmese as third-class citizens behind the 'second-class' Indians.

This was too much to bear for many Burmese who had long been prejudiced against Indians because of the Hindu caste system and resented the support given by Indian troops to the British during the three Anglo–Burmese wars of the nineteenth century. The British appeared to do their best to alienate the Burmese in a number of other ways. They undermined the local system of Buddhist schools by encouraging the establishment of mission schools and by creating a number of government schools. These schools provided no training in science and as a consequence the Burmese found many professions closed to them. Those Burmese who did manage to advance themselves usually entered the Civil Service in relatively junior positions with little hope of advancement.

A few outstanding Burmese managed to go to Britain to study law. On their return to their native land, they came to be looked upon as natural leaders by the Burmese people. In 1906, a group of these British trained lawyers formed the Young Men's Buddhist Association which, although not initially an anti-British organisation, was later to become a breeding ground for such sentiments.

Burmese nationalism began to grow in parallel with the older but similar movement in India, but when, in 1920, Burma was excluded from the political reforms introduced in the sub-continent to pacify the Indian National Congress, it began to take on a momentum of its own.

British professors were put in charge of Rangoon College in 1921. This was the final straw for the Burmese. Students at the college went on strike with the backing of the now openly dissident YMBA. Schoolchildren all over the country joined in and the strike received widespread support from among the Buddhist clergy and the general public, who staged a boycott of British goods. The groundswell of opinion against Britain grew rapidly, culminating in the formation in 1923 of the nationalist *Thakin* movement which began striking for independence.

This, then, was the Burma in which Patrick Heenan grew up. How much he identified with the general disenchantment with the British felt by many of the Burmese is impossible to tell. But the evidence of his later life suggests that he had a deep hatred of racism and it seems likely that he acquired this in Burma. For, in all probability, Patrick's own complexion, and his dead father's lowly position in society, led both him and his mother to being treated as second-class citizens. In his resentment at this, any Irish republican sympathies he may have inherited from his father, the stigma of his illegitimacy, and the lack of a formal education all gave Patrick problems of 'fitting in' when he arrived in England. Both at school and later in his army career, he was to remain very much the 'odd man out'.

CHAPTER 5

'WE HAVE NOT SECURED A SCHOLAR'

The young Patrick Heenan and his mother left Burma and moved to England some time in either 1922 or 1923. It is not clear why Annie Heenan decided to come to England. Perhaps she followed the Carroll family as their governess or house-keeper. Perhaps it was Bernard Carroll she was following. Whatever the reason, she would not have found things easy.

Britain in the early 1920s was not a good place to be a widow with a young son, or for that matter anything else. The country would never again regain the pre-eminent international trading position of the years before the 1914–18 War. The immediate post-war boom designed to make Britain 'a fit country for heroes to live in', had come and gone, leaving behind it a nation in which inflation was widespread and where strikes had become endemic. The slump which had begun in 1921 caused unemployment to rise so high that right through until the eve of World War Two, unemployment was to be the fate of one in seven Britons.

The old structures of society were breaking down, altered forever by 'the war that was to end all wars'. This manifested itself in a number of different ways. After Lloyd George resigned as prime minister in 1922, Britain had three changes of government inside three years. And it was not only governments that were changing. So too, was just about everything else, or so it seemed to the man in the street.

As anyone who has gone through the experience will recall, when someone returns to Britain after years spent in the colonies there are problems in making adjustments to their lifestyle. In the troubled times of the 1920s these problems of adaptation would have been magnified. This would have been particularly true in Annie Heenan's case for, on top of everything else, she was arriving in a strange country. Her parents had been born in Britain, but she had spent the whole of her life, prior to going to Burma, in New Zealand, the country of her birth. Neither she nor Patrick had ever visited Britain before.

Her financial position at the time is unclear, as is her employment. Maybe the Carrolls, now living off the Balham High Road in south London, helped her. The three addresses Annie is known to have stayed at – two in the Earl's Court area of London, at Courtfield Gardens and Marloes Road, and the third at Sunbury-on-Thames – were all boarding houses, and she never stayed at any of them long enough to appear in any electoral roll. It must have been an unsettled and unsettling time for both the forty-year-old woman and her son.

Whatever her circumstances, Annie Heenan was set on giving him a public school education and was somehow able to fund it. Perhaps she obtained help in this from Bernard Carroll, but wherever the funds came from, Patrick Heenan entered Sevenoaks School as a fee-paying boarder in 1923.

Why Annie Heenan chose to send her son to this particular school is not known. It was certainly not because he was expected to make his career in the army, for Sevenoaks, unlike some other public schools, had no great military tradition. Nevertheless Sevenoaks had a good reputation and was certainly not a bad choice. It lies in attractive grounds bordering Knole Park. It was established in 1418 by Sir William Sevenoke, a former foundling who had risen to be Lord Mayor of London. (He held that office immediately prior to Richard 'Dick' Whittington's third term.) Sir William endowed a Grammar School, to 'teach and instruct poor children . . . taking nothing of them or their parents and friends for the teaching . . . them'. In 1560, Queen Elizabeth issued Letters of Patent which provided a new constitution for the school, and granted it the use of her name. This title was later discarded as the school developed into one of the most respected, if one of the less famous, of Britain's public schools.

One local legend surrounding the school has survived. It is commonly believed in the town that when the rebel Jack Cade accused Lord Say in William Shakespeare's *King Henry VI*,

Part II, with the words, 'Thou hast most traitorously corrupted the youth of the realm by erecting a grammar school', he was referring to Sevenoaks.

Whatever schools Patrick had attended in Burma, the indications are that the standard of tuition there had not been particularly high. As a result, throughout his schooling in England he was to struggle to keep up with other boys academically. After he joined School House at Sevenoaks at the age of thirteen, his only recorded academic success was the winning of a prize for history in his second year. History seemed to be the only subject for which he had any aptitude.

During his first year he took a female part in a Chekhov play. Most schoolboys do not relish such quirks of casting, and as Patrick was described in a school report as 'growing fast', it seems likely that he would not have liked it.[1] One old Sennockian recalls Patrick as being a bit of a loner and says, 'He looked half foreign, but I didn't know him well for I was a Day-boy and he was School House.'

Although he did not excel at academic studies, Patrick was a fine natural athlete. Perhaps his very lack of academic brilliance drove him on to success in sport, at a school where sport played an important part in the overall activities. Patrick's sporting achievements were highly valued and carefully documented in the school records.

During his first year, he won a novice's swimming prize. The next year, he won the Junior three-lengths race and second place in diving. But these results in the swimming-pool were to pale to insignificance alongside his other sporting successes. He was awarded his house colours after the 1925 school cross-country, which School House won, and commended for his running in that race. The same year saw the first success of many in the boxing ring, when he won the under-ten-stone competition. He also did well in athletics, winning the under-fifteens' 220 yards and coming second in the 880 yards.

But he really came into his own the next year. He did well at rugby, playing first for the school 2nd XV and then for the 1st XV. He was growing into a well-built young man and was something of a utility player, and perhaps something of a rough one, for he was described in the school records as 'a thrusting forward who must be careful – somewhat headstrong, growing quickly'. But boxing was to be his main sport and that year he won the school's 'Class I' boxing championship and was the mainstay of the school team, scoring the school's only victory in the match against the City of London School. 'HEENAN BEAT MUMFORD (CLS)', announced the school magazine. Patrick's strength appears to have brought an early end to the fight, for the magazine's report ends with the words, 'the referee interfered'.

Patrick ran for the school cross-country team that year and, in the athletics championships, won both the under-sixteens' 880-yard and 440-yard races as well as proving his sporting versatility by coming second in the High Jump.

In the British public school system, academically backward students are often given positions of responsibility in an attempt to bolster their confidence. So it was at Sevenoaks. The school put Patrick on its library committee, and in 1926 he was on both the boxing and swimming committees as school captain in both sports.

There is some mystery about why Patrick left Sevenoaks in 1926, at the age of nearly sixteen. A present member of the school staff suggested that he may have been expelled, though there is now no evidence of this in the school files. But perhaps the more likely explanation is that Annie Heenan, having read reports of Patrick's lack of academic success, decided he needed some personal tutoring. So, she sent him away for some cramming, first to G. Hewlett at Portishead near Bristol, and then to W. R. Heaton of Downs Farm, Barham, near Canterbury. This tutoring lasted for almost a year, and then Annie sent Patrick to Cheltenham College.

When Patrick arrived there, in January 1927, he was already sixteen-and-a-half years old, over three years older than most new joiners. The fact that he was placed in Form 4B along with boys of thirteen and fourteen, indicates that his private tutors, Hewlett and Heaton, had not had much success with him. So why did Cheltenham accept a boy much older than the norm, and who was not at all academically bright?

There are two possible reasons. One is that most fee-charging schools at that time were experiencing 'recruitment' problems due to the drop in the number of thirteen-year-olds caused by the effects of the 1914 War on the national birthrate. The second, and possibly more important reason, was that George Heenan had been an Old Cheltonian. Both of these factors are likely to have influenced the headmaster, Henry Hardy, in taking the boy on. Perhaps Patrick's sporting achievements at Sevenoaks also played a role.

Cheltenham College is a much younger school than Sevenoaks.² Its present main buildings stand impressively on the eastern side of the Bath Road, not far from the town centre. This very proximity to the town has been the cause of a few problems over the years. The school has periodically published lists of 'forbidden premises' in the school magazine, banning boys from visiting grocers and other shops which were licensed to sell alcoholic beverages. There were also the potential distractions of the local girls. Indeed, it is here that the first signs of Patrick's interest in women – an interest that was to be much in evidence in later life – emerge.

The College, which began its existence in other premises, dates from 1841, and prides itself in being the most senior of the public schools created in the Victorian era. It also takes pride in the fact that, during the first years of its life, it played a leading part in liberalising the education of the period, by setting out to teach modern languages and science in addition to the classics and mathematics. But such liberal thinking scarcely extended to other matters. The original memorandum regarding shareholding in the school carefully defined the status of would-be shareholders. No person was eligible 'who should not be moving in the order of gentlemen'. Under no circumstances were retail traders to be considered, a rider that must have annoyed some of the upwardly mobile burghers of the home town itself.

The school had always had a large proportion of Irish boys

among its students. Many of these came from Irish families who had settled in Cheltenham, a town traditionally popular with the Irish, not least for its National Hunt racing traditions. (The Gold Cup race week still attracts many Irish visitors.) Indeed, so many Irishmen had taken up residence there that one local wit in the early part of this century penned the lines:

'The Churchyard's so small and the Irish so many,
They ought to be pickled and sent to Kilkenny.'

Boys also came to the school direct from homes in Ireland as boarders, especially after the railway steamer service from Holyhead to Dublin began in 1848. George Heenan was among these when he arrived in 1869 to join the College's Hazelwell House.

Later, the college became famous for its military emphasis, a factor which was to play a major part in Patrick's life. The school then became organised into three departments, the Classical and Modern, the Military, and the Juniors. It was usual for at least half the boys to be in the Military Department, where extra stress was placed on mathematics – 'Maths, maths, and yet more maths,' groaned one Military boy – and on chemistry. Boys in Military did not study Greek but they did learn to draw. (It was said that the only art taught in the college was the art of drawing military panoramas.)

Both the British and Indian Armies considered that the public school system produced the best officer material. At Cheltenham, boys were prepared for the Royal Military College, Sandhurst, and the Royal Military Academy, Woolwich, and it was considered a bad year when Cheltonians did not gain most of the top entrance places in both lists. The College's record in this respect has perhaps only been equalled by Wellington.

No less than 675 of the school's old boys died in World War One, and the then Principal, Dean Waterfield, took it upon himself to write to the parents of each of them.[3] Spread out over the four years of that war, this meant he was writing one such letter every two days. World War Two was to bring with it many more school casualties.

Over the years, Cheltonians have earned at least fifteen Victoria and George Crosses and an Albert Medal, in addition to many other honours for gallantry and distinguished service. Two old boys have risen to become Chiefs of the Imperial General Staff. One of these was perhaps the school's most distinguished soldier, Field Marshal Sir John Dill.[4]

For a school with such military traditions, it is perhaps surprising that dress in Patrick's day was very informal except for the black jackets and pin-striped trousers worn on Sundays and special occasions. Everyday wear at the school consisted of a tweed jacket of no prescribed pattern, and grey flannels of varying shades. In winter, pullovers in the fashionable and colourful range of Fair Isle patterns were worn. The only uniform item of dress was the mortar-board with a cherry-red tassel, and even these were not exactly the same, the velvet cap of the mortar-boards of sixth-formers and prefects being decorated with various insignia of status. (It was the custom to doff this headgear when entering the classroom and then nonchalantly spin it across the room, hopefully to land fair and square on the hat racks. This took a great deal of practice and a well-battered mortar-board was a prized possession – a sign of seniority.)

There was not even a standard strip for rugby. Players who had obtained their colours played in dark blue shorts with rows of mother-of-pearl buttons down the sides. The others wore white shorts. Not even the jerseys were uniform, each department having different stripes on a cerise background. When the College XV took to the field, it had 'somewhat the air of a scratch side'. This was considered an endearing eccentricity, except perhaps by the opposite side who must have found the buttons rather painful in the ruck. Perhaps Patrick put them to good use when he played for the 1st XV in his last year there, for when he later played for an Army XV he was noted for his dirty tricks in the pack.[5]

Henry Hardy, the Headmaster during Patrick Heenan's time, who was later to endorse Patrick's application for the Army, was a man of singular force of character. He had served in the Rifle Brigade during the war and been mentioned in despatches. An energetic man with an unyielding adherence to his principles, he insisted on rigorous standards of discipline and ensured that hours were long and liberties few. He leavened this slightly by his reputed close concern for each individual boy. It was said that he knew every Cheltonian by sight – or at least the boys believed he did. He was a keen sportsman, and took a great interest in the Officers' Training Corps (OTC) unit at the school. These two interests may have caused young Heenan to come to his attention from time to time, for Patrick was to maintain and improve on the sporting prowess he had shown at Sevenoaks and also joined the OTC, as did all boys on the Military side.

Many Old Cheltonians from Hardy's time do not look back on their schooldays as the happiest days of their lives. This seems to go beyond the normal love–hate relationship with their school which most ex-public schoolboys have. Discipline at Cheltenham was severe and the prefects reportedly used hunting whips to back up their authority. Junior boys were referred to as 'scum'.

It was not solely the strict discipline that made the college a depressing place. The classrooms were archaically fitted out – dim, dank and gloomy, and often windowless. A young schoolmaster who joined the staff a couple of years later said that it was as if those responsible for designing the college had planned a fine main building but had forgotten to provide classrooms or laboratories, and that these had to be fitted in afterwards in any old space that was available.

The food was nothing to write home about either, except perhaps in complaints to Mother. So boys who could afford to, made good use of the school's 'tuck shop'. This was presided over by an ex-army sergeant-major who had no truck with the normal public school system of seniority, and insisted on working on a 'first come, first served' basis. The queue must have been a rare haven of 'justice' for the smaller boys.

Patrick Heenan came to the school as a 'day boy' and would therefore have been somewhat looked down upon by those who boarded at the school. In British public schools, 'boarders' tend to envy day boys, who go home and escape from the school every night, while looking down on them because their parents pay lower fees. But Patrick did not go home every night. He was an 'East Day Boy', one of those who lodged in a private boarding house.[6] He did not have the compensation of a nightly visit 'home'. He was also a Roman Catholic. In a school with a policy of no religious discrimination, this should not have mattered, but school policy is one thing, the attitudes of boys to one who is in some way different to the norm quite another.

But the factor that sealed his fate as an 'odd one out' and made him so decidedly different from most of the other boys was his poor showing in the classroom. When he joined the school he had been placed in a class of boys two or three years younger than himself. 'I think we have not secured a scholar,' said the author of Patrick's first term report, leaving no doubt that the decision to place him in a low form was correct from an academic point of view. But as one contemporary who remembers Patrick well points out, 'It must have riled him.'

So Patrick, already a tall, well-built young man, found himself in a class of boys not only junior to him in years but considerably smaller than him in size. The situation appears to have affected him badly. Perhaps a boy of different character and better disposition confronted with similar circumstances might have managed to contend with the situation, but Patrick was not that boy. 'It was difficult to get him to smile,' says another contemporary. He is remembered as being 'unusual in looks and manners, graceless and a bore with a saturnine gloomy face'. He was 'a strange boy. Very good at sports but not much else.' He was 'a dunderhead'. And perhaps most tellingly of all, 'He did not fit in. His skin was sallow, his manner of speech was rather rough, and nobody liked him.'[7] This was to be the pattern of Patrick's life. He made few friends during it, and apparently none at school.

There is probably no cruelty so deeply cutting or so long remembered as that inflicted on an 'odd one' by a group of youngsters. At public schools with no parental control and

where self-reliance is the order of the day, this cruelty is accentu-
ated as groups of boys gang up on anyone in any way different.
From the physically slight to the overweight, from the 'wetbeds'
to the 'dunces', anyone who becomes a target is made to suffer,
and as a 'dunderhead' Patrick would have presented an obvious
target. Given his size and strength it is unlikely that he was on
the wrong end of any physical bullying. But there are other
ways, even more painful perhaps, of ganging up, and in view
of the report that he had no friends, it seems that the method
used in his case was to keep out of his way.[8]

Patrick joined the school's Officers' Training Corps in 1927.
Doing well in the OTC could help anyone with Army aspirations
and there was a special part of the Army application form set
aside for details of a boy's OTC career. At least three of Patrick's
contemporaries at Cheltenham, who were also in the OTC, were
to have splendid records in the Indian Army. A fourteen-year-
old 'exhibitioner', who was in Form 4B with Patrick, rose to
the rank of Lieutenant-Colonel in one of the Mountain Regiments of Artillery. Another, James Lawford, who joined the
college in the same year that Patrick left it, later served alongside
him in a regiment in India. Lawford won the Military Cross
and also rose to the rank of Lieutenant-Colonel. Colonel G.
Bartley-Dennis was also at school with Patrick. He served in
10 (Abbottabad) Mountain Battery and fought in the Malayan
campaign before being captured by the Japanese.

His experience in the OTC appears to have persuaded Patrick
that he should try for a military career. There was no mention
of any such ambition on his application form for the school.
Against the question, 'For what profession is he destined?', Annie
had rather optimistically written, 'To be decided later, possibly
he may go on to Oxford or Cambridge'.

Patrick attended OTC camp in each of his three years at the
school and was passed as 'efficient' in 1928 and 1929. In March
1928 he gained the 'Certificate A. Infantry', and in the same
year attended an army physical training course at Aldershot.
By the time he left the OTC he had risen to the rank of sergeant.
The officer commanding the unit, Major J. R. Holland, was

later to sign the certificate on Patrick's application form for a commission in the Supplementary Reserve stating that 'he was a fit and proper person to hold such an appointment'.[9]

The Head of Military when Patrick was at the school was John Mercer. He was an unusually humane master for the time, who had managed to introduce an element of freedom and a touch of culture into the rigorous curriculum laid down by his 'merciless' predecessor in the post, which some believed had come close to a regime of perpetual cramming.

Mercer would have written Patrick's reports in conjunction with the 'East Day Boys' housemaster, J. S. Bond, and he appears to have been extremely astute. It did not take him long to have Patrick's character and temperament summed up. The reports do not start out badly, although they naturally make note of his lack of academic prowess. 'Sound start', is the assessment in his first half-term report, followed by 'A really good boy with patchy knowledge'. At the end of his first term comes the remark noted earlier – 'I think we have not secured a scholar'. Nevertheless, he is still seen as having compensatory qualities, for the report continues, 'But a good straight fellow anyhow, and he is working well.' According to the report, he appears at the time to have been marked down for a career with the American Tobacco Company, which had connections with India and Burma. Perhaps he had a yearning to return to the East of his childhood, and only later decided that joining the Indian Army was his best hope of achieving this?

During Patrick's second term at the school, the report writer's assessment retains the initial positive flavour. 'Confirms good impression,' he writes, adding, 'making good obviously, old as he is for his place.' The only real criticism appears to be about his French which is described as 'poor'. He won the Navy League Prize that term, but there appear to be no records of what this was awarded for.

It was during Patrick's third term that the assessor begins to have his doubts about him. 'Old for his place, but doing well; I gladly accept his housemaster's generous estimate of him. Next term he must show that it is justified.' Clearly Mercer has spotted something that he feels Bond might have missed. Possibly there is a clue in a few words of Greek jotted down on the report – '*Parthenorastios enokos tupes*'.

Parthenorastios is a made-up word from *parthenos* meaning virgins and *rastios* – love. So, freely translated, the note says, 'Struck by his devotion to young girls.' Possibly, as one present Cheltenham College master has suggested, the writer of the report 'is being a little coy in his comment on a perfectly normal problem of growing up!'[10] But in Patrick's case it implied probably a bit more than that.

It is during this third term that Patrick wins the Tredhill History Prize. History is still the only academic subject for which he shows any aptitude, but the prize is only available to boys in his form and below, and he is at least two years older than other candidates.

The fourth term sees a decline in the previous standards and a first indication of a nastier side of his character. 'Quite satisfactory,' the half-term report states. But at the end of term comes a hint that Patrick had difficulty controlling his temperament. 'History, Boxing, Running have all shewn him in good light, very welcome. Let him master his moods and all will go well.'

As at Sevenoaks, Patrick is much better on the sports field, in the gym and in the swimming-pool, than he is in the classroom, and in his first year he comes second in a half-mile swimming race. His running is also well regarded but it is at boxing that he is most successful. He boxes at lightweight initially, winning his school boxing colours in 1928. His boxing instructor, Sergeant Dyer, must have been highly pleased when Patrick appeared on the scene. He is a boxing natural and Dyer trains him well.

In his fifth term Patrick fails his School Certificate Examination (the examination that was replaced in 1951 by the General Certificate of Education or GCE). He is to take it three times, failing on each occasion. At half-term, his work is described as being satisfactory, but with French and Mathematics lagging far behind. At the end of term Mercer appears to lean over backwards to give Patrick a good report: 'A great deal of good in him, with many activities, mental and physical. Let him only control his temperament and he will prove a fine fellow.' But no indication is given of how Patrick's lack of self-control is manifesting itself.

Patrick is seen as 'very active' in English, Football and Boxing, during his sixth term but with 'other matters unduly defective'. He is however congratulated on winning the school's Jex Blake Prize for 'below sixth', although he is now nearly seventeen and should on age already be a sixth-former. 'Now I wish he would earn one for mastering the waywardness that tends to spoil him,' bemoans Mercer. Patrick has by now been made 'Assistant Head' of his private boarding house, perhaps in the hope that the extra responsibility might do him good.

The reference to football refers to Patrick's selection for the school 1st XV at rugby. He has no great skill but he knows how to make his strength count – 'not a polished forward, but he went hard and saved well in defence'. It is yet again in the boxing ring that Patrick is at his best. The local newspaper, the *Gloucester Echo*, reporting on the school boxing finals held a fortnight before Christmas 1928, notes that 'the contests were good and fast. Heenan, in the welter class, and O'Dwyer, the heavy champion, both showed excellent skill. Heenan has improved on his fine form of last year.'

The detailed report of the match headlined 'P. S. V. Heenan (Day Boys) beat P. J. Rowe (Newick)' shows Patrick's determination to come out on top. 'This was a fast bout, with the competitors standing up to one another. Both hit hard to the body and head. Heenan handed out a lot of punishment, but with a big punch in the face, Rowe steadied him. After this, Heenan had the best of the fight, and with great spirit and style fought his man to a standstill. Heenan is a quick and clever boxer and was a very good winner.'

In his penultimate term, he again stars in the ring. Since 1925 there had been an annual boxing tournament between Cheltenham, Clifton, Downside and Malvern. On 5th March 1929, it is held at Downside and for the first time it is won outright by a visiting team. Cheltenham win by four clear points, winning flyweight, featherweight, light-heavyweight and heavyweight titles. Patrick, who has now moved up to the light-heavyweight division, takes the title for Cheltenham. According to the report, he 'won his fights against Milne of Downside and subsequently Richards of Clifton. He did not appear to be fully extended, though the first fight was the more even. Heenan has the makings of a good boxer, having good style.' It is perhaps a pity that it was not 'on' for gentlemen to take up the sport professionally, for it might have provided him with an acceptable way of displaying and dispelling the aggression boiling inside him.

Although he has done well at sport, Patrick is still far from succeeding in the classroom. He is 'very sensitive on his weak subjects'. His work is seen as 'not wholehearted', but he does win the Duke of Devonshire Prize for some form of academic achievement, although it is no longer known what this was. It was certainly worth winning for it carried with it £21, a not inconsiderable sum in those days. It was in this term that he became one of the hated house prefects, and his report again indicates the now familiar problems with his temper. 'His Devonshire Prize is a good mixture with his athletic successes, but he still does not wholly command his temperament. That is his final task next term before he leaves.'

It was during the Easter holidays that his mother married Bernard Carroll. Patrick was one of the witnesses to the ceremony which was held at St Anselm's Roman Catholic Church in Balham High Road on 27th April 1929. Bernard Carroll's first wife, Lena, had died at Balham in August 1927. Bernard seemed to have a penchant for older women. Lena had been eight years older than he was, and although he was only forty-one when he married Annie Heenan, she was now well into her forty-seventh year. She recorded her age in the register as forty-two, however, but she was probably a well-preserved woman anyway, and there is no doubt that Bernard loved her a great deal. When he died in 1948, he left 'to my beloved wife, Anne Carroll, all that I possess'.[11] After the wedding ceremony, the Carrolls lived in Surrey, where Bernard had bought a pleasant detached villa in Manor Road, Cheam. It was called 'Rocklands' and in the early thirties, when the houses were allocated numbers, it became number 46.[12]

After the wedding Patrick returned to school for his final term. The fact that at the age of eighteen and a half he was still in Form Middle 5A, Military, speaks for itself. He takes his School Certificate Examination for the last time, and fails once more. And his temper again lets him down. 'We have had some rows and there is a real danger of him having some in the future,' Mercer predicts. 'But I respect him and I hope he is glad of his two-and-a-half years here which have brought him some successes of various kinds.'

Patrick left Cheltenham College at the end of the summer term of 1929 with no formal qualifications. He was nineteen years old. Without the School Certificate or a pass in their entrance examinations, there was no opening for him at Sandhurst or Woolwich, let alone Oxford or Cambridge. But he appears to have given up any idea of becoming a soldier for a while, because his final report records that he is to join Steel Brothers, a trading company with extensive interests in the Far East and offices in London and Burma.

Annie Heenan Carroll had tried her best for her son, but despite his sporting achievements, Patrick's time at school had not been a success. The failure to pass the School Certificate would put a block on any hopes of a good career, and his failure to make friends meant he was not affiliated to the 'old boy network' which has helped so many other former public schoolboys in the same position.

If Patrick had arrived at Cheltenham with a chip on his shoulder, that chip had now become a plank. He had failed to fit in at school and had been put into classes with boys considerably younger than himself. Worse, his classmates had made no secret of their dislike for the 'strange looking' boy with 'a sallow, sullen face and a rough sounding voice' who was prone to throwing his weight around. Even the popularity normally at the disposal of a good school athlete had not come his way.

All this added to the growing number of charges Patrick held against society. His illegitimate birth, the early death of the man he regarded as his father, the difficulties he and his mother must have faced during his formative years in Burma, the change in schools – in itself something of a trauma – and now his treatment at the hands of masters and schoolmates. Patrick Heenan had been scarred by his experiences. From being 'odd boy out' he was now 'odd man out'.

'Let him only control his temperament and he will prove a fine fellow,' Mr Mercer had written. But Mercer's final judgement was to prove more accurate. 'We have had some rows and there is real danger of him having some in the future.'

CHAPTER 6

GOING BACK OUT EAST

Patrick Heenan left Cheltenham College at the end of the summer term of 1929, joining Steel Brothers' London offices almost immediately as a very junior assistant. The headquarters in Fenchurch Street was one of the company's two main offices, the other being in Rangoon, the Burmese capital.

Steel Brothers Ltd – a well-known and highly respected trading company – had been formed in 1870, and sixty years later was running a network of branch offices throughout Burma, India and Thailand. In Rangoon and a number of other Far East ports, the company held the agencies for the leading shipping lines whose very names remain evocative of the great days of the Raj – British India, Blue Funnel, Anchor, Elder Dempster and Union Castle. They also held the agencies for the Royal and the Atlas insurance companies. But most importantly, they were the Lloyd's agents in Rangoon, which in itself meant that they were one of the leading companies doing business in Burma.[1]

The main role of the Fenchurch Street offices was to act as the firm's principal centre for buying and selling in the West. It traded in almost anything that would bring in a profit, a range of goods and services that extended from the export of large pieces of British machinery and equipment to the import of the small Burmese cheroots popular among smokers at the time.

The company was the leading importer of rice from Burma, then known as the rice-bowl of the world, and the Fenchurch Street offices had a rice sampling room with a long counter displaying samples of the latest batches. It was also well entrenched in Burma's logging[2] and oil industries. Steel Brothers had formed the Indo-Burma Petroleum Company in 1908 and had oilfields at Yenangyaung and Lanywa, both in the general area of Pauk, where Patrick's father, George, had died in 1912.

Possibly George Heenan, the self-described geologist, had worked for them and it was the family connection that got the poorly qualified Patrick his first job.

Working in the city offices of an import–export company may not sound as exciting as a career in the services, but for a young man looking for a chance to travel, it was a good choice. After an initial period in the Fenchurch Street offices, single men were sent for a further period of apprenticeship in Rangoon, where they had the opportunity to live the bachelor life to the full, enjoying the exotic pleasures of the Far East in the company of the firm's other trainees.

It was in his first months at the company that Patrick met Donald Morrison Harper. Harper left Steels in January 1930, a few months after Patrick arrived. He worked in 'the piece goods department' as a junior assistant. He knew Patrick 'for a few weeks or two months' but cannot recall which department he worked in. Harper went up to Cambridge, where he gained a degree before joining the priesthood. The two men were to meet again in 1941, when as a chaplain in the Royal Air Force Volunteer Reserve, Harper, by now a Squadron Leader, was posted to Malaya.[3]

If Patrick did join Steels in the hope of returning to the Far East, he was unsuccessful. For just over three years later, in early 1933, he was still working in the Fenchurch Street offices. It is possible that he remained with the company in London until he gained his commission in the army in February 1935. But at least two fellow officers recall hearing that he had spent some time in a police force. 'Rumour had it, as far as I can remember, that he had once been in the Metropolitan Police,' one of them says.[4] The second officer, Major S. T. A. Longley, who knew Patrick in 1940 when they served together on the North-West Frontier, writes: 'It was said that he had been in the London Police Force.'[5] The Metropolitan Police records of 'joiners and leavers' for the time do not include Patrick's name, although this is inconclusive evidence since they are not comprehensive, and neither do those of the separate City of London Police force.[6]

However, Patrick certainly enjoyed the bachelor life in London. It is not clear if he lived with his mother and her new husband in the house in Cheam, although it was certainly the address he put on his application to join the Army. His name does not appear on the local electoral roll, however, and at some point, towards the end of 1932, he was lodging in a boarding house at 77, West Cromwell Road, Earl's Court.

Perhaps he did not get on with his stepfather, or possibly there was just not room. Bernard Carroll's two children from his first marriage, a daughter and a son who were both still quite young, were living there. But from the stories he later told his fellow officers of his time in London, it is probable that he preferred a more independent existence than living under the same roof as his mother and her new family.

Patrick was to regale one of his mess mates in the sub-continent with tales of his sexual exploits across London. Clearly his former master's assessment – 'struck by his devotion to young girls' – was accurate, for he was a frequent visitor to a number of establishments in Jermyn Street, in the West End, where 'gentlemen' willing to pay a price could procure the services of discreet young women. From the eighteenth century right up until the Second World War Jermyn Street had a reputation for loose-living and debauchery.

In the early 1930s, the street contained a number of Turkish Baths – the Savoy Turkish Baths at no. 91, and the nearby Hammuns, originally the London and Provincial Steam Bath Company, among them – but Patrick's interest was not in the steam baths themselves, for it is his accounts of the 'extras' he received that his fellow officer remembers most clearly. Patrick told him that he often stayed the night at the baths and the experience obviously left a deep impression on him for, ten years later, he was still recounting in graphic detail the 'French techniques' of the young women with whom he spent those nights.[7]

Certainly, these were not the sort of women he would have wanted to bring home to his mother's house in Cheam, but the reaction of his neighbours in Earl's Court might also have been interesting. For next door to 77, West Cromwell Road, at no. 79, was a home for sisters and novitiates of the Community of the Holy Family.

With no apparent opportunity to move to Rangoon, life at Steel Brothers must have palled and Patrick's interest in an Army career revived. But he faced a major problem. There were only a limited number of commissions to the British and Indian Armies in any one year and most of these would have gone to successful graduates of the Royal Military College (RMC) at Sandhurst and the Royal Military Academy (RMA) at Woolwich. The rest would have been contested by direct entrants from the universities and officers from the reserve forces – the Territorial Army and the Supplementary Reserve.[8]

Given his lack of academic qualifications, the Supplementary Reserve was the only course open to Patrick Heenan. Established in August 1924 by Royal Warrant, to supply 'on mobilisation the requirements of certain arms and branches of the Regular Army not provided for by the Regular Army Reserve', the Supplementary Reserve was split into three separate lists.[9] Category 'A' and Category 'C' were highly specialised: the first consisted of Royal Engineers reserves who needed to keep up their training in peacetime; the second was made up of officers with professions, such as solicitors and accountants, who would be required in the event of war to perform similar duties for the Army.

It was Category 'B' which Patrick joined. According to the regulations, these were 'personnel required to undergo training in peace. Those not in units will form a reserve for the corps to which they belong, being available for use on mobilisation as required. The personnel of Category "B" will, with certain exceptions, be attached to and supplementary to, the establishment of the Territorial Army.'

But even here, Patrick's poor school results formed a barrier to his progress. Applicants had to have passed either the matriculation or an entrance examination to a recognised university or either the RMA, Woolwich, or the RMC, Sandhurst.

There was only one other way in, a certificate signed by 'the headmaster of a secondary school or other competent educational establishment, regarding his educational attainments'.

It was the only way open to Patrick, the only way he could have got himself placed on the Supplementary List and put himself in with a chance of eventually receiving a regular commission; so, with the endorsement of Major J. R. Holland, the officer commanding the OTC at Cheltenham, and Henry Hardy, his old headmaster, he took it. But his academic shortcomings were not his only obstacle. There were still two further problems: persuading the recruiting officer that his sallow skin was not, as many tended to believe, the result 'of mixed blood' – that he was, in the words of the regulations 'a British subject and of pure European descent' – and hiding his illegitimacy, which would, at that time, have disqualified him from the role of 'officer and gentleman'.

To Patrick, it must have seemed that nothing in life would ever come easily for him, but his determination to win through ensured he succeeded. Instead of his birth certificate, which he had no doubt 'lost', he produced the certificate of baptism that listed George and Annie Heenan as his parents and so disguised his real origins. He would have had an ideal excuse for not producing a birth certificate – obtaining a copy from New Zealand would have taken months.

His application for 'Appointment to a Commission in the Supplementary Reserve of Officers', was dated 29th December 1932. On 6th January 1933, when he was called forward for a medical examination, at Queen Alexandra's Military Hospital at Millbank in London, Patrick was twenty-two years old, 6ft 1in. tall, weighed 12½ stone (175 lbs) and had perfect '6/6' vision. Two months later his commission into the Supplementary Reserve was confirmed.

Having passed the Officer Training Corps 'Certificate A' at Cheltenham, Patrick only needed to undergo eight weeks' basic training – for those without such a certificate, there was a thirteen-week training period – and since he was attached to the Bedfordshire and Hertfordshire Regiment, his training took place at the regimental depot in Bedford. Thereafter, officers on the Supplementary Reserve were required to do three weeks of training a year. They could also attend weekend camps with their units, or the Territorial Army unit to which they were affiliated, and were paid for all the days they underwent such training.

Both of his possible employers at this time, Steel Brothers or the Police, would have allowed him time off for this training and in all probability he would not have lost any of his salary – Steel Brothers, who had a reputation as a generous employer, was one of the first companies in London to introduce luncheon vouchers for their staff – so the army pay would have been a bonus. For Patrick there would also be the opportunity to play rugby and box competitively that association with an army unit would provide.

But the prime objective was to become an officer in the Regular Army and on 1st February 1935, at the age of twenty-five, Second-Lieutenant Patrick Stanley Vaughan Heenan was commissioned into the British Army and placed on the unattached list of the Indian Army.

The Army in India was made up of two separate bodies: the British Army units stationed there – which in 1935 amounted to around fifty battalions, mostly infantry, plus a large number of artillery units – and the Indian Army, which by now was about three times the size of the British Army in India. Its officer corps was mainly British but was gradually being Indianised with three different types of Indian officers. These were King's Commissioned Officers (KCOs), who had been through Sandhurst, and Indian Commissioned Officers (ICOs), who had studied at Dehra Dun, 'the Indian Sandhurst' – both types of officer were treated as equivalent to British officers – and Viceroy's Commissioned Officers (VCOs). The vast majority of Indian officers were VCOs and, no matter how senior, were subordinate to the most junior of British officers.

The Commander-in-Chief of the Army in India was a British officer selected in turn from the Indian and the British Armies. As a legacy of the Indian Mutiny, brigades were normally made up of one British and two Indian battalions, a pattern that was followed among most of the Indian Army Brigades which served in the Malayan campaign.

British officers destined for the Indian Army spent their first year on the sub-continent attached to a British battalion – Patrick was to join the 1st Battalion, The Royal Warwickshire Regiment, at Poona, some 75 miles south-east of Bombay.

Officers waiting to join a troopship to India generally spent the last few weeks prior to embarkation in a round of fond farewells to relatives and friends. The majority would be gone for four years at least – and some would never return – so there were many riotous parties. But, apart from his mother and his step-relatives, with whom he appears not to have had a close relationship, there would not have been many people to whom Patrick would want to wish goodbye. During his time in England he had made few friends.

It was a dull, grey and overcast day on 15th February 1935 when Annie Heenan saw her only son off from the dockside at Southampton. She never saw him again.

There were forty-five other newly commissioned Indian Army subalterns with Patrick aboard His Majesty's troopship *Neuralia*, together with ten sapper, signals, and gunner officers on attachment to the Indian Army, and a group of new subalterns being sent out to their British regiments in India. At nearly twenty-five Patrick was the eldest of the entire group. Like Patrick, three others in the Indian Army contingent had been commissioned through the Supplementary Reserve, and four through the Territorial Army. The rest had passed through Sandhurst or Woolwich and, in the way that seniority was determined in the army, those officers were considered one day senior to anyone who was commissioned on the same day but via another route. And while one day may not appear to amount to much, in peacetime, with promotion a tediously slow progress and, up to the rank of Major, based purely on seniority, it could make a considerable difference in the time it took to reach the next rung of the ladder.

One of the other junior officers on board *Neuralia* was Peter

Adams. He was commissioned on the same day as Patrick, but had passed through Sandhurst and was therefore a day senior to him, even though he was only nineteen.[10] To Patrick it must have seemed like Cheltenham all over again.

There was a general air of excitement among the young officers, Adams recalls. Some were going to the sub-continent for the first time. Others were returning to the country where they had been born or brought up. As the men split into groups, making friends with their fellow officers, Patrick, ever the odd man out, maintained a sullen silence. 'He was unpleasant and unpopular, with no friends,' Adams says. Perhaps worst of all, he was 'a sponger'. Adams remembers that Patrick took part in a light-heavyweight boxing exhibition on board, fighting a sergeant, but otherwise seemed unable to join in with the excited conversations of his fellow officers as they discussed India, the Indian Army, and the respective merits of the various British regiments stationed there.

Another of the subalterns on board, John King-Martin (later Brigadier J. D. King-Martin, CBE, DSO, MC) also recalls Patrick. 'Heenan was heavily built and good-looking. Always reminded me a bit of Errol Flynn. I remember that he gave a boxing exhibition on board.'[11]

So too does Gawain Douglas. 'If my memory serves me correctly,' Douglas says, 'Pat Heenan was about six feet. Well set up, with dark brown hair. Clean shaven and no moustache. Handsome in a way, with a slightly darker skin than the rest of us – almost olive-coloured, as though he might have had a Mediterranean ancestry, or was of mixed Irish/Spanish Armada blood. Not quite a gentleman. He was twenty-four whereas the rest of us were just turning twenty.

'One event does stick in my mind which involved him and many of us equally which one wouldn't want to boast about. Before we reached Port Said, word went around the ship about the infamous Café d'Or and its "exheebeetions", and without saying anything to anyone out of one's own particular little group of six or eight officers, it was decided that it must be paid a visit. What none of us knew was that there were some seven or eight other groups also planning to visit the Café d'Or in the "Out-of-Bounds" Arab quarter under the same conditions of utmost secrecy.

'Well, after an hour or so ashore, the eight of us set off in two taxis by what appeared to be opposite routes, and a few minutes later we met again – in a near head-on crash at a crossroads. A crowd collected, and while the two taxi-drivers were cursing each other's female ancestors and nearly coming to blows, we hopped out of the taxis and jumped into another passing one and, hilariously, continued on our way to our destination. Judge, therefore, our surprise, when as we arrived, at finding another group from the ship just departing. It was the same when we left – two groups arrived with much chaffing and badinage when they saw us.

'Of the show itself little need be said except that the "girls" were all fat and ugly. There was only one rather neat little piece, probably a Somali or a Nubian, who was quite different from the others, and I remember Pat Heenan taking quite a shine to her, though there was no sexual contact. He seemed more assured and an "homme d'affaires" than the rest of us which isn't really surprising as he was four years older.

'That is my last real memory of him. Gradually, I forgot him as there was a Paddy Keenan in Hodson's Horse, whose name was almost similar, and my memory of him gradually supplanted that of Heenan.'[12]

The Royal Warwickshire Regiment, which Patrick now joined, was not a popular regiment among senior Army officers in India, largely due to the abrasive character of the man who had been its commanding officer since January 1931 and who was to become the British Army's most famous Second World War soldier, Lieutenant-Colonel Bernard Law Montgomery. He had brought the regiment to India from Egypt in January 1934 having built up a reputation for being fanatical about combat training and intensely disliking the ceremonial side of the army, from drill parades to regimental dinners. This was anathema to the other regiments of the Army in India who, away from the rigours of the North-West Frontier in what was traditionally known as 'the Sloth Belt', indulged themselves in magnificent ceremonial parades, regimental balls and Officers' Mess cocktail parties.

Then, in the words of his biographer, Nigel Hamilton, 'into an Indian station whose performance at the King's Parade was legendary marched Lieutenant-Colonel B. L. Montgomery and his thousand men'.[13] Monty, who had written the section in the Infantry Training Manual dedicated to infantry training and tactics, immediately fell foul of General Sir George Jeffreys, GOC Southern India Command, who not only had little interest in tactical training but also believed passionately in square-bashing and had written the section in the manual on military drill.

No sooner had the regiment landed in India than Jeffreys arrived to inspect them performing a complicated drill procedure which ended in complete and utter shambles, leaving relations between the two men extremely strained. The situation was only saved by Montgomery's decision to take some leave, sailing with his wife on a cruise of the Far East which included a fortnight's stay in Japan. It was during this cruise that he received the offer of a staff job at Quetta, in northern India, out of Jeffreys's command.

Lieutenant-Colonel J. P. Duke took over the regiment, immediately facing a scandal as it was discovered that a reputation for first-class marksmanship gained in Egypt, where units marked their own scores, had been based on cards altered to please Montgomery's insistence on good combat training. In India the scorecards had to be marked by members of another regiment and the Warwicks were now uncovered as a collection of very poor marksmen.

Such was the regiment to which Patrick Heenan was attached, and joined in the spring of 1935. Most attached officers were treated reasonably well, although at least one Officers' Mess had a special rule that forced attachees to eat at a separate table, and there was sometimes an undercurrent of ill-feeling caused by the better pay received by Indian Army officers. But life as an army officer was, and still is in many regiments, governed by peculiar regulations and traditions which a junior subaltern ignored at his peril.

There were rules, both written and unwritten, about everything to do with 'The Mess' – the way one dressed, the subjects that could be discussed and the behaviour that could be accepted. There was to be no mention of politics or of ladies' names. Bar bills were to be kept within certain limits and 'spongers', which Patrick had already gained a reputation for being, were considered to be the lowest of the low. He was also to get a name for another cardinal sin, talking behind his fellow officers' backs, which did nothing to increase his popularity.

Public school no doubt provided good training for the traditions of the Mess, but for many the new rules and the derogatory way in which young subalterns were treated when they first arrived in a regiment provided a traumatic experience. 'It came as a shock as I had imagined my schooldays were behind me and that I had entered an adult world,' said one contemporary of Patrick who was attached to a different regiment. 'But far from it; it was worse than school had ever been.'[14]

One of the more traumatic experiences recounted by officers who went through similar attachments was the co-called 'Subaltern's Court-Martial'.[15] This was a longstanding device for punishing young officers who transgressed any part of the traditional code of behaviour. It was reminiscent of the bullying that many officers had experienced at school and those, like Patrick, who failed to fit in, were frequently the victims of these kangaroo courts, which were run along the lines of proper courts-martial and resulted in punishments ranging from a verbal berating through to tarring and feathering. Senior officers tended to turn a blind eye, although technically the holding of these tribunals was a court-martial offence in its own right.

Patrick's reputation as 'a sponger', his propensity to talk behind his fellow officers' backs and his general unpopularity would have made him an obvious target. His sullen, rough manner – he was considered 'uncouth' by many of his contemporaries – did nothing to endear him to them. But the most damning fault of all in the eyes of many of them would have been his sallow complexion. Major S. T. A. Longley, who knew him in 1940 when they served together on the North-West Frontier, says: 'Heenan was, I think, of mixed blood.'

But there was some consolation for Patrick in the emphasis placed on sport – his contemporaries recall him spending a lot of time keeping fit – and in the social life. For a good-looking twenty-five-year-old there were no shortage of invitations to parties organised by mothers with single daughters to marry off, although most Indian regiments of the time had strict customs about an officer not marrying until he reached the rank of captain. At the least, any officer wishing to do so, had to obtain the permission of his CO, and officers under the rank of captain were never given such permission.

Patrick, like all young attached officers, was expected to be extra keen and demonstrate that he was worthy of his commission. He had to hire a local teacher, a *Munshi*, to teach him Urdu, the standard language of communication within the Indian Army. He took his regular turn as regimental orderly officer and at being drilled under the watchful eye of the Regimental Sergeant-Major. He also had to spend time on the ranges practising shooting, and he attended minor courts-martial as an observer to prepare him for the time when he might have to sit in judgement himself.

During his year with the Warwicks he also had to decide which Indian regiment he should apply to join. His application had to be supported by a good report from his commanding officer and he would then have to be vetted by his chosen regiment. Whenever an officer retired, or was posted out of one of the best regiments, there was a flood of applications to replace him. Each applicant received an invitation to spend ten days with the regiment and was placed in the charge of a junior subaltern who escorted him constantly. His every move would be closely monitored and the junior officers would attempt to get him drunk, for as John Masters said of his own similar experience '*in vino* there is *veritas*'.

But something went wrong. Quite exceptionally, Patrick was forced to undergo a further six months with another British battalion. Perhaps he was rejected by the Indian regiment of his choice. But it seems more likely that Colonel Duke, unconvinced that he was worth his commission, simply refused to recommend him. 'The Warwicks' CO had doubts about Heenan's ability to fit into the Indian Army,' one former officer says. 'Heenan was a difficult chap to fit into anything.'

It was a devastating blow. Former Indian Army officers say they remember no other instance of it happening and it could not be kept quiet to prevent any embarrassment on Patrick's part. The details were included in the annual Indian Army lists where any of his contemporaries would see them. These were closely monitored by officers watching for the chance of promotion and memsahibs seeking husbands for their daughters. They would all now know that Patrick had either failed to make the grade with the Royal Warwicks or that no Indian regiment wanted him.

On 8th March 1936, the first anniversary of his starting date with the Royal Warwicks, Patrick was attached to the 1st Battalion, The Royal Norfolk Regiment. He was to stay with them until October of that year when his application to join the 16th Punjab Regiment was accepted.

But for Patrick himself, the earlier rejection by his fellow officers was the latest victory for the British establishment in the personal war it appeared to be waging against him. By now he was convinced that, no matter what he did, it would not be good enough. He would never fit in, he would never be allowed to fit in. The way in which he had been ostracised by his fellow officers and their suspicion that his sallow complexion indicated 'a touch of the tar-brush' had been added to the mounting litany of his own charges against the establishment. As one fellow officer in the 16th Punjab Regiment said: 'Heenan had a huge grudge against society and was out to get his revenge.'[16]

CHAPTER 7

ODD MAN OUT

The 16th Punjab Regiment was one of the many proud infantry regiments of the Indian Army. Although it had only come into existence in 1922, as the result of a major reorganisation of the Indian Army, it traced its origins back to the early nineteenth century.

This reorganisation regrouped five battalions together into the 16th Punjab Regiment. The battalions were the 30th Punjabis, which became the 1st Bn, the 31st Punjabis, the 2nd Bn, the 33rd Punjabis, the 3rd Bn, 9th Bhopal Infantry, the 4th Bn, and the 46th Punjabis, which became the 10th Bn.[1] It was the 4th Battalion, the so-called Bhopal Contingent, which had the oldest traditions, dating back to 1818. But Patrick was to join the old 30th Punjabis, the 1st Battalion of the 16th Punjab Regiment, better known as the 1/16th.

The 16th Punjab Regiment's campaign and battle honours followed an illustrious tradition. Elements of what became the regiment had fought in many campaigns on the North-West Frontier, been part of the China Expeditionary Force of 1902, and been present at some of the most famous battles of the First World War, including Neuve Chapelle, Givenchy and Ypres. During that war alone, officers and men of the regiment had won a Victoria Cross, 13 Military Crosses and bars, 12 Distinguished Service Orders, and 39 Indian Distinguished Service Medals.

The battalions of an Indian Army regiment were linked by common regimental dress and traditions but not by any single system of command. Each battalion had its own commanding officer, a lieutenant-colonel, but there was no overall commanding officer for the regiment. All regiments had a Colonel-in-Chief, but he was usually a retired senior officer and his role was largely that of a figurehead. He was nevertheless the final arbiter on all matters pertaining to regimental tradition and custom and he sometimes had a say in the selection of new officers.

The Viceroy's Commissioned Officers and other ranks of a battalion usually stayed with it for life. British officers also tended to stay with the same battalion until they were appointed to the General Staff or promoted beyond the rank of lieutenant-colonel. But these traditions were broken when the Second World War forced the expansion of the Indian Army and experienced personnel, both Indian and British, had to be posted out to supplement the newly formed battalions.

So despite the reorganisation into regiments, the battalion remained at the heart of the Indian Army and the unit with which both officers and men identified, sometimes even to the extent of still referring to it by its pre-1922 title – even now former officers of the 5th Bn, 14th Punjab Regiment still look upon their old unit as the 40th Pathans, its original name.

A year before Patrick joined the 1/16th, it had moved from an isolated garrison in a square mile of British territory in the state of Baroda, to Fort Sandeman in Baluchistan, just to the south of the area known as the North-West Frontier. The battalion's new base made it part of the Zhob (Independent) Brigade under Western Command and, in the words of the regimental history, it was there 'to shake off the sloth of the plains on 14-day columns in that mountainous border country'.[2]

Fort Sandeman was one of a series of garrison towns, or cantonments, which dotted the mountainous border areas that stretched for four hundred miles from the Khyber Pass in the north to the Bolan Pass in Baluchistan in the south. It was far from 'the Sloth Belt' and the battalion would spend most of the time when it was not fighting in training exercises and long route marches.[3]

The area was the home of the proud and war-loving Pathan tribesmen. They lived in the area of the border between India and Afghanistan – a border whose existence they did not recognise – and made a living from the booty of armed raids on each other and on neighbouring tribes, and by exacting tolls from passing traders.

The British had never succeeded in subjugating them and resorted instead to building forts linked by road at strategic points throughout the border area and stationing larger contingents of troops in nearby garrison towns like Fort Sandeman. But they had great admiration for the fighting capabilities of the Pathan, so much so that, when they could, they recruited him into the ranks of the Indian Army. There were periods of relative peace along the North-West Frontier when the British let the tribesmen carry on their feuds without interference. But frequently the soldiers intervened, mainly, the cynics said, to give the Indian and British Armies the opportunity to gain experience of real war.

By the time Patrick Heenan joined the battalion, in October 1936, his dogged determination to win through and his skill in the boxing ring had finally brought him his first success on the sub-continent – as Heavyweight Boxing Champion of India. His fellow officers may not have liked him but few argued with him. For while he lacked the intellectual ability to put across his point of view, he was over six foot tall, built like an ox and not averse to throwing his weight around. He was a bully with a tendency to pick on his fellow officers, in particular the smaller ones.

A fellow member of the regiment recalls one particular mess anecdote that illustrates this side to his character. 'I was told shortly after joining that Patrick Heenan was very unpopular generally and could be very aggressive particularly when having imbibed well or too well on guest nights,' he says. 'I got the impression that he was probably actively disliked, but I may be wrong as it was quite a time ago.

'No-one wished to have to mix matters with him physically in self-defence, but it appears he did tend to pick on certain individuals. On one such occasion, well into the evening, it appears that he cornered an intended victim, who decided to stand his ground. He was confronted close by a fireplace in the room, but near at hand was a poker! The intended victim brought this down with some force on Heenan's shoulder which stopped him short and saved the evening. Whether or not this curbed Heenan's aggression towards that particular officer thereafter was not related as far as I can remember. Yes, he was a big and powerful man physically. He was reasonably well-spoken, certainly grammatically, though his accent was not what I would describe in those times as being Public School.'[4]

The lack of an upper-class accent was enough on its own to set him apart. Mercer at Cheltenham had described him as 'a good straight fellow' but this could have been a euphemism for 'too blunt for his own good'. Certainly he had a massive chip on his shoulder, a rough and abrupt manner, and an uncontrollable temper.

But he was also good-looking and, while his fellow officers found it difficult to get a smile out of him, women had no such problems. His tanned looks may have caused suspicion among his colleagues but together with his well-developed physique, they made him extremely attractive to the opposite sex. And Fort Sandeman may have been remote, but there were women there. In most places in India, the charms of a certain class of Indian girl could be bought providing an officer was circumspect and was not caught at it. And during the hot season, when the memsahibs left their husbands to the heat of the cities and plains and retreated to hill stations like Simla and Ranikhet to become grass widows, those places became a temporary paradise for any subaltern lucky enough to get permission from his commanding officer to spend his leave there. Some of the officers' wives dropped the high morals of the plains as they were transported up into the hills and many a young officer took full advantage of the opportunities available.

At Fort Sandeman, Patrick would have had a tiny room in one of the bungalows allocated to subalterns. The small bed, the chest of drawers, the couple of chairs and the table would all have to be rented and would have left the room looking extremely crowded. Jutting out of the room would have been his private bathroom, but one which included none of the modern conveniences. A small zinc tub would serve as a bath once it had been filled by the Bhisti, or water-carrier, with water heated in empty kerosene cans over an open fire in the compound. The water ran away through a hole in the wall which also acted as a convenient entry point for snakes and scorpions. And the toilet was a 'thunderbox', a wooden seat with a hole cut in it, under which was placed a large enamel pot, which the low-caste untouchable known as a Mehta, or sweeper, would empty when called.

John Masters, in his book *Bugles and a Tiger*, described one of these bathrooms as 'a fine miniature of the Indian scene – barren, ramshackle, by turns too hot or too cold, yet full of interesting corners, strange expectations, and a mixed smell of wood smoke and human excrement'.[5] Anyone who has ever visited India will appreciate how evocative those words are of the country.

Life for an Indian Army officer revolved around the mess. By today's values, the pre-war Indian Army might appear hidebound with tradition, but it was this that transformed men from all over the sub-continent, who might otherwise have ended up fighting among themselves, into such a cohesive force. There was little else to bind white British officer to lowly Indian Sepoy, Muslim to Hindu, or Sikh to the many other ethnic and religious strands that made up the Indian Army.[6]

Officers were expected to stick rigidly to these traditions and in the mess they followed an elaborate code of conduct. There were strict rules about dressing for dinner, for example. Suits could be worn only on a Sunday. On Thursday and Saturday, dinner-jackets had to be worn. On every other night, mess kit was obligatory. The Thursday night dinner-jacket was a legacy of the death of Queen Victoria; she died on a Tuesday but news of it did not reach India until the following Thursday.

Some of the rules would have given Patrick a number of problems. An officer had to learn to drink a lot but anyone who became boastful or quarrelsome in the process could find himself in serious trouble. Getting into debt was acceptable, in a country where just about everything was purchased by signing a chit, but this was not to be taken to excess. The Commanding

Officer of the 1/16th was Lieutenant-Colonel Donald Powell, 'a splendid officer. A nice chap, well thought of by everyone'. He was then forty years old, with twenty-two years of soldiering behind him, but from all accounts he must have regretted allowing Patrick into his mess. The misfit with the darkish complexion appeared to have more in common with the Indian officers than with the British officers. Any trace of native blood was looked down on by the majority of white officers and, had they discovered his illegitimacy, he would have been completely ostracised.

The decision in 1918 to give King's Commissions to Indians had cut across the prejudices of the British officers who believed that their leadership qualities had been instilled in them during their years at school. They saw the British public school system as the ideal training ground for officers and imagined that anyone who had not been through that system would not have the necessary qualities of bravery, team spirit and leadership. This was, of course, quite apart from the considerations of race.

Nor was any special account taken of the religious customs of the various Indian officers. Muslims were expected to drink the loyal toast in whisky and the presence of Hindu officers in the mess did not prevent the appearance of roast beef on the menu, although the cow is a sacred animal to the Hindu. These things must have caused niggling tensions among the more zealously religious Indian officers and sometimes there was racial friction. Traditionally British and Indian officers had been kept apart and some of the white officers had never fully adjusted to having Indians in the mess. This seems to have caused further problems for Patrick in getting on with his fellow British officers. For despite all his faults, he appears to have been quick to defend the underdog.

His closeness to the Indian officers did not help him pass the Lower Standard Examination in Preliminary Urdu. It took him longer than most to master the language and he did not pass the test until April 1937, more than two years after he had arrived in India. This was naturally an important element in how quickly any officer was accepted by the Indian troops, but it was not the only factor. No-one who has passed through this process has ever been able to define satisfactorily what was required. It did not depend on whether the officer was liked, for thoroughly unpopular officers found themselves accepted, and it seemed to have nothing to do with military expertise. It just happened. One day an officer was still trying to gain acceptance and the next, for no apparent reason, he knew without being told that he was at last a member of the regimental family. Patrick must have passed through this process. But acceptance by the men was one thing, acceptance by his fellow British officers quite another.

One of the few officers who appears to have got anywhere near close to Patrick was Major Alisdair Ramsey Tainsh, MBE, who arrived at the battalion in the summer of 1937 as a lowly second-lieutenant. A well-built man, he had served his attached year with the East Kent Regiment, better known as the Buffs, at Lucknow. 'I had been a bit of a misfit in the Buffs,' he said. 'I had been up at Cambridge, and travelled around Europe a lot. I knew there was about to be a Second World War, and spoke openly about it. When the Buffs told us attached officers that we would have to give a ten-minute lecture, I said off-hand I would speak on "Europe Today". This upset them because it was political.' Eventually, he was seen by the colonel and agreed to talk on a less contentious subject.[7]

'Later, I opened my mouth about the Japanese and quoted from the translation of a 1921 Japanese text I had bought for sixpence which outlined their plans to take over Siam, Malaya, and Singapore. This caused more trouble.[8]

'I tell you this because I was an odd man out, and was to meet at Fort Sandeman, "Odd Man Heenan". He arrived in my quarters without warning soon after my arrival, and seemed for some reason to want to have a row or make trouble. He boasted about being the boxing champion of India. But I was not worried and asked whom he had fought. I told him I had boxed for the Buffs and had run the boxing tournaments for them.'

This seems to have impressed Patrick, who became more friendly. 'I told him that I needed his help as I had been given the company accounts to do,' said Ramsey Tainsh. 'Within minutes he was sitting helping me, and that association went on for some months until I got posted away to the training battalion at Sialkot.'

By July 1937, Patrick had passed the examination for the *Higher* Standard in Preliminary Urdu, which was part of the retention test needed to have his posting to the Indian Army confirmed. It also included tests in tactical and ceremonial competence and he must have passed the test by October of that year, the anniversary of his joining the regiment, since it had to be passed within an officer's first year.

Periods of peace on the North-West Frontier were dominated by military training. There was individual training for the Indian Other Ranks in drill, weapons training and how to set up temporary fortifications in the hills. Officers not involved in such training would be taught map-reading and the use of field codes or would carry out 'paper exercises', or TEWTs (Tactical Exercises Without Troops). There would then be section training, with soldiers being taught to work together in small teams; this would progress to tactical platoon training, in which a company's various platoons would fight mock battles against each other.

Officers were also given special firearms training at the Small Arms School in Pachmari in the Central Provinces. The six-week Pachmari course was compulsory and aimed to make officers expert marksmen with the pistol, the rifle and the light machine-gun. It was also a good opportunity to meet officers from other regiments and, since each one's uniform, drills and mess customs were different, it frequently turned into a very enjoyable 'circus' as each officer attempted to show that his regiment was better than any of the others.

In October 1937, the 1/16th moved north to become part of the 3rd Jhelum Brigade, based in the frontier town of the same name, taking up what were known as 'watch and ward' duties along the Bannu–Razmak road in northern Waziristan. It was shortly after this that Colonel Powell appears to have decided he had had quite enough of his problem officer. Peter Adams,

(*Above*) Sevenoaks School, July 1924. Patrick sixth from left in back row.
(*Below*) Cheltenham College East Day Boys, 1929. Master in charge, J.S. Bond.
Patrick second from left in front row, talking.

Action on the North-West Frontier, in the Ahmedzai Salient.
(*Above*) Patrick standing on left of canvas shelter, with,
on right, Major (then Lieutenant) Alisdair Ramsey Tainsh;
(*below*) troops of 1/16th Punjab fan out as they advance
against the Pathans.

(*Above*) A further scene from the battle for Gomati Tangi, on the North-West Frontier.
(*Below left*) C.J. Windsor, the planter turned naval officer,
and Mrs Windsor, a photograph taken in the early 1960s outside their house in Kuantan;
(*Below right*) 'Pinka' Robertson Scott, who lived in the Cameron Highlands of Malaya
and became, after the war, an influential member of the Jockey Club of Malaya.

Alor Star – the airfield and officers' mess (*above*), and home in 1941 to No. 62 Squadron.
(*Below*) Some of the officers and men of 'A' Flight, taken at RAF Tengah, 1940,
including, from the left in front row, (1st) F/Lt 'Pongo' Scarf, VC; (2nd) F/Lt Duncan, Flight commander;
(3rd) S/Ldr Gatheral, Squadron commander; (4th) F/O Keegan;
and (6th) Flt/Sgt Swindlehurst, frequently consulted by Patrick on aircraft movements.

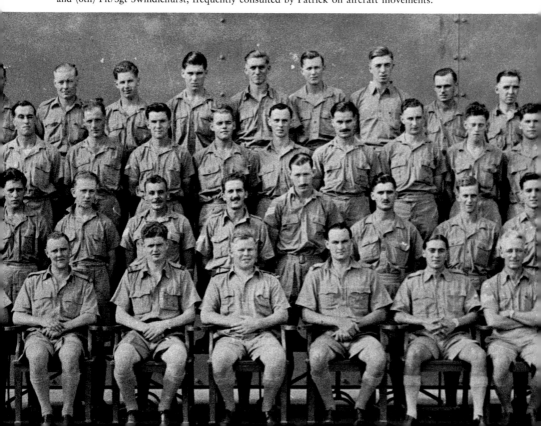

(*Above*) Major James Cable France, CO of 300 Air Liaison Section, Malaya 1941–42.
(*Below*) France's despatch rider Private Jack 'Bladder' Wells; and Wells'
close friend Private Fred Cox who drove Patrick to plantations near the Thai border.

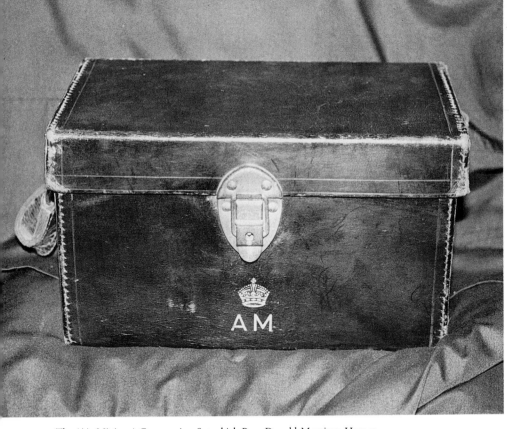

The (Air Ministry) Communion Set which Rev. Donald Morrison Harper
passed over to Major France.

(*Left*) Lt-Col. B.K. Castor,
Deputy Provost Marshal, Malaya,
in early 1942.
Before the war he was
Secretary of Essex County
Cricket Club.
Later he became Secretary
of Surrey CCC.

(*Below*) The home of Mrs B.J. Carroll, Patrick's mother,
at 46 Manor Road, Cheam, Surrey.

QUENTIN GARDEN   CLAUDE WALLER GOLDSMITH
ANTHONY JULIAN CLAUDE GARDINER · JOHN GARDNER
PATRICK GRATTAN GEARY   GUY WORDSWORTH GIBSON
GERALD WILLIAM CHEVALLIER GLEED · PATRICK JOHN GOOD
THOMAS ARTHUR GLOSTER · EDWARD THOMAS GODDARD
OLIVER GODFREY   JOHN MICHAEL McVEAN GUBBINS
PETER LESLIE GOSSAGE   HUGH DESMOND GRUNDY
DONALD KENNETH GORDON · ROBERT DIGHTON GORDON
HUMPHREY TRENCH GILBERT   LESLIE FRANK HANCOCK
FREIHERR VON VINZEN KARL MARIA E. P. G. HAAS-TEICHEN
FREDERICK FENTON H. HALL   FRANK MICHAEL M. HALL
RONALD FRANK HARRIS · HERBERT BERKELEY HARRISON
JOHN WYNDHAM HARTIGAN · JOHN O. COBBOLD HASTED
GEOFFREY HARRISON-BROADLEY   PATRICK S. V. HEENAN
ARTHUR N. O. P. HILL-LOWE   JULIAN HURLSTONE HORTIN
PATRICK HOWARD HAVERS   FRANK LANKESTER HAYNES
BRUCE LYNDON HAYNES · MAURICE GEORGE OAKLEY HILL
MARCUS HUGH HAWKINS · CHRISTOPHER JOHN HODGSON
CHARLES GODFREY HINTON   ERIC McCAULLY HECTOR
ALAN ARTHUR HOFFMAN · DOUGLAS ALFRED K. HOMAN
JOHN REGINALD HORNBY   JAMES HEATHCOTE HUMPHRIS
DOUGLAS WALSHAM HOW · REGINALD GORDON P. HUNTER
          FRANCIS LIONEL HUDSON

(*Above*) Part of the Roll of Honour at Cheltenham College for the first and second world wars.
(*Below*) Portion of Column 263 of Kranji War Cemetery, Singapore.

16TH PUNJAB REGIMENT

LIEUT-COLONEL   JEMADAR
MOORHEAD   ABDUL HAMID
H. D.. D. S. O.   AJMER SINGH
          CHANAN SHAH
MAJOR   DALIP SINGH
WAKEFIELD G. C.   FAIZ AHMAD
          GURBAKHSH
CAPTAIN   SINGH
BELCHEM J.   INDAR SINGH
HEENAN P. S. V.   MAHBUB ALAM
JARMAN J. D.   SHAH
McLENNAN K. L.   MAULA BAKHSH
SHARP J. M.   MUHAMMAD
THATCHER J. A. R.   AFZAL

who had arrived in India with Patrick on *Neuralia* and was now with the 1st Battalion, the 8th Punjab Regiment, recalls that Patrick was 'transferred because he didn't fit in'.

Another officer who served with the 3rd Jhelum Brigade, remembers meeting Patrick shortly before he was posted out of the battalion. 'It was during the winter of 1937–38. I was stationed at Jhelum, Punjab. At Jhelum in those days we had a complete Indian Infantry Brigade, one of whose units was the 1st Battalion, 16th Punjab Regiment. One evening, I had occasion to call on one or two officers of this battalion – their mess was practically opposite ours – and I vaguely recall meeting someone called Heenan; a tall, well-built subaltern of ruddy complexion. He seemed somewhat ill-at-ease or stand-offish, possibly both. What his business was in his battalion I had no idea, but his stay in Jhelum was apparently so brief that, before anyone realised he was there, he had left. I gathered that he was most unpopular and his commanding officer had got him transferred to the Royal Indian Army Service Corps.'⁹

Ironically, if Patrick had been allowed to stay on at the regiment, he might finally have earned his spurs, for within a very short time of his transfer, the 1/16th were to see active service, and in a later action on the North-West Frontier he was to earn praise from his fellow officers for his bravery. Fighting against the hill tribesmen of the North-West Frontier always gave young subalterns a chance to shine and while Patrick missed out, one of his fellow officers grasped his opportunity. Second-Lieutenant David Potts, who was seen by his fellow officers as having the qualities they believed Patrick lacked, acquitted himself well and found himself marked down for promotion.

As Patrick began his enforced secondment to what was rather disparagingly called 'the Rice Corps', the battalion he had left under a cloud moved into a camp at Mir Ali, guarding a stretch of the Bannu–Razmak road. A Pathan leader known as the Fakir of Ipi had organised a large *lashkar*, or armed band of tribesmen, which was carrying out raids on convoys passing along the Bannu–Razmak road. In April 1938, the Fakir's men blockaded an outpost manned by members of the famous Tochi

Scouts and the 3rd Jhelum Brigade came together with the Razmak Brigade to form a force known as 'Wastrike' to end the Fakir's uprising.

In the ensuing fierce fighting, 'C' company of the 1/16th distinguished itself. Several soldiers were killed or wounded and a Subadar (a Viceroy's Commissioned Officer) and a Naik (Corporal) from the battalion were later awarded Indian Distinguished Service Medals for their part in the battle.[10]

Transfers are a traditional method of dispensing with an officer who does not 'fit in'. But a posting to 'the Rice Corps' was a double-blow for Patrick – one further humiliation to heap on top of all the others he had suffered. The RIASC was short of officers at the time and captains from infantry and cavalry regiments were being offered promotion to major if they transferred to the corps. For those approaching retirement, this was a tempting offer but it did not apply to Patrick, who remained a lowly subaltern, attached to the RIASC until late 1939.

It was around this time that he became engaged to an English girl. Technically, however, Patrick was still an officer of the 16th Punjabis and the custom in that regiment, as in all infantry regiments, was that no officer under the rank of captain was ever given permission to marry. Even engagements were frowned upon as interfering with an officer's military life, so the chances are that this liaison was kept secret. But if Patrick was serious enough about the relationship to apply to Colonel Powell for permission to get married it would have been refused, giving him yet another grievance against authority.

It was a little later that Patrick took the 'long leave' that was due to him. We do not know the exact dates of this leave, but it is likely to have taken place between the autumn of 1938 and the spring of 1939. He would have had about six months' 'long leave' plus any periods of local leave that he had not used and, like many officers based in India, he chose to go to Japan. Sometimes this was just a stopover on the way back to England, but others spent all their leave there, taking the opportunity to learn Japanese. On their return to India, they then took an interpreter's examination and were listed as such in the Indian Army List. With war in the Far East looming, the shortage of officers who spoke Japanese was well recognised and some Japanese-speaking civilians were later given war commissions in the Indian Army.[11]

Perhaps Patrick intended merely to use his visit to Japan as a stopover before travelling on to England. He had not seen his mother for some time but, if that was his intention, something made him change his mind, for he spent the whole of his long leave in Japan.

With war inevitable, British officers visiting Japan at this time frequently found themselves the target of the Japanese secret service. John Masters, who stopped over in Japan on leave in 1938, found himself accosted by two secret servicemen on a train as he travelled from the port of Kobe to Tokyo, before going on to Yokohama where he was to rejoin his ship. 'I eagerly awaited the next step as any student of John Buchan can readily foresee,' said Masters, who at the time was only twenty-four and keen for adventure.

He had decided not to travel first-class and was in a rather scruffy compartment with an old lady with whom he was getting on famously by means of sign language. By this time he was surprised not already to have been approached by the secret service, but when the train stopped in Osaka, two men in business suits came up the aisle and, although there were plenty of seats, scared the little old lady off. One of the men then took her place. 'I decided that the secret service had been looking for me in the upper classes, and that was what caused the delay,' Masters said.

The Japanese began to speak to Masters in English, asking him a lot of questions. 'He was most interested in the Indian Army, and I gave him some interesting information about it. He told me of a British officer who had recently visited Japan and gone climbing on Fujiyama and there disappeared. He looked at me. I said it was very interesting and tried to help him guess what had happened to the poor chap. I said that our theory was that he had been murdered by the Japanese Secret Service who were such fools that they didn't know that the officer was a leading proponent of friendship with the Japanese. None of this was true, but my companion's smug expression faltered and he was silent for a long time.'[12]

Whether Patrick Heenan deliberately went out of his way to get in touch with the Japanese secret service or was himself approached in a similar way to Masters is not clear. Neither the Intelligence Department of the Ground Staff Office of the Japanese Defence Agency nor the Military History Department of the National Institute for Defence Studies in Tokyo have files on him, but this is scarcely surprising.[13] Any such secret files would in all probability have been destroyed before the Japanese capitulation. Possibly, sex was the bait that brought Patrick into the Japanese fold. One of his fellow officers remembers hearing later about a liaison between Patrick and a Japanese woman during his time there.

Possibly this woman was used to recruit him, or perhaps she was merely assigned to watch over him while his new masters debriefed him – to discover what gaps in their Intelligence picture of the British defences in India he could plug – and while they taught him the 'tradecraft' of the spy. It was probably here that he was taught to use radio equipment. He certainly did not gain this knowledge in India. The Indian Army signals school at Poona did not give instruction on the use of radio equipment until 1941. Heenan would have needed to be taught to use Japanese codes and how best to take pictures of military installations – he was later to demonstrate a surprising expertise at photography. He was also to have contacts in Malaya with the anti-British Indian Independence League, which may have been cultivated initially in Japan, where many members of the League were living in exile.[14] At this stage neither the Japanese authorities nor Patrick himself could possibly have known quite how valuable he could prove to be. But even a subaltern would have had a store of Intelligence useful to the Japanese military machine. Patrick would have been able to tell them of the current disposition and strengths of the British and Indian Army units in India, one of the targets of the proposed Japanese-dominated 'Greater East Asia Co-Prosperity Sphere', and would have had a knowledge of the equipment and stores available to those forces. He would also have known something of the RAF squadrons in India and of how many and what type of aircraft they had.

All the time his Japanese mistress could have been helping him build up his knowledge of Japanese, using what has often been described as the most effective method of learning any language – a 'sleeping dictionary'. Surprisingly perhaps, given Patrick's propensity for bragging about his conquests, not much is known about his relationship with the Japanese woman but if it was the key to his recruitment it would not have been the only attraction. Working for the Japanese was certainly fraught with danger but for Patrick it would be highly rewarding, not just financially but also in terms of the satisfaction to be had from wreaking revenge on a society that had treated him badly and, as far as he was concerned, was about to get its just desserts.

He returned to India at the end of his leave with a new-found interest in all things Japanese and there was no shortage of Japanese agents on the sub-continent to maintain that interest and keep control over their new Intelligence asset. 'There was a Japanese dentist in every garrison town in India looking after the teeth of the BORs (British Other Ranks) and their families,' Ramsey Tainsh says. 'They provided cheap and excellent treatment and no doubt learned much military information.' On one occasion Tainsh found himself being questioned by a Japanese attaché. 'I was travelling by train to Simla. The Japanese Imperial Military attaché and his wife joined the train at Ambala. He lost no time in asking for my name, rank and regiment.'[15]

Patrick was now twenty-nine. He had spent most of his life, from his fatherless youth, through his unhappy public school years, to his time in the Indian Army, in a fruitless search for acceptance and recognition from those around him. Now in the Japanese, the future enemy, he had found people who seemed to value him. In his lowly post with the Indian 'Rice Corps', he must have been a very small cog in the Japanese Intelligence machine, but at least they seemed to want him. The Japanese had won a friend for life. Their investment in him had cost them little, but within the space of a year it was to pay dramatic dividends.

CHAPTER 8

ON THE NORTH-WEST FRONTIER

His long leave over, Patrick returned to the 'Rice Corps' and by July 1939 was serving with the 15th Motor Transport Company based at Bareilly, a town about 140 miles east of Delhi. But whatever else he had learned in Japan it was not to control his temper, and within a few months he was in trouble again.

Patrick tried to intervene in a dispute between some British Other Ranks and military policemen at Bareilly in September 1939. 'I met Heenan again at the outbreak of the war [with Germany in September 1939],' says Alisdair Ramsey Tainsh. 'He arrived in Jhelum. He had been seconded to the RIASC. There was some trouble with BORs and the Military Police arrested someone – Heenan had tried to intervene and was posted back to the 1/16th Punjabis.'[1]

Another of Patrick's contemporaries confirms the story. 'Heenan evidently poked his nose into business that was not his on behalf of some British soldiers. He was in serious trouble with the Military Police. He was moved away from Bareilly very smartly.'[2]

As far as the Indian Army was concerned, Patrick would have been exceeding his authority even if he merely attempted to mediate between the Military Police and the British soldiers, for the men involved are unlikely to have been under his command and, even if they had been, such an intervention would have had to be done through 'the proper channels'. But given his inability to control his temper and the apparently serious nature of his offence, it seems likely that his intervention involved something more than arbitration.

So Patrick arrived back with the 1/16th Punjabis, unwanted, unpopular and generally disliked, to renew his acquaintance with Colonel Powell, and with Second-Lieutenant Ramsey Tainsh, who had arrived back with the battalion after his stint with the training battalion, the 10/16th Punjabis, in Sialkot. 'We had many long talks, as he could talk to me,' Ramsey Tainsh recalls. 'We had long chats on Japan and how the British Government and Army failed to see the obvious. I told him that the Singapore authorities had failed to protect the water supplies of the so-called fortress as if the Japs would attack from the sea. I said I disagreed with the training, and that the UK government had neglected South-east Asia and the Japanese realised this.'

The two men used to talk well into the night, sharing experiences and beliefs, and it was at Jhelum that Patrick told Ramsey Tainsh about the women he used to sleep with in the Turkish Baths of Jermyn Street and about the sexual acts they would perform, including what he described as *gamahuche* – a word popularly used at the time to describe oral sex. But even these intimate conversations and the time the two men spent together did not turn their relationship into true friendship. 'Heenan and I were not friends but we both realised that we were not the type that was wanted in the regiment,' Ramsey Tainsh explains.

'It was in Jhelum that I realised that he was very angry and wanted to have his own back. I told the Adjutant [Lieutenant I. Pringle] that Heenan should be removed from the Army. But I was not taken seriously as I was in the process myself of trying to leave the regiment to get into the Political Service. Heenan should never have been sent to a key post, in fact he should not have been commissioned in the first place. He must have known that Malaya and Singapore were lost as soon as he set foot there. He knew the 1/16th were going to kick him upstairs and it was obvious to me he should not be put in any key place as he was a deeply hurt man.'

But Indian Army officers' memories of Patrick are not all bad. For he was soon involved in action on the North-West Frontier that was to lead those who served with him to express admiration for him. Major S. T. A. Longley, a retired officer, had been recalled to the Indian Army just before the war with Germany began. 'When I got back to my battalion, the 1/16th,

Heenan was one of the officers there,' Longley says. 'He was with me in a minor action which took place on the North-West Frontier.'[3]

In February 1940, following a series of marauding raids by a *lashkar*, or band of warring Pathans, 3rd (Jhelum) Brigade, which now comprised the 1/16th Punjabis, the 1/3rd Queen Alexandra's Own Gurkha Rifles, the 1/10th Baluch Regiment and a number of mountain artillery units, was ordered immediately to Bannu, deep inside Waziristan, and Patrick Heenan finally had the opportunity to prove himself to his fellow officers.

As the brigade moved out of Jhelum, the garrison town was alive with the movement of troops, animals and equipment. All Indian cities and towns pulsate with life no matter what the time of day but in a garrison town with the army on the move, the hustle and bustle had to be seen to be believed. The ground itself seemed to move under the pounding of many feet as company after company marched to the troop trains waiting in the railway station, the senior NCOs barking out orders to their men. Behind them came the large Missouri mules of the mountain artillery units, each animal capable of carrying up to 350lb. of pack howitzer, their hooves clattering on the ground and their harnesses and disassembled gun parts jangling and clanking. Finally came the host of camp-followers, the syces or grooms, the bhistis and the dhobi-wallahs, the washermen, all chattering excitedly under the watchful eye of the kotwal or head man.[4]

But no-one would have been more excited at the prospect of long-awaited action than the young subalterns, many of them going into action for the first time. Here at last was the chance to gain their spurs. They were off to fight the Pathans, among the most formidable fighting men in the world, for whom fighting was a way of life. The Pathan was a mountain Will o' the wisp, expert at ambushes and hit-and-run attacks, and against such tactics the Army, for all its superior firepower, its armoured cars, its artillery and its aircraft, had no answer. Only when the Army managed to create the conditions for a set-piece battle did it achieve any real success and then the Pathans were usually crushed.

The tribesmen were ruthless fighters. Most of their captives and any wounded inadvertently left behind were castrated and flayed alive. Even the dead were barbarously mutilated so it had become a point of honour in the Indian and British armies that their dead and wounded were never left behind to the mercies of the Pathans.

And the ruthlessness was not all one-sided. There are recorded instances, after mutilated corpses of soldiers had been found, of Army commanders issuing orders to their men that no prisoners were to be taken. More often than not it was a case of no quarter asked and none given.

Despite the cold-blooded approach displayed by both sides, the British played 'the game' to certain rules. Over the years, a systematic pattern of war had developed between the two sides. The British knew that, once the current bout of fighting had been put down, they could look forward to a period of relative quiet, during which the Political Agents based in the Tribal Territories would manage to sit on any new trouble for a while. But these spells of comparative calm were unlikely to come about if Pathan women and children had been harmed, wells and water channels blown up, or the Pathans' fragile attempts at agriculture had been destroyed. So there was never all-out war and certainly no scorched-earth policy.

After one battle, Ramsey Tainsh and his orderly went around destroying Pathan hand mills and baking stones, and holing every water container they could lay their hands on, but he was stopped by the Political Officer who admonished him for such behaviour. The argument put forward by Ramsey Tainsh that if you got rid of these essential items, or better still of the masons who made them, there would be no more trouble in Waziristan for the rest of the war, was frowned upon. It was just not 'playing the game'.

Under the rules of the game, the British were never permitted to open hostilities and were therefore robbed of one of the most effective of military tactics, the pre-emptive strike. They always had to wait until the Pathans had actually committed some offence, even when there had been indications or intelligence that trouble was on the way.

But now a *lashkar* was on the loose and the 1/16th and the rest of 3rd Brigade were on their way to sort it out. The excitement at the forthcoming action combined with an understandable fear of what might lie ahead produced a heady mix and as the troops entrained at Jhelum station there was an undoubted tension in the air.

And it was as the train carrying the 1/16th prepared to leave on the long journey through the night to Bannu that Patrick became embroiled in yet another incident that demonstrated his remarkable ability to upset his fellow officers, his propensity for finding trouble where none had previously existed and – possibly the only laudable side to his character – his obsession with protecting the underdog.

The other British officer involved in the incident, which demonstrated how Patrick tended to relate more to the Indian officers than to his fellow Britons, remembers it clearly. 'A very recently attached Indian Commissioned Officer from a State Force was to accompany our battalion to Waziristan where operations against the Pathans in the Tribal Territory were soon to begin,' the officer says. 'On the regimental special train due to leave Jhelum station that particular night in February 1940, he and I were allocated by the officer i/c travelling arrangements a two-berth compartment to share (top and bottom bunks). I told my bearer that if he got to the train reasonably early he could probably get my bed made up on the bottom bunk [always the favourite], unless my travelling companion had already taken it, in which case, he should prepare my bed on the top bunk.

'In due course, my bearer reported back to me, as instructed, to tell me that all was well and my bed had been made up on the lower bunk, as by the time he had left the carriage, neither the other occupant nor his bedding had arrived. Eventually, having completed my entraining duties, and just as the train was about to depart, I reached my compartment. Imagine my surprise and extreme irritation to find my bedding was in a heap in the middle of the carriage floor with the attached officer, looking distinctly uncomfortable, sitting on the lower bunk made up with bedding for him to sleep on!

'On questioning, he told me straight out that Lieutenant Heenan had come into the compartment just as he was having the top bunk made up for himself and, learning who was sharing the compartment, had thrown my bedding from the lower bunk on to the floor. He further gave a direct instruction to the attached officer that under no circumstances was he to agree to nor allow any change from what had been done.

'Although I had not seen the incident actually happening, I believed the attached officer's explanation completely and utterly as, from my short experience, I knew that no other officer in the regiment would have done such a thing, nor would a newly attached officer of an obvious gentle disposition have risked antagonising, without any good reason, a brother officer of a battalion he had only just joined.

'The action described to me was one that I had no doubt was the sort that Heenan was quite capable of perpetrating, particularly as he was named clearly and without hesitation by the attached officer concerned. To avoid any further embarrassment to my Indian Officer colleague, I decided to accept the situation and do nothing further about it.

'Heenan had no right nor business to take it upon himself to interfere as he did as to how two junior officers of equal rank (both lieutenants) should arrange to share the train accommodation allocated to them. He was not my company commander nor was he even in the same company as myself. Suffice it to say that he never subsequently broached this episode to me and after much thought I concluded that I should treat the whole episode with the contempt it deserved. It served however as a warning to me and I never forgot this revealing, and unpleasant to me, aspect of his character.'

There was undoubtedly an inherent racism in the Indian Army but if Patrick was seeking to put right some perceived wrong, there was none committed here. In this case the 'bagging' of the lower bunk was nothing more than a question of 'first come, first served' which the officer concerned had specifically instructed his bearer to accept. But the officer's lack of surprise at Patrick's action, his reluctance to challenge him on it and his long memory of the incident are clear indications of the deep antagonism the mess bully evoked among his fellow officers.

Bannu lies about three hundred miles up-country from Jhelum as the crow flies, but by rail the distance is considerably longer and the journey took the rest of the night and much of the following morning. At Bannu, the battalion disembarked and then marched a few further miles into the hills to a place called Kurram Ghari where it was to set up camp.

The brigade was generally lucky with the weather. Winter on the North-West Frontier could be extremely bad and the area was frequently covered in ice and snow. Since the Indian Army infantry always wore knee-length shorts and never wore rain capes in combat because of the difficulty of handling weapons, it could prove very uncomfortable indeed even without the threat from the Pathans. But on this occasion the worst the battalion suffered was occasional heavy thunderstorms. Most of these were at night and one in particular was spectacular. The lightning turned the night into brilliant day as the thunder roared and cracked overhead, echoing off the surrounding mountains. The accompanying rain lasted for several hours and was so heavy that the camp was flooded out, with only a few of the tents and bivouacs surviving the torrential downpour. But apart from the storms, the weather remained relatively good throughout the campaign. It was bitterly cold at night and early in the morning, but as the sun rose the temperatures became quite comfortable.

The *lashkar* of warring Pathans had based itself in a protected area known as the Ahmedzai Salient which it was using as a hideout from which to carry out raids into the surrounding countryside. The brigade's primary objective was to bring the Pathans out into the open, engage them in battle, and destroy them. Once this had been achieved, it was to build roads to make future troop movements easier and then it was to carry out patrols along the road, a duty known as RP, 'road protection'.

The camp at Kurram Ghari was well protected by outlying pickets based at strategic points on the surrounding hills. Some of these were armed with Vickers machine-guns, some were permanent and reinforced each night. Others were moved around. But whatever the troops did, they followed the golden rule of the frontier – never make the same move twice. For the Pathans had a nasty habit of carefully watching and noting any signs of regular troop movements and were expert at laying ambushes and booby-traps, which were made from stolen grenades and shells discarded by the army as dud. They were also expert snipers and it was not unknown for them to use dum-dum bullets which would break up in the victim's body, ripping his internal organs apart.

The defenders of the camp at Kurram Ghari were well aware of the danger from Pathan snipers, particularly at night, and took appropriate measures to minimise the danger to the camp and its surrounding outposts, but one night the Pathans made a change to their usual mode of attack, carrying out a determined raid on the camp itself.

'I was off duty and asleep in my "dug-down" bivouac tent,' says one of the officers who was at Kurram Ghari that night.[5] 'I found myself suddenly wide awake having been aroused by what appeared to be the father and mother of a battle raging. The noise seemed to indicate that every soldier manning the perimeter armed with small arms, Very lights, etc. was engaged in "rapid fire". By the time I reached my battle position on the perimeter, the noise and volume of fire began to diminish, fire discipline was restored and silence fell.'

As the sun came up, the full strength of the attack became apparent. A strong force of Pathans had infiltrated the outlying pickets and had got within thirty yards of the camp perimeter before being spotted. Spent cartridges at the point where they had been stopped told the tale. It was impossible to say how many Pathans had been killed or wounded for, like the British, the tribesmen carried their casualties away with them whenever they could, although sometimes details emerged later through established intelligence sources.

On Wednesday 14th February, 3rd Brigade set out on a 'reconnaissance in force' and it was in the ensuing actions that Patrick was to distinguish himself, although even here his temper was to lead to a needless altercation with one of his fellow officers.

There were two main routes, some miles apart, into the Ahmedzai Salient where the Pathan *lashkar* was hiding out. Both were through very narrow defiles overlooked on both sides by high, and in places precipitous, hills which provided the tribesmen with excellent opportunity to attack the approaching Indian Army troops. It was important to keep the enemy guessing as to which of the two gorges was to be used to approach the salient so that he needed to divide his forces. The brigade planned a feint advance towards Mirza Khel which lay in the hills opposite one of the two approaches to the salient and then down to the defile itself, the plan being then to advance along the other approach a few days later.

As an additional diversion, the RAF flew overt aerial reconnaissance missions over the whole area, using Westland Wapitis and Hawker Hart light day-bombers armed with 25lb. Cooper bombs which they carried under their wings. Given the Pathans' habit of castrating and flaying their captives, the RAF aircrew all carried notices — popularly known as 'gooly chits' — which offered substantial rewards to the tribesmen for their safe return to British lines alive and, perhaps just as importantly, physically intact.

Having reached the mouth of the first defile, the diversionary force began to withdraw but 'A' Company of the 1/16th, the Sikh company, which was commanded by Lieutenant David Potts and had led the approach into the mouth of the defile, found itself cut off from the rest of the force. It then came under attack from several hundred well-concealed Pathan tribesmen who had been lying in wait for them. It suffered immediate casualties including Potts, who was killed outright. He was one of the most promising of the battalion's young subalterns.

What happened next is far from clear. 'My company was in reserve,' Ramsey Tainsh says. 'Lieutenant Heenan went forward to try and help Potts.' Another officer who was there remembers meeting Patrick as he returned from trying to help his fallen comrade. 'The Punjabi Mussalman "C" Company [of the 1/16th], of which I was second-in-command, was ordered forward literally at the double to help extricate our Sikh company, which was pinned to the ground it had been forced to retake in order to recover its casualties. On the way forward, I passed the body of David Potts being carried back on a stretcher, as well as a wounded sepoy. Somewhere around this time, I saw Heenan, who was not in my company [he was in 'B' company, the Dogra company], and I noticed he had blood on his hands and slightly up one forearm.

'Somewhat concerned, I went up to him and asked if he was all right or had been injured? His response, I could best describe as "savage" and, whilst I can't remember his precise comments, it was clear that my inquiry had somewhat infuriated him. He expressed himself in no uncertain unfriendly terms. We were all upset at the turn of events that afternoon but it was beyond me why he should react in the way he did.'

A few days later, on Tuesday 20th February, the Brigade left the Kurram Ghari camp under cover of night leaving only a skeleton force behind as a decoy. The troops marched ten miles through the night to the second defile, known as Gomati Tangi, in order to be ready to advance along it at first light. They were supported by the Rolls-Royce armoured cars of a cavalry regiment and the mountain artillery units. The Indian Army's mountain artillery had a formidable reputation and the sight of the giant Missouri mules trotting into position with the pieces of the 3.7-inch pack howitzers on their back which the tindals, or gunners, would then reassemble ready to fire, within the space of a minute, was always impressive.

The battle for Gomati Tangi began at dawn as heavy 6-inch howitzers opened fire from the brigade's rear on what appeared to be the *lashkar*'s headquarters high up on a pinnacle of rock above the gorge. 'Here they flew their standards, one in particular distinctly larger than the rest,' one officer recalls. 'This was eventually captured by the 1/3rd Gurkhas.'

The light howitzers of the mountain artillery opened up, bombarding the hilltop defences for the best part of an hour, and then eventually the infantry battalions moved forward, covered by machine-gun fire. There was little in the way of natural cover in the undulating slope of the approach to the defile and instead of charging straight down it, the troops began to climb to get to grips with the enemy.

Throughout the morning, the battle for control of the hilltops raged, and once again Patrick's fitness and courage impressed his fellow officers. 'I was an eyewitness to his courage, dash and agility, when the Dogra "B" Company was the battalion's leading company, attacking the crucial objective line leading into the Ahmedzai Salient territory,' one of the officers says. 'Contrary to normal practice, the tribesmen were so confident that they stood to fight a defensive battle on a "set-piece" basis. The objective which "B" Company had to take was an extremely difficult one, i.e. almost vertical rock-surfaced hills hundreds of feet above the open ground which had to be covered before reaching the foot of this formidable objective. Heenan, who was either the company commander or second-in-command, I can't recall which, was always in the forefront of this attack which I could observe clearly but at some distance from where my company, "C", was in reserve awaiting the second phase of the attack. I can remember at the time being impressed with the determination and courage with which this successful attack was executed and this certainly included Heenan.'

In the face of heavy fire from some of the world's toughest fighting men, Patrick had shown considerable courage. Whatever else he was, he was certainly not a coward.

The fighting was extremely fierce everywhere. When a platoon of the 1/10th Baluchis reached a strongly defended post high up on a plateau, they were held up by heavy fire. A popular Viceroy's Commissioned Officer led the attack against the enemy position but was shot and mortally wounded. Stung to fury by the sight of the officer falling, the platoon charged forward into the teeth of the enemy's fire. The Pathans kept firing until the last moment, then dropped their weapons and raised their hands in surrender. But by now there was no stopping the angry Indian troops who showed no mercy and took no prisoners.

By the early afternoon, the brigade had secured its initial objectives, with the Pathans, who had suffered very heavy casualties, retreating deep into their territory. 'C' Company of the 1/16th then took over the forward positions captured by Patrick's sub-unit, 'B' Company. But before he and his men fell back into a reserve position, they had one more objective.

'There were a number of caves between our position and some of the high ground immediately to the front. In the retreat from our original defensive position, certainly one and perhaps two or three Pathans had taken up a new position in a cave some two hundred yards to our immediate front. We came under intermittent sniper fire from it and despite every effort to neutralise the occupant or occupants by continuous LMG [light machine-gun] fire penetrating the entrance, 3.7-inch howitzer fire from the mountain artillery being brought down just two hundred yards away from us with great accuracy, the hostile fire continued in defiant response!'

By this time, the entrance of the cave had been virtually sealed off by artillery fire, but even this did not prevent the Pathans trapped inside from firing on the attackers. 'It was then decided to send a section of "B" Company Dogras to attack the cave with hand-grenades. A gallant Lance-Naik, moving over most difficult terrain eventually reached the entrance but, before he could throw a grenade in, he was promptly shot through the face at close range. Fortunately he survived, though badly wounded, being rescued by his comrades from where he had fallen. It was then decided to call off further action as it was obvious the cave dweller or dwellers would not surrender and would probably slip away that night if any wounds allowed.'

The Pathans' wounds did allow them to slip away in the night, for a search of the cave the next day found only some blood-stained clothing, a number of shell splinters and expended British bullets. But this was the last determined resistance from the Pathans. The Battle of Gomati Tangi ended in a victory for 3rd Brigade. Patrick had passed his first test under fire with flying colours. 'Given a chance he did well in Waziristan,' Ramsey Tainsh summed up. 'He acquitted himself well.'

The entire brigade had done well too. The deception plan had worked brilliantly and by scaling the sides of the gorge, the Indian troops had avoided the warm reception of boiling oil and large boulders that the Pathans had been preparing for them further along it. Next day, the brigade marched into the Ahmedzai Salient, set up Gomati camp and started building roads to make future policing of the territory easier.

It was to be the last engagement that both Patrick Heenan and Ramsey Tainsh fought with the 1/16th. 'I was at Lieutenant Potts's funeral and Heenan was standing by me,' Tainsh says. 'That was the last time I saw him. I got stomach trouble and left the 1/16th Punjabis and joined the RIASC.' Within a month of the end of the Waziristan Campaign, Colonel Powell also left the battalion. His place was taken by Lieutenant-Colonel C. P. Clarke. Two months after he took over, the battalion moved with the rest of 3rd Brigade to nearby Damdil, where they were engaged in routine road protection duties. In October 1940, the 1/16th was detached from the brigade and moved to Nicholson Lines at Kohat, closer to the Khyber Pass. But by now Patrick Heenan also was no longer with them.

Colonel Clarke was a popular commanding officer but, like his predecessor, he had soon had enough of the mess misfit. Patrick's exploits at the Battle of Gomati Tangi had not been enough to change the battalion's opinion of him and when the opportunity came to make him someone else's problem, Clarke grabbed it with both hands.

CHAPTER 9

'A HOTBED FOR JAPANESE SPIES'

As the Indian Army expanded to make up for the loss of British and Indian regiments sent to reinforce the troops in Europe and North Africa, experienced officers were at a premium. Those with any length of service in the Indian Army were spread around among various battalions and, in spite of his record and the fact that he was still more than four hundred places down the lieutenants' seniority list, Patrick was promoted to the temporary rank of captain and transferred to the 2nd Battalion of the 16th Punjab Regiment, commanded by Lieutenant-Colonel F. M. Moore.

The battalion was off to Malaya as part of the 6th Indian Infantry Brigade to reinforce the British and Indian troops there. The 12th Indian Brigade – Force Emu – under Brigadier A. C. M. Paris, had been despatched to Malaya a year earlier to placate the Australian and New Zealand governments who were understandably worried by the possibility of a Japanese offensive in South-east Asia.[1]

But the reassignment of the British units to the war in Europe, which was being given a higher priority by the government in London, meant that no British battalion could this time be spared to go to Malaya as part of the 6th Brigade. So it was made up of three Indian Army battalions – the 1/8th Punjab Regiment, the 2/15th Punjab Regiment, and the 2/16th Punjab Regiment, Patrick's new unit.

It is possible that Patrick requested the transfer after hearing that the 2/16th were off to Malaya, where he was bound to be more useful to Japanese intelligence, or indeed that his controllers told him to apply for the posting. The other possibility is that he was transferred in order to get a troublesome officer away from India. By now his reputation as a trouble-maker had spread beyond the messes of the 16th Punjab Regiment. Several

Indian Army officers of the period who had never met Patrick, had heard of him in distinctly unfavourable terms. Brigadier John King-Martin, who did not see Patrick again after the voyage out on the *Neuralia*, says that he heard mention of Patrick's bad reputation several times. But whatever the reason for his departure, there was no doubt a collective sigh of relief in the 1/16th to be rid of the battalion's least popular officer.

The brigade, codenamed Force Abnormal, began to assemble near Bombay on 13th October 1940. Six days later, Patrick and the rest of the 2/16th set sail for Malaya on board the troop transport *Santhia*. The brigade headquarters contingent were on the *Dunera*, and the other two battalions were on the *Islami* and the *Talma*, while their motor transport unit was loaded aboard the *Jala Mohan*. The convoy was protected from the German surface raiders and submarines that were known to be operating in the Indian Ocean by the 'D' class cruiser HMS *Danae* and the armed merchant cruiser HMS *Hector*.[2] Perhaps it was comparisons with the merchant cruiser's substantial superstructure that caused the officers of the 2/16th to dub their new, well-built messmate 'Hector' Heenan, a nickname he had never had in the 1/16th, but it seems more probable that it was because he was already known as a swaggering bully.[3]

The convoy arrived off Penang on 27th October, but it was three days until Patrick's battalion disembarked and a week before it had settled into its new camp at Ipoh. By early 1941, it had moved to Tanjong Pao, before settling close to the Thai border at Arau in Perlis, the most northern of the Malay States. The battalion carried out some jungle training but, in a move typical of the complacency which characterised most of the Allied preparations for war in Malaya, 'training was seriously handicapped by restrictions on cross-country movement to avoid damage to rubber trees, and the medical authorities put a stop to night operations for fear of malaria'.[4]

The proximity of the battalion to the Malay/Thai border facilitated Patrick's contacts with his new principal controller, who appears to have wasted no time in putting him to work. Patrick made a number of clandestine trips into Thailand during his time at Arau, and began passing on secret information. He is known to have had a number of meetings with a mysterious 'Dutchman', a cover frequently used by German agents, telling the British soldier who drove him to meet the man that it was 'not necessary to mention it to anyone'. Perhaps this 'Dutchman' was his 'local controller', but undoubtedly any information he supplied would have been passed back to Tokyo via the Japanese embassy in Bangkok, a well-established route for Intelligence from northern Malaya.

The Japanese espionage system on the Malay peninsula was an extremely complex and loose-knit affair. For a long time before they attacked in December 1941, the Japanese had been building up their intelligence information about Malaya. Much of this was of a commercial nature but a large part of it was military and it was all being relayed back to Tokyo.

The intelligence was not collected through any single network of spies. It came mainly in the form of various small pieces of a large jigsaw collected separately by groups or individuals from within the 5,600-strong Japanese community. These agents were united only by similar aims and targets, sometimes passing information on to each other but generally passing it across the border into Thailand to the Japanese embassy in Bangkok, or to the Japanese Consulate-General in Singapore. There was no clear-cut method of coordinating the activities of these groups, but Singapore Special Branch believed that the man in charge of at least part of this operation was Dr Tsune Ouchi, the Japanese Deputy Director of the League of Nations Health Bureau in Singapore.

No full examination of the espionage, counter-espionage and fifth-column activities in Malaya has ever been published, largely because many of the British official files remain locked away under the government's stringent secrecy rules. Some have been closed until the year 2015, while, even now, one intelligence file containing a 'black list' of enemy agents in the Far East is still marked 'retained in department', a method used by government departments to prevent files from being opened to the public.[5] The information that is available in open files lies scattered among various Foreign, Colonial, Admiralty and War Office documents in the Public Records Office at Kew. Nevertheless, what is available clearly shows that, in the two years leading up to the Japanese entry into the war, Malaya and Singapore were awash with anti-British spies and fifth-columnists, most of them Japanese.

Harry Miller, a journalist on the *Straits Times* during that period and later to become the newspaper's editor, recalls that rumours of spies were rife.[6] As early as February 1938, one Foreign Office official in London wrote that Singapore was apparently becoming 'more of a hotbed for Japanese spies'.[7] This was no exaggeration, and the main plank of the Japanese intelligence effort was the massive network of Japanese nationals living and working in Malaya and Singapore.

The Japanese had been actively setting up a string of 'sleeper' agents across the region since the First World War, which they entered on the side of the Allies. Part of Japan's First World War role was to help ensure that the Indian Ocean was kept clear of German naval units, and Britain readily made port facilities in Penang available to the Japanese Navy.

From then on, every Malay township had its Japanese photographer, its Japanese barber or its Japanese storekeeper, and every seaport received regular visits by Japanese fishermen who would routinely send home reports of what they saw. Japanese brothels, initially staffed by Japanese girls, but later by locals, blossomed in every large town in Malaya in the twenties and early thirties. In Singapore these 'happy houses' were centred around Malay and Malabar Streets off Middle Road. They became extremely popular not only with members of the British forces but also, for somewhat different reasons, with Japanese agents. Middle Road was famous for its many Japanese stores, the largest of which, K. Baba & Company, rivalled the British department stores in Raffles Place. Japanese companies invested heavily in Malayan rubber estates and other property. Some of this land was around the major routes into and out of Singapore, allowing troop movements and exercises to be monitored. The small port of Batu Pahat on the west coast of Johore – which was to be the site of a major Japanese landing – was virtually encircled by Japanese-owned rubber estates.

By 1940, with the British war effort largely committed to Europe, Japanese intelligence gathering in the region was becoming increasingly aggressive, particularly in Thailand. Just a month before the invasion, the Far East Combined Bureau (FECB), the body which controlled British intelligence gathering in the region, reported that 'Japanese espionage and intelligence activities are widespread, efficient and comprehensive. . . It can be assumed that their reconnaissance of the country has been largely completed; there can be no doubt whatever that their information is much more complete than ours'.[8]

The FECB said the intensification of Japanese intelligence activities was believed to have begun with a tour of Thailand by Rear Admiral Maeda, the Japanese equivalent of the British Director of Naval Intelligence, in April 1941. All available evidence indicated that the Japanese had thoroughly covered every field of commercial, economic and military intelligence, and that its agents were suitably placed to obtain information on every subject likely to be of value to the Japanese General Staff.

In 1939 the Japanese Legation in Bangkok was only seven strong, of which two were service attachés. In March 1941 they opened a consulate at Singora in the south, and in the following month another at Chiengmai in the north. In August of that year the Legation was upgraded to Embassy status. By November, the staff had grown to forty-eight, and no fewer than twenty-six of those were service attachés. The latter included a group of eight 'special' military attachés led by General S. Takagi. There was also a 'special' naval attaché, Rear Admiral S. Sakamoto, in addition to the naval attaché himself, Rear Admiral Naomasa Sakonju, and his staff of four assistants. A man posing as a secretary at the Singora Consulate, Saburu Shiro, was known to be a military officer, and at both Singora and Chiengmai there were other unidentified service officers.

The military attaché at the Japanese Embassy, Colonel Hiroshi Tamura, was in charge of all intelligence gathering matters, and all military intelligence reports concerning British possessions in South-east Asia passed through his hands. He would have had a channel of communications with Dr Tsune Ouchi, and the Japanese Consulate-General in Singapore.

The FECB considered that the Japanese Consulate at Chiengmai was suitably placed to control intelligence matters in North Thailand and Burma, while the Singora Consulate was established to control intelligence gathering in South Thailand and Malaya. Situated only fifty miles to the north of the nearest point on the Malayan border, Singora was almost certainly the centre from which Heenan's activities were directed. Saburu Shiro, the military officer there posing as a secretary, would have been either Patrick's main controller, or at the very least, in charge of the officer who was. One of the undercover men was a Major Osone, who had the responsibility for setting up a guide system in the area.

The FECB estimated that the Japanese spent £50,000 monthly on propaganda matters within Thailand. That was a vast sum, and the Japanese must have spent additional large sums on their espionage network. There were several reports during the months prior to the war that Japanese commercial companies in South-east Asia were busy extending their activities in the espionage field. One rubber firm, Nomura and Company, which was known to be a cover for espionage activities, opened new offices in Bangkok and at Sungei Golok a few miles from the Malay border in Thailand. The company's manager in Sungei Golok was arrested by the Thai authorities in January 1941 after being caught mapping the surrounding countryside.

Large numbers of Japanese agents were rounded up in Operations 'Collar' and 'Trousers' within hours of the start of the war with Japan, but by then they had already done their job. Every weakness in the British defences had been pinpointed, from the numbers and quality of troops and aircraft to Singapore's lack of defences against an attacker approaching by land.[9]

Much of the intelligence collected in Singapore and Malaya was sent in code in the diplomatic traffic between Singapore and Tokyo and was intercepted by the Allies. Because of the intense secrecy that even now still surrounds some aspects of the Bletchley Park operation few of the British intercepts of Japanese signals are available. But far more examples of MAGIC, the codename given by the Americans to the Japanese intercepts, have been made public and a translation of one diplomatic message from Singapore to Tokyo on 16th February 1941 shows just how much information was being sent back:

REPORT ON DEFENCES FOLLOWING FRONTIER INSPECTION BY SHIMANUKI 7TH-14TH FEBRUARY. ROUTE: PENANG, ALOR STAR, HAADYAI, SINGORA (S. THAILAND), KOTA BHARU*

ABOUT 6000 TROOPS IN SUNGEI PATANI (WESTERN AND CENTRAL BORDER DEFENCE PIVOT) 1000 AUSTRALIANS, 500 MALAYAN AND HALF CASTE REST INDIAN. 1000 IN PENANG: 3000 SU PA (JAP SPELLING) 1000 ALOR STAR, 1000 MATU AERU (JAP SPELLING) (PERLIS STATE): 200 ATTACHED TROOP TRANSPORT LORRIES (TRUCKS?) 100 MUNITION LORRIES (TRUCKS?); NUMBER TANKS MINED AREAS; ROADS AND BRIDGES OVER FRONTIER. CENTRAL DISTRICT, PLACES FROM ONE POINT 2 MILES EAST OF BALING (KEDAH) TO KROH (5 MILES IN PERAK). WESTERN DISTRICT PLACES UP TO ONE MILE SOUTH OF FRONTIER.

300 INDIANS IN KROH AND 400 NEAR AERODROME (3 HANGARS) 8 MILES NORTH OF ALOR STAR ON ROAD. 50 NEW BARRACKS IN PLANTATIONS NEAR ROAD 10 MILES NORTH ALOR STAR AND SOME AT MATU AERU (JAP SPELLING) ACCOMMODATING 40 PER BARRACK. NO ONE OBSERVED, APPARENTLY PREPARATORY TO DESPATCH OF TROOPS.[10]

There were several reports of unidentified radio transmitters in Malaya in the run-up to the Japanese invasion. General

* The notes in brackets were inserted by the intelligence analyst who processed the report. The tanks referred to were probably armoured vehicles of some kind. There were no British tanks in Malaya.

Percival, G O C Malaya Command, said a powerful transmitter based in Malaya which had been sending messages to Japan for a long time had never been discovered. Four months before the war, on 2nd July 1941, the Signals Section of the 22nd Indian Brigade at Kuantan picked up signals from a radio station located outside the brigade's area and using the call-sign 'B C A'. The army operators were instructed not to attempt to contact the station.[11]

All the information gathered by the spies in the south was passed by the Japanese Consulate-General at Singapore on to the *Toa Keizai Chosa Kyoku*, the East Asiatic Economic Investigation Bureau in Tokyo, which in turn passed any relevant intelligence on to Japanese Military Intelligence and to the Imperial High Command. In the north, it was passed back to the Japanese Embassy in Bangkok and fed straight through to Military Intelligence.

Not all espionage operations conducted in Malaya by Japanese nationals were carried out by actual residents. Some Japanese were sent in for special operations. Early in 1941, disguised as a native, a Major Asaeda was infiltrated into Thailand before crossing into northern Malaya. He returned with a detailed report on the sea coast at Kota Bharu where the Japanese were to make their first landings. Four months before the invasion, two submarines were seen berthed alongside the wharves of a Japanese mining company at Endau on the east coast of Johore. The submarines came in by night on 7th and 8th August, landing several men and leaving behind a number of boxes of equipment. No attempt appears to have been made to stop them although only two months earlier the Navy had warned that Japanese ships loading iron ore overnight at Endau could easily be used to land troops.[12]

This surprisingly relaxed, some would say careless, approach seems to have typified the British attitude to the Japanese intelligence efforts. The Japanese were not to be taken seriously. The cartoon image of little men with buck teeth and large spectacles prevailed. Only four days before the Japanese invasion the C-in-C Far East, Air Chief Marshal Sir Robert Brooke-Popham, was telling a press conference: 'There are clear signs that Japan does not know which way to turn. Tojo is scratching his head.'

Japanese agents armed with pencils and notebooks openly followed members of the Argyll & Sutherland Highlanders about as they constructed the Kota Tinggi Line – a series of Maginot-line-style defensive emplacements about sixty miles north of Singapore. They did little to disguise their intentions and it was as if the British could not believe that the Japanese would do anything worth worrying about. The agents were apparently allowed to carry on about their business unimpeded, although the Argylls took great delight in planting bogus markers to confuse them.

'Laying out the Kota Tinggi Line was always an entertaining pastime, as it was invariably done to the accompaniment of Japanese agents,' said Major Angus Rose of the Argylls. 'These nips would follow along behind us taking all the measurements and carefully writing them down in their notebooks; so, in order to give the little men more home-work, we used to stick in extra pegs. So much for British anti-espionage, although there are a lot more stories that could be told.'[13]

It was widely regarded in Singapore as a huge joke that the clubhouse of the Japanese Golf Club, near the junction of Tanglin and Alexandra Roads in Singapore, had a grandstand view of the fortifications and gun emplacements on the island's Pasir Panjang Hills.

Singapore's Deputy Chief of Police, Mervyn Llewellyn Wynne, found his preoccupation with writing reports on Japanese subversion dismissed as paranoia in some quarters, but information gathered by Singapore Special Branch left little room for such accusations, and Operations 'Collar' and 'Trousers' showed quite how concerned the British Colonial authorities were over the activities of the Japanese residents. A few days before the invasion, the War Office sent the following MOST SECRET signal to General Percival, for the attention of the Deputy Director of Military Intelligence, Far East:[14]

JAPANESE ESPIONAGE ACTIVITIES IN MALAYA EVI-
DENTLY LARGELY DIRECTED FROM BANGKOK SEEM
LATELY TO HAVE BEEN GREATLY INTENSIFIED.
FOREIGN OFFICE ASK WHETHER ANYTHING CAN BE
DONE TO PREVENT ALL JAPANESE FROM TRAVEL-
LING BETWEEN MALAYA AND THAILAND BY LAND?

The activities of Japanese agents operating out of Bangkok
were indeed causing a great deal of concern. A secret circular
on Preventative Security sent out by the Far East Combined
Bureau, which coordinated Allied intelligence and counter-
intelligence matters, warned that a member of the local staff
working in the Dutch mission in Bangkok, and known to have
had indirect contact with the Japanese military attaché, had
been found with duplicate keys to all the mission's safes.

According to correspondence between the Straits Settlements
Government and the Colonial Office in London, there were
5,600 Japanese in Malaya in July 1940, of whom 3,600 were
men. Singapore Special Branch estimated that a large number
of these were involved in some form of intelligence gathering
activity. Employees of shipping and mining companies were
particularly likely to be involved in such work, as were many
visiting 'tourists', diplomats, scientists, and members of the Japanese armed services.

Patrick Heenan's position within this ad hoc collection of
spies is not difficult to guess. Of all the individual agents he
must have become one of the most important – a spy not just
within the Allied forces themselves, but one who was to have
access to secrets vital to the Japanese in the opening hours of
the planned invasion and which would pave the way for an
inevitable victory.

But while few other individual Japanese agents had access
to the kind of information Patrick would be able to supply,
collectively they constituted a formidable intelligence effort.
General Heath, Commander of III Corps, was in no doubt that
the Japanese knew as much about British war preparations and
troop dispositions as the British knew themselves, and he was

scathing about the restrictions on the British counter-espionage effort.

'The Japanese received the most valuable assistance in. the form of guides and other intelligence agents,' he said in his unpublished private papers, adding that they had 'obviously seeded the western area with spies and agents. It would not be out of place to refer here to the striking advantage which before and during the campaign accrued to the Japanese through the superior facilities they enjoyed for obtaining accurate and timely information regarding all our military activities and for ingratiating themselves with and for obtaining timely assistance from local inhabitants.' Heath could have added that Japan was seen by them as an Asian power, operating on Asian soil, ostensibly in Asian interests, which was of untold advantage.

General Heath railed against Allied inactivity in the face of the Japanese intelligence effort – 'our authorities not ignorant of Japanese espionage activities' – and complained of the 'crabbed work of our Secret Service and counter-intelligence services. Though certain subterranean counter-espionage was conducted by us,' Heath said, 'it was not considered it would be politic to take measures before the outbreak of hostilities of a nature defamatory and outwardly inimical to a particular power.'[15]

British intelligence operations in the region were impeded not only by political constraints. They were hampered by their own fragmented nature. They were coordinated by the Far East Combined Bureau. The FECB had been set up in Hong Kong in 1934 but was now based at the Singapore Naval Base and controlled by C-in-C, China Fleet. Staffed by officers from all three services, it was responsible for the collection and collation of all intelligence information from Burma, Malaya, and Hong Kong. It had links with the Pacific Naval Intelligence Organisation, which itself collated information from naval sources from the east coast of Africa to the west coast of North and South America.

The FECB had set up a Security Intelligence Section in 1940 'to build up a comprehensive picture of the persons and organisations working against British security in the Far East, and to convey this to the various organisations who are in a position to make use of it'.[16] It was also involved in the monitoring of enemy radio traffic. British Intelligence had broken the main Japanese naval cipher, JN25, before the war and former FECB codebreakers say they anticipated the Japanese attack on Pearl Harbor and attempted to warn the Americans.[17] There was a military 'Y' SIGINT monitoring station at Kranji linked to a naval and military cryptanalysis section at Seletar in Singapore, and a Royal Navy organisation known as the Operational Intelligence Centre which had counterparts in the Admiralty and the Mediterranean and coordinated, controlled and promulgated all Navy intelligence. It was closely linked to the FECB and was based at Fort Canning in Singapore.

Headquarters, Malaya Command, had its own intelligence branch but its remit covered only military intelligence matters inside Malaya. In 1936, at the request of the then GOC Malaya, Major-General W. G. S. Dobbie, the War Office despatched Colonel F. Hayley-Bell to Singapore as head of military intelligence. Hayley-Bell's team uncovered a number of Japanese espionage operations and predicted with considerable accuracy where Japanese troops would land, but it was disbanded in 1939, just when it was most needed, by Dobbie's successor, Major-General L. V. Bond.[18]

For much of their Malayan intelligence, the services were dependent upon the intelligence branches of the Civil Police. The link between the military and civil authorities was the Defence Security Office of the Singapore Government. There was also a Malayan Intelligence Committee, the members of which were representatives of the services, the Civil Police and the Defence Security Office.

The fragmentation did not end there however. Malaya was not one country, but a group of sultanates. These had been divided into two administrative groupings by the British, and called, respectively, the Federated Malay States (FMS) and the Unfederated Malay States (UMS). Then there was the Straits Settlements (SS), a British colony covering Singapore, Penang and Malacca. Both the FMS and the SS had their separate police forces. So did each of the five constituent sultanates which made up the UMS, although these state police forces were under the command of officers seconded from either the SS or FMS.

In theory, the Head of the Straits Settlements Police was responsible for intelligence gathering throughout the country, but with such a complicated political structure, there was a considerable lack of coordination. There are more than a few indications that rivalry between the various branches hampered the overall intelligence and counter-intelligence effort. To make matters worse, some of those involved in British intelligence operations appeared to be as dismissive of the Japanese threat as Air Chief Marshal Brooke-Popham.

In the months before the war began, the military authorities had been busy sending their own agents across the border into Thailand on reconnaissance missions. Between June and the end of October 1941, a total of 36 British officers had travelled into Thailand on intelligence 'recces' with a further 15 planned to go there before December. But the officers, who travelled in civilian clothes on passports describing them variously as schoolteachers, retired civil servants or musicians, appeared to regard the whole exercise as a joke.

The profession of at least one of the officers was given on his passport as 'comedian', while another was described as a 'retired tight-rope acrobat'. Not surprisingly this latter aroused the suspicions of the Thai police who stopped him for questioning. Fortunately, in an exercise that must have been the verbal equivalent of his supposed former trade, the officer managed to lie his way out of trouble. On another occasion, British officers actually met up with Japanese officers, also in civilian clothes. The Japanese were checking details of their planned advance south from their future landing sites at Singora and Patani, while the British were checking over the same ground for their proposed advance north from Malaya!

The Secret Intelligence Service (SIS), perhaps better known as MI6, was active in Singapore, but reported directly to London. From a few months before the Japanese invasion, the Special Operations Executive (SOE) was also represented, and set up a jungle training centre at Tanjong Balai at the mouth of the Jurong river. This camp was only ten miles from Singapore itself but was almost inaccessible except from the sea. In August 1941 the SOE put forward provisional plans for sabotage behind enemy lines in the event of a Japanese invasion. It would be carried out by what were to become known as 'stay-behind' units. These units were to consist not just of Asians, who could merge into the local population, but also of European planters and policemen with a deep knowledge of the country.

The plan was initially turned down by High Command in Singapore who believed that the very existence of such units would imply that a Japanese invasion was not just likely but expected to be successful. Nor were the generals too keen on the idea of arming Chinese communists who were likely to make up the bulk of the Asian recruits for the units. But the SOE pressed on regardless. One of those trained at Tanjong Balai was a French planter, Pierre Boulle, who carried out a hazardous mission in Indochina. He was captured and imprisoned but lived to write *The Bridge over the River Kwai*. Another was Freddie Spencer Chapman, who emerged after two years in the jungle leaving a trail of 1,000 dead Japanese behind him. When the Japanese invaded, the authorities did a swift U-turn. 'By this time it was too late for the plan to be effective,' wrote Spencer Chapman in *The Jungle is Neutral*. 'We had to improvise at the last moment what we hoped to organise beforehand in a careful and orderly manner.'

The 'crabbed' behaviour of the British, which stalled the SOE's plans for 'stay-behind' units and so frustrated General Heath, is partly explained by the reluctance in London to do anything that might bring Japan into the war. During the 1930s, with ominous signs of a war looming in Europe, the government in London was anxious not to risk the possibility of confrontation on another front.

The Japanese had shown themselves very sensitive to accusations of spying and not afraid to provoke diplomatic incidents given the opportunity. There was an angry diplomatic exchange in November 1938 when Assistant Superintendent J. S. H. Brett of Singapore Special Branch boarded a Japanese ship, the *Hakone Maru*, berthed at Singapore, and searched the baggage of a passenger, Akiyama Motoichu, who, unfortunately for the British, held a diplomatic passport.[19] As a consequence, right up until the time of the Japanese landings at Kota Bharu, Britain remained extremely sensitive to the possible diplomatic repercussions of any action against what was still, at least in theory, a friendly country.

In most of the cases where there was confirmed evidence of Japanese espionage, the authorities 'hushed it up', quietly deporting the people concerned. Sometimes this was unnecessary. A Japanese businessman called Nishimura, who was arrested in 1934 after being caught attempting to buy plans of the RAF air base at Seletar, swallowed a cyanide pill rather than face questioning. Another alleged Japanese spy killed himself by jumping out of a window at the CID headquarters on Robinson Road, Singapore – no easy task given that the building was only two storeys high.

But even deporting those Japanese found involved in espionage activities led inevitably to diplomatic rows between London and Tokyo. In February 1938 five Japanese men – Shohei Goma, Masaji Kosaka, Tamizo Tsujimori, Ippei Kai and Sakahiko Shirai – were deported following a report on their activities by Leonard K. Knight, the acting Director of the Singapore Special Branch.[20] One of the main official Japanese complaints against the Singapore authorities was that, while held prior to deportation, the five were given a special diet for Chinese prisoners rather than the meals given to European prisoners. But the anger in Tokyo over the deportations was more likely to have been due to the importance of the men within the Japanese espionage system.

Of the five, 'Shohei Goma' appears to have been the most important. The name was an alias. He was an officer in the Imperial Armed Forces and the younger brother of the Japanese transport minister, Nakajima Tsunekichi. According to the Knight report Shohei Goma employed Tamils and Malays as agents to monitor the movements, locations, organisation and training of British troops. Tamizo Tsujimori was alleged to have had links with Joseph Hassan, a well-known Sumatran communist. Hassan had visited Japan, where he was in contact with Rash Behari Ghose, the exiled Indian nationalist described in the Foreign Office files of the time as the 'No. 1 enemy of British rule in India'. Ghose had fled India for Japan in 1912 after attempting to assassinate the then Viceroy, Baron Hardinge of Penshurst, who was wounded in the attack. Another of the five, Sakahiko Shirai, was allegedly an ex-army officer skilled in the use of explosives.

The Knight report said that the 2,000-strong Japanese male community on Singapore island was highly organised into vocational, commercial and social groups all of which were engaged in obtaining as much information as possible concerning the most vulnerable points of the town and fortress. These were to be sabotaged in the event of war. Knight also named Dr Tsuni Ouchi, of the League of Nations Health Bureau in Singapore, as a Japanese spy. Tsuni had been part of the Japanese espionage operation since 1934 and had been involved in Nishimura's attempt to get the plans for RAF Seletar, Knight said. Three Singapore government agents, acting independently of each other and unaware of each others' existence, had reported in 1937 that Tsuni was actually the head of Japanese intelligence in Malaya. But since he enjoyed diplomatic status, the police had been unable to touch him. The League headquarters in Geneva should be contacted with a view to making him *persona non grata*, Knight added.

In another such case, the Japanese head of the local Domei News Agency, Ishiro Kobayashi, was deported in November 1940. He was also the manager of the Japanese Eastern News Agency. He was arrested on 4th August 1940 and accused of circulating 'false information' about unrest among Indian troops stationed in Singapore, at least some of which turned out to be true. Also a Formosan, Ko Tsui Kim, alias Tomoda, who worked for the Southern Godown Company, a subsidiary of the Japanese firm *Ishihara Sangyo Koshi*, was deported in

November 1940. He had been seen contacting visiting Japanese officers and was alleged to have been involved in fomenting unrest among the ethnic Chinese in Singapore since 1934.

Only occasionally did the Singapore authorities take firmer action against Japanese residents or visitors, the most famous case being that of Shinozaki Mamoru, a press attaché at the Japanese Consulate-General in Singapore.[21] When Shinozaki arrived in Singapore in late 1938, he set about building up social contacts with British servicemen. Inevitably his notoriously lavish parties began to attract the attention of the Japanese section of Singapore Special Branch. In August 1940, under surveillance from Special Branch officers, he was seen meeting several times with Gunner Frank Gardner of the Royal Artillery. Gardner was subsequently detained for questioning.

Then, in early September, Shinozaki took two visiting Japanese army officers on a guided tour of military areas in Singapore and Johore. The officers, Lieutenant-Colonel Tanikawa and Captain Kunitake, subsequently supplied information gleaned during their visit to Colonel Masanobu Tsuji, Chief of Operations and Planning Staff of the Japanese 25th Army and the main architect of the Japanese victory in Malaya.[22]

In late September, with Colonial Office approval, Shinozaki was arrested. Six other Japanese were also held but only Shinozaki himself was charged. He was formally accused of collecting military information from a gunner in the Royal Artillery, collecting information on the movements of British troops, and obtaining information from a corporal in the RAF about types of British aircraft – 'all of which information might prove useful to a foreign power'.

The Japanese made strong representations to the British government and threatened to take reprisals. Shinozaki always maintained his innocence, saying his detention was itself in response to the earlier arrests of fourteen Britons living in Japan, one of whom, Melville Cox, Reuter's correspondent in Tokyo, later fell to his death in suspicious circumstances from the window of the police station where he was being interrogated.[23]

But during Shinozaki's trial at the Singapore Assizes that

November, the Singapore police produced evidence that he had tried to obtain information about troopship movements, the positions of minefields and gun batteries, the movement of naval vessels and the types of planes deployed in Malaya. He was found guilty on two charges, of collecting information from the gunner and on the movements of British troops, fined and sentenced to three-and-a-half years 'rigorous imprisonment' in Changi Jail. (Shinozaki was released in February 1942 by the victorious Japanese army and later went to work in the Japanese administration of Singapore, issuing 'protection cards', the name given to the identity cards issued to neutral and Axis residents of Singapore. He took an Eurasian mistress, whose name was Mrs Siddons.)

A Formosan called Wee Twee Kim was linked to Shinozaki and deported by the British, only to return with the Japanese occupation forces. He became one of the so-called 'Three Wees', a group of gangsters who, under the 'benevolent' eyes of the Japanese, were allowed to terrorise the local Chinese population during the Occupation. Despite having the same name – the others being Wee Sian It and Wee Kim Chuan – the three men were not related. The last-named was already well acquainted with the Singapore criminal fraternity, having been a policeman under the British.

The information collected by the Japanese agents was shared extensively with German and Italian intelligence services via the three countries' consulates and intelligence posts. Japanese and German military intelligence had been exchanging information on the Red Army since as early as 1932, meeting annually in alternate capitals to swap military assessments. At the 1939 meeting, held in Tokyo in April, this exchange was expanded to include intelligence reports on Britain, the United States and France.[24]

The extent of this exchange of information is not entirely clear, but the *Abwehr* – the German military intelligence – and the Japanese Army were certainly sharing information on British and US diplomatic codes for at least two months before the attacks on Malaya and Pearl Harbor. Gustav Mand, a member of the *Abwehr* working in Shanghai under cover as a German businessman, is known to have played an important part in coordinating German–Japanese intelligence operations in Malaya and across South-east Asia.

One FECB report, No. 5106 dated 12th October 1941, entitled 'Axis intrigues in Thailand', dealt with German–Japanese liaison, but this appears not to be in the 'open' files at the Public Records Office. But the FECB report on Japanese intelligence activities in November 1941 said there was evidence that German influence was on the increase in Thailand. Several notorious German 'intriguers' were based in that country, including Baron Leopold von Plessen, described as 'the recently appointed Chancellor to the German Legation in Bangkok'. The military attaché there had previously held the same post in the German Embassy in Tokyo and a Gestapo officer, Major Franz Hueber, was also based in Bangkok.

The FECB knew that these men were in close touch with Japanese officials in Thailand. 'It can be taken for granted that if Japanese occupation of Thailand is in Germany's interest, any plans which have been made for this eventuality will receive the active advice and support of the German General Staff through their representatives in the country,' the report said.[25]

There were many reports of German nationals being active on the Malay peninsula and in other parts of South-east Asia, some of them said to be posing as neutrals. They were able to infiltrate Malaya from Thailand in the north or across the Malacca Strait from Sumatra in the Dutch East Indies. Shortly before the war with Japan, a beautiful 'Dutch' girl and her mother took up residence at the Sea View Hotel in Singapore. This hotel, at Tanjong Katong, was one of the most popular rendezvous for planters and their wives from up-country, and for unaccompanied military officers. From its grounds, there was a romantic view through palm trees over the sea and the Roads, where the many ships that plied the routes to the spice islands of the Indies lay at anchor. The hotel's dance band, sometimes Italian, sometimes Filipino, was very popular and the Sea View was one of the 'in' places to go for Sunday tiffin.

The Dutch girl and her mother claimed to be refugees and received a great deal of sympathy and attention from unattached males, most of whom were service officers. She became known as 'Hollow-legs' by officers who supplied her with drinks in abortive attempts to get her to bed. She, on the other hand, was far more successful in getting what she wanted. Eventually, she and her mother were arrested as spies, accused of persuading a number of RAF officers to give them secret information.

The Germans had a significant presence in the Dutch East Indies (DEI), which was neutral until Germany attacked Holland on 10th May 1940. According to three-cornered correspondence between the British Embassy in Batavia, the authorities in Singapore, and London, more than seven thousand Germans and Austrians were resident in Batavia, including some four hundred in senior positions in the Army, Police Force, and civil administration.

In 1940 Julius Ruckenbrod, the German Trade Commissioner in Batavia the capital (now Jakarta), was the main Gestapo officer in the DEI. A year before that, the chief police officer on the island of Banka was a German. When the Germans attacked Holland, the DEI authorities arrested a number of Germans and Dutch collaborators, including the Dutch Police Commissioner, U. J. A. Piepers, a fanatical member of the Nazi organisation the *National Socialistische Beveging*.

The Italian consulate in pre-war Singapore was heavily involved in Axis espionage activities and an intelligence file on the consulate held in the Public Records Office at Kew remains closed to this day.[26] Italian businesses aided the pre-war Axis intelligence effort, and the closed file might relate to the subversive activities of the management of the Fiat assembly plant in Orchard Road, Singapore.

Perhaps one of the best examples of cooperation between the various Axis intelligence services was the capture, on 12th November 1940, of secret British documents and codes from a British merchantman, the *Automedon*. The British ship was carrying 120 mail bags, two of which contained a number of top-secret documents including Cabinet papers on proposals for defence plans in the Far East. There were also top-secret messages to the British C-in-C Far East, Air Chief Marshal Sir Robert Brooke-Popham, and to British intelligence posts in Hong Kong, Shanghai and Tokyo, from the War Office, the Air Ministry and MI6.

The *Automedon*'s movements were monitored by Italian signals intelligence units in East Africa and passed on to Kapitän zur See Bernhard Rogge, of the German armed merchant raider *Atlantis* which had no problem intercepting and sinking a vessel which had a top speed of only 14 knots.[27] When the captured documents arrived in Berlin, copies were handed to the Japanese naval attaché, Captain Yokoi Tadao, who was the main liaison man between the *Abwehr* and Japanese naval intelligence. But anxious to impress the Japanese with their ability to penetrate British security at the highest levels, the Germans held back the source of the information with the result that some sections of the Japanese intelligence community believed the documents were too good to be true and must be fakes.

The success of the *Automedon* operation led the *Abwehr* to put pressure on Captain Yokoi to provide it with as much information as possible from Japanese espionage networks across South-east Asia on British shipping movements, in the hope of repeating the success of what was by any standards a spectacular intelligence coup.

After the hostilities in Malaya began, there were a number of reported sightings of German agents by retreating British troops. General Percival told General Wavell, the Allied Commander in the Far East, that independent reports from various units that Germans were operating alongside the Japanese seemed to confirm their presence but that it was impossible to estimate the scale or precise nature of their assistance, since there had been no mention of them in captured documents or by prisoners-of-war. Given that the rapidly retreating Allied forces captured few documents and even fewer prisoners, this is hardly surprising.

The failure to capture many Japanese prisoners-of-war – the total number sent back to Singapore was variously put at twelve or fourteen – has always been blamed on the speed of the retreat and the scale of the Japanese victory. But in fact some troops shot captured Japanese soldiers, in contravention of the Geneva Convention, rather than face the difficulty of taking them back. Intelligence officers, who had hoped to glean details of the Japanese order of battle and plans of attack from the interrogation of PoWs, urged that troops should be made more aware of the potential intelligence value of captured Japanese soldiers.

'The conduct of the forces in this respect is still somewhat of a mystery,' one senior staff officer wrote in a Most Secret report on the campaign. 'Units did not realise the importance of going out and getting information for themselves by sending out patrols, particularly by capturing prisoners. The reason for the lack of prisoners has been proved to be that units shot any prisoners taken in order to avoid the trouble of sending them back to the rear.'

All units had to be made to realise that prisoners were 'a very valuable source of information' and had to be sent back for interrogation by Intelligence officers, wrote Lieutenant-Colonel H. C. Phillips, RA, then GSOI (Ops) Malaya Command. Japanese prisoners were particularly useful because they were so keen to save their honour by committing hara-kiri that they would give away information in exchange for a weapon with which to kill themselves, he said. 'It is a matter of training until every officer and man down to the youngest realises that all information, however trivial, is important.'[28]

But despite the lack of prisoners, there were reports of Germans with the Japanese troops. Major Cyril Wild, an Intelligence officer on General Heath's staff, recorded one such report of an encounter with a German by members of an Indian battalion – '1400 hrs on 16 Dec, party of enemy in Malay dress headed by German try to cross Pataka bridge, reported by 5/2 Punjabs'.[29]

In what may have been the same encounter, an Indian Army jemadar reported that a white man in a strange khaki uniform had tried to cross a bridge shortly before it was to be demolished. The man told the jemadar that he was British but since he was acting suspiciously he was refused permission to cross the bridge. He ignored the order not to approach and was shot in the ensuing fight with the jemadar. Japanese troops hidden in the jungle immediately opened fire on the Indian officer, who was later decorated for his courage. (When the Indians later tried to recover the white man's body for intelligence purposes, it had been removed by the Japanese.)

After the fall of Singapore, the Germans had full use of the port facilities there. German submarines were often in port and their crews used the recreational facilities of the German Club on Singapore's Pasir Panjang Road. The club was exclusive to the Germans who wore small swastika badges on their shirts. A local police officer who, in his own words, was 'not willing to serve the Japanese and stayed away from work from 15th February 1942 to 5th September 1945, fishing and trishaw riding for a living', often saw German seamen as he rode past.[30]

Once France had fallen, Vichy-French agents based in French Indochina became active on the Axis side. British censors intercepted pro-Vichy material written by Commandant Maurice Lenormand who had arrived in Singapore from Hanoi in June 1941. He was arrested in January 1942, interrogated, and placed in Outram Road Prison, Singapore. In a series of articles he wrote after the Japanese victory in the *Syonan Shimbun* (the Japanese successor to the *Straits Times*) he claimed to have been badly treated by his British and Free French interrogators. This is denied by the British police officer who was responsible for Lenormand's arrest, who says that 'at no time did we mistreat him'. Lenormand also claimed in the newspaper that he was sentenced to death by the Free French in Singapore. He was due to be executed on 17th February, and only the Japanese victory on the 15th saved him, he said.[31]

Another Frenchman to be arrested was Monsieur Letondu, a chicken farmer with a German wife, but there is no record of the charges brought against him.[32]

In the run-up to the war, the Japanese also spent a considerable amount of effort encouraging Asian independence movements. In October 1941, Major Fujiwara Iwaichi, a Japanese army officer, arrived in Bangkok to set up the *F-Kikan* unit which ran a network of subversives across northern Malaya, among Indian nationals. (The 'F' stood for Fujiwara. Kikan can be translated as organisation. Several other Japanese subversive organisations had codenames based on the first letter of their commanders' names.) In Singapore itself, the Japanese Consulate-General was known to be the paymaster for subversive elements, much of the money coming from drugs smuggling and other illegal activities. After the war broke out, it was discovered that staff there had earlier provided Ibrahim bin Haji Ya'acob, a noted Malay nationalist, with $40,000 to purchase an anti-government newspaper, *Warta Malaya*.

Malay nationalism was strong among some sections of the community, particularly teachers. Some like Ya'acob were recruited by the Japanese. He was in fact a double agent who also worked for Singapore Special Branch. The British only discovered the nature of his association with the Japanese in August 1941. A secret report by two Singapore Special Branch officers on the fifth-column in Malaya, dated 11th March 1942 and written in India after their escape, says that until he was arrested at the outbreak of the war with Japan, Ya'acob was kept in ignorance of the discovery that he was a double-agent. He was among a group of 110 Malays detained by the British on suspicion of subversive activity on 8th December 1941.

The main vehicle for Ya'acob's subversion was the anti-British youth organisation, *Kematuan Malaya Muda*, of which he was president. This, together with the Singapore branch of an Indonesian independence movement, and a group of anti-British Malay secret societies, formed the basis of the Japanese fifth-column movement among the Malays. It was given the code-name 'Kame', the Japanese word for 'tortoise'. Later – following Major Fujiwara's arrival in Thailand in October 1941 – the codename 'Fujiwara' was used. The Special Branch officers who wrote this report thought that 'Fujiwara' referred to Japanese subversive operations over the whole of the southern sphere of Japanese interests, and that 'Kame' referred particularly to

Malays. The second part of their theory is correct. 'Fujiwara', on the other hand, referred particularly to Major Fujiwara's activities among the Indians in Malaya.

The secret report states that members of 'Kame' had made caches of stores and transport well behind British lines, so it seems there may be some truth in the persistent reports that the Japanese were able to make use of such stockpiles. One such report, mentioned earlier and in several books, is that bridge repair equipment was stockpiled close to strategic road bridges. While these particular reports have never been confirmed, and there is some evidence to suggest that the stockpiles were placed there by Public Works Department engineers in case the Japanese bombed the bridges, it goes some way to explaining the speed with which Japanese army engineers repaired bridges blown up by retreating troops.

The Special Branch officers also refer to Axis agents who were discovered among European military and RAF officers, 'some of whom were shot in the field'. Some of the detail in that part of the report is now known to be incorrect, but there can be little doubt that they had somehow caught a whisper of the Patrick Heenan affair, which was covered up by the military authorities, and perhaps also that of the Royal Artillery officer shot for refusing to order his troops to shoot down Japanese aircraft.[33]

There was also considerable Japanese pressure to turn Chinese feeling in Malaya against the British. According to a report by the Director of the Straits Settlements Special Branch, the case of the Formosan agent 'Tomoda', deported for fomenting unrest, was not an isolated incident. A number of Chinese from the Japanese-occupied Hainan Island were blackmailed into acting as agents with the threat of action against their families back home. Other Chinese were loyal to Wang Ching-wei, Japan's puppet leader in occupied Manchuria. They were mainly employed to spread anti-British propaganda and subversion among the ethnic Chinese population but also acted as spies and even guides for the advancing Japanese after the war began.[34]

In his private papers General Heath reported that a Chinese smuggler used lights to guide the invading Japanese troops on to the best landing points at Kota Bharu. The authorities had tried to arrest the man months earlier but there had been insufficient evidence against him.

But the bulk of subversion efforts were aimed against the Indians in Malaya, both civilian and in the Indian Army, whom the Japanese had identified as being most vulnerable to anti-British propaganda. And Patrick Heenan, who as a white Indian Army officer showed considerable sympathy for the Indian officers and men, and a dislike for the inherently racialist system within which he served, had his full part to play in that propaganda campaign.

CHAPTER 10

SUBVERSION

More than half the regular Allied troops serving in Malaya at the time of the Kota Bharu landing were Indian, and large numbers of Indian civilians, mostly Tamils, worked on the rubber plantations.[1] So in early 1941 the Japanese stepped up the frequency and aggressiveness of broadcasts from radio stations based on the island of Formosa, reporting unrest among Indian troops stationed near the border between Malaya and Thailand and claiming that the troops resented their treatment by their British officers. At the same time, the Japanese increased their support for the Indian Independence League which was seeking independence from Britain and had for some time had a number of active cells in Malaya.

One of the most effective of the Japanese *boryaku*, or subversion, operations among the Indian population took place in May 1941 when agitators used a strike by Tamil rubber workers to provoke a serious outbreak of fighting and troops had to be called in to quell the unrest. The workers at estates in the Klang and Port Swettenham areas of Malaya had a number of genuine grievances, including abysmally low wages, and when their demands were refused they went on strike. Members of the Central Indian Association – an offshoot of the Indian Independence League – stirred up the workers and fighting broke out with representatives of the European plantation managements. Telephone lines were cut and bridges damaged as the Tamil workers ran riot. The authorities were forced to send in Indian Army troops from the 1/13 Frontier Force Rifles and give them emergency powers to halt the fighting.

Then in October 1941, a Japanese army intelligence officer, Major Fujiwara Iwaichi, was despatched to Thailand to set up *F-Kikan*, the special department which exploited similar grievances and other opportunities for *boryaku* among the Indian troops and civil population in northern Malaya. The work he did formed the basis, after the war began, for the formation of *Azad Hind Fauj*, the Indian National Army (INA), a pro-Japanese force that was the League's military wing.[2,3]

Following the creation of the INA, the Japanese began dropping pamphlets telling the Indian troops that, while they braved the dangers at the front, British officers were hiding in safety. It was untrue, of course, but combined with messages from the INA commander, Mohan Singh, telling them how well the Japanese were treating their PoWs, the leaflets had a damaging effect on morale.

Low morale among the Indian troops is often cited as one of the reasons for the rapid Japanese advance down the peninsula but the reports of pre-war unrest among the Indian troops are normally discounted as propaganda. Certainly, many of the Indian soldiers captured by the Japanese remained loyal to the British Raj, but many others quickly volunteered to join the Indian National Army. There is considerable evidence to show that there was substantial sympathy for the League's aims among the Indian State Forces in particular, and also in the Indian Army itself.

Lieutenant-Colonel E. L. Sawyer of the 4/22 Mountain Regiment of Artillery, who spent much of his time in Japanese captivity documenting the Indian National Army, wrote at the end of a comprehensive list of INA officers that 'on the surface, it appears likely from the foregoing and also from subsequent events that the Indian Army, especially among certain units, was subject to Indian Independence propaganda prior to the outbreak of war in Greater East Asia'.[4] There is much evidence to support this in the war diaries of Indian units based in Malaya, which give many instances of unrest.

At the time of the Japanese landings, there was a total of 23 battalions of Indian troops in Malaya, eighteen of which were Indian Army units and five Indian State Forces, troops raised by Indian Rajahs and Nawabs. The five State Forces battalions were the 1st Bahawalpurs, the 1st Hyderabads, the 1st Mysores, the Kapurthalas and the Jinds. Each of these battalions was commanded by a British lieutenant-colonel but most of the remainder of their officers were Indian and the units were not trusted to perform anything other than support roles. The impression that, because they had few British officers, they were only second-class soldiers – an accurate reflection of British and Indian Army thinking at the time – did little to curb dissension among these battalions.

The Indian Army itself had been largely insulated from the rise of nationalism, but the demand for an end to colonial rule was now so strong on the sub-continent that it inevitably had its backers within the army. To make matters worse, the rapid expansion of the Indian Army had brought many more national-ists into its ranks and had led to a dramatic reduction in the ability of the British officers to man-manage their troops. Also, when experienced officers were moved to new battalions, many of their replacements could not even speak Urdu, let alone relate to the average sepoy.

The Japanese played on these weaknesses and Patrick Heenan, who had found it easier to get on with his Indian colleagues than with the British officers, was quickly in touch with anti-British elements within one of the Indian State Forces battalions. His main contact among these nationalist sympath-isers appears to have been Captain A. D. Jahangir, of the 1st Bahawalpur Battalion, who was described by one of his fellow officers, Captain Mahmood Khan Durrani, as 'a zealous advo-cate of independence'.[5] Both men later joined the Indian National Army and Jahangir went on to become the General Secretary of the Indian Independence League in Singapore.[6] Many of their fellow Bahawalpur officers had contacts with the League.

The 1st Bahawalpurs arrived in Malaya at the beginning of March 1941 with a new commanding officer, Lieutenant-Colonel Roger Fletcher, who had served with distinction in the First World War, Russia, Waziristan and Burma, and had three times been mentioned in despatches. He clearly saw his new command as a demotion and took it out on the officers and men of the 1st Bahawalpurs.

The battalion had been riddled with dissension for some time and one Indian officer had deserted two nights before they set sail. Fletcher's ill-tempered behaviour – he found fault with almost anything his troops did, often spoke of the battalion in disparaging terms, and adopted a racist and bullying approach to both officers and men – exacerbated the situation still further.

Immediately on arrival in Malaya, the Bahawalpurs were put under the wing of a 'parent' battalion, the 5/14th Punjabis, and assigned to airfield perimeter defence at Sungei Patani in north-west Malaya, a lowly task that everyone from Fletcher down saw as an implied criticism of their military ability. The combination of latent nationalism, a racist commanding officer in whom they had no confidence, and the fact that they were not trusted with anything other than a menial duty provided the ingredients for serious unrest.

But worse was to follow. The battalion set up camp under canvas near Sungei Patani but the site was poorly chosen and three days after they arrived a torrential downpour inundated it under two feet of water. When news of what had happened reached Fletcher, who was not in the camp at the time, he rushed back. Morale not surprisingly was low and a good man-manager would have dispensed sympathy and encouragement but Fletcher lashed out, swearing and bawling at everyone in sight and physically kicking both officers and men.

The next day was spent in 'improvement of camp site', says the battalion's war diary for 20th March 1941[7] but once the camp had been cleared up, the battalion's officers made a joint complaint to their most senior Indian officer, Lieutenant-Colonel G. Qasim Gilani, who agreed to see the CO on their behalf. An unrepentant Fletcher threatened furiously to take every one of those who had complained up in front of the commander of 11th Indian Division, Brigadier (later Major-General) D. M. Murray-Lyon. He followed up this threat by calling a meeting of all the officers during which he denounced them as 'coolies' and, waving his swagger-stick in the air, threatened to use it on them in future instead of his feet.

The Bahawalpur officers saw this as not only besmirching their honour, but that of the battalion and the Nawab of Bahawalpur who had commissioned them, and they threatened to take the matter to Murray-Lyon themselves. Gilani managed to calm them down by saying that Fletcher, who had spent several months in hospital prior to the battalion's departure for Malaya, was not a well man. But two days later, the situation boiled over again, a petition was raised and a telegram of complaint sent off to divisional headquarters.

Murray-Lyon went to Sungei Patani in person and, after hearing both sides of the argument, urged Gilani to get the complaints withdrawn and to hush the affair up since it was damaging to all involved. But it had gone too far. Either Fletcher had to go or they would demand to be sent home, the officers said, and Murray-Lyon had no option but to relieve Fletcher of his command and send him back to India.

His replacement came from Patrick Heenan's battalion, the 2/16th Punjabis, who were stationed close by. Major H. E. Tyrrell was promoted to acting lieutenant-colonel and ordered to restore morale among the Bahawalpurs. But it was an impossible task since the Indian Independence League's supporters now dominated opinion among the Indian officers and men. They accused two other British officers attached to the unit, Major Thompson and Captain Macdonald, of poisoning Tyrrell's mind against them. Eventually, four of the Indian officers were sent home and Major-General F. Gwatkin, Military Adviser-in-Chief to the Indian State Forces, was called over to Malaya to try to calm the situation. But there were continued problems.[8] Another Indian officer had to be shipped back to India, and then two service revolvers went missing and were found in the home of a local civilian.

Jahangir and Durrani were not among the dissident officers who were sent home. Nor were a number of other Bahawalpur officers who went on to join the Indian National Army, including Colonel Gilani himself and three others who feature in Sawyer's list: Captain Shaukat A. Malik and Lieutenant Sanuallah, who both went on to become instructors at the

Japanese sabotage school at Sandicroft in Penang which trained saboteurs to be sent back to India, and Major Barar.

But it was not just the Indian State Forces which suffered from problems with nationalism. The most famous Indian officer to join the Indian National Army was its commander Mohan Singh, who was a captain in the 1st Battalion of the Indian Army's 14th Punjab Regiment when he was captured by the Japanese but, in what must have been one of the most rapid promotions in history, instantly became a general in charge of the pro-Japanese force.[9]

Another officer in the 1/14th, Captain Mohammed Zaman Kiani, who was on Murray-Lyon's staff at Penang, also became a prominent member of the INA. He was closely associated with an Indian woman living in Penang, a Mrs Lakhsami who, following the fall of Singapore, became 'Captain Mrs' Lakhsami and formed a women's regiment within the INA. She named it The Ranee of Jhansi Regiment after a famous Indian princess who had opposed British rule and was killed by British troops in 1858. Later Allied prisoners-of-war on work parties in Singapore, who often saw the women marching through the town wearing their mauve sari uniforms and carrying captured British rifles, used to refer to them jocularly as 'whores-de-combat'.

One of the most serious cases of unrest among Indian troops took place in the 4th Battalion 19th Hyderabad Regiment, an Indian Army unit based at Tyersall Park Camp in Singapore and part of Force Emu, the 12th Infantry Brigade. It occurred after an Indian lieutenant was ordered home for expressing pro-independence views in the mess and inculcating such views among his men. At one point the 2nd Battalion Argyll & Sutherland Highlanders was put on standby in case the troops mutinied.

The unrest began on 7th May 1940, the day after the lieutenant was told to prepare for transfer to India 'as a result of highly undesirable conduct of the officer concerned who had expressed views which were considered to be highly objectionable'. Yet again the battalion had only recently acquired a new CO,

Lieutenant-Colonel E. L. Wilson-Haffenden, who had taken over in March of that year. Nor was it the first problem under his command. On 6th April, a sentry shot his post commander and then committed suicide.

The men of the battalion were Ahirs, Jats and Kumaonis. The lieutenant concerned, Lieutenant Mohammed Zahir-ud-Din, was an officer in 'A' Company which was made up entirely of Ahirs, an ethnic community from Rajasthan, in northern India, and Sindh, in what is now Pakistan. The Jats and Kumaonis were two martial tribes from the hill country of Northern India. It was Indian Army policy to fill a company with men from one ethnic group. The battalion was due to move to Kuala Lumpur for a three-week training camp the next day, the 7th, but one Ahir platoon and two sections of another refused to load their kit on to the lorries and threatened not to march to the railway station. This disaffection spread rapidly until all Ahirs were refusing to obey orders.

At 1100 hours, the Brigade Quartermaster-General put the Argylls, who were based in the same barracks, on standby in case there was further trouble. A platoon of the Argylls was then called out for immediate duty, and the rest put on fifteen minutes' notice. Half-an-hour later orders were issued to the OCs of 'B' and 'C' companies of the Argylls, but only these two officers and the Adjutant were informed of the real reason for the Company standby. All others were told that the reason was the possibility of a strike in the town. By mid-afternoon, the situation was clearly showing signs of getting worse and approximately 60,000 rounds of ammunition was taken out of the Hyderabads' armoury and placed in the Argylls' guardroom for safe custody. A platoon of Argylls was then ordered to mount guard on the Hyderabads' weapons and two more platoons told to remain on standby.

The next day the trouble spread to the Jats of 'B' Company who refused to turn out for physical training. They resumed normal duty after being allowed an interview with the camp commandant and seeing the platoon of Argylls relieved by a guard of officers from the Hyderabads themselves. But the battalion's Ahirs were still refusing to obey orders and one company of Argylls was kept on standby.

That afternoon the situation was defused by a decision to allow Lieutenant Zahir-ud-Din to say farewell to the men of 'A' Company, at a parade attended by most of the battalion's Ahirs, and next morning all members of the battalion resumed their duties. But the battalion's problems did not end there. In July 1940, a sepoy was sentenced to a year's imprisonment for disobedience and given a dishonourable discharge. A year later one sepoy attempted to stab a lance-naik and another sepoy hanged himself. A court of inquiry failed to explain the suicide.

There were persistent disciplinary problems with the Indian regiments in Malaya. In the four-month period between May and September 1941 alone, at least sixteen Indian soldiers were court-martialled, including several from the 5th Sikh Regiment. So large was the problem that the scarcity of officers with sufficient service to act on courts-martial was considered acute.

But the worst case by far occurred in the 1st Hyderabad Battalion, one of the five Indian State Forces (ISF) battalions. Like its fellow ISF battalion, the 1st Bahawalpurs, it was on airfield perimeter defence duties, but over on the east coast rather than the west. Pre-war, the battalion suffered many instances of unrest, numerous changes in officers, including attached British officers, and several courts-martial among other ranks. In October 1941 one of the battalion's Indian officers was arrested for refusing to go on a reconnaissance mission. As in the case of the 1st Bahawalpurs, the battalion was heavily infiltrated by the Indian Independence League. But unlike the Bahawalpurs, there is no evidence that the battalion's commanding officer, Lieutenant-Colonel C. A. Hendricks, did anything to exacerbate that situation.

When the Japanese landed at Kota Bharu, the 1st Hyderabads, who were guarding Kota Bharu airfield, suddenly found themselves in the front line. What happened next can only be pieced together from fragments of information which back up a story originally heard by some of the Allied troops as they tried to fight off the Japanese attack.

About an hour after dusk on Monday 8th December, the day the Japanese invaded, Hendricks went to the Wireless Station at Kota Bharu airfield with an escort 'for his own protection', an indication that trouble of some sort had developed. Hendricks then arranged for pillboxes previously manned by his own troops to be taken over by an Indian Army battalion, the 1/13th Field Force Rifles. Then, at 2200 hours, he called up all the reserve Hyderabads from their camp and ordered them into the RAF barracks.

About fifteen minutes later, and after some fighting with the Japanese, the Hyderabads withdrew under the orders of the Adjutant, Captain D. R. Munro, Hendricks having been 'lost' during that short time. Around noon on the following day, Tuesday 9th, the battalion's medical officer, Lieutenant H. E. Adams, collected some stragglers together and took them to Machang, about thirty-two miles south of Kota Bharu.

The next two fragments of information appear in the diary of events written by Major Cyril Wild, the Staff Officer who was to become famous as the man who carried the white flag at the capitulation of Singapore. In his entry for Tuesday 9th December, he wrote: 'Kota Bharu aerodrome. Panic evacuation by RAAF without kits or any demolitions. Demoralisation of Hyderabad ISF followed, Col Hendricks and Ajt. killed.' His entry for Sunday 14th December records that a Line of Communication Provost unit sent up-country specially from Singapore had 'disarmed the 1st Hyderabads' at Bangsar railway siding near Kuala Lumpur.[10]

The final piece of evidence appears in a report on the same day by General Murray-Lyon, GOC 11th Indian Division, that a company of 130 Indian other ranks from the 1st Hyderabads had arrived at Penang as a labour force.[11]

The Hyderabads, already subverted by the Indian Independence League members in their midst, had apparently watched in horror as, at around 1600 hours on Monday 8th December, the Australian airmen panicked following an unfounded rumour that the Japanese had reached the perimeter of the airfield. They were ordered by Hendricks to stand firm and fight, but seemed to have seen little reason why they should die while the Australians turned and ran.

Hendricks therefore went to the wireless station to inform his superiors of what was going on and then called in regular Indian Army troops to man the pillboxes on the airfield perimeter. The Hyderabads, who were by now so close to mutiny that Hendricks had to have a guard to protect him from them, tried to persuade him to allow them to pull out, but he ordered them all into the air base and told them to stand firm ready to fight.

When the Japanese troops arrived at the airfield shortly after 2200 hours and Hendricks still refused to allow the Hyderabads to withdraw, again ordering them to stand firm, they mutinied and shot him, leaving Munro with little choice other than to order a retreat. The leaderless troops then fled but were arrested and disarmed at Bangsar by a special Provost unit sent from Singapore and 130 of them were forced to work in labour gangs, an unusual move when every available fighting man was urgently needed. Despite the statement in Wild's diary that Munro was killed, he survived, was captured, and was interned in Changi prison.

Reports of what had happened circulated among the Allied troops as they attempted to hold back the Japanese advance, but they had other things on their minds and as they withdrew the incident was covered up and forgotten – until now – just one more cover-up in a campaign that was to be full of them.

The effects of Japanese subversion caused immense problems for the Allied forces, and the attitude towards fifth columnists, which at the start of the invasion had been remarkably complacent – '5th Column more active, but it is hoped they can be kept within bounds', noted one war diary – hardened considerably. By Saturday 13th December the following MOST SECRET signal was being sent out from 3rd Indian Corps to all commands:

FIFTH COLUMNISTS CAUGHT IN THE ACT WITH DEFI-
NITE PROOF WILL BE TREATED AS COMBATANTS NOT
WEARING UNIFORM. SUCH INDIVIDUALS WILL BE
SUMMARILY LIQUIDATED BY CMDS AND THEY ARE
ON NO ACCOUNT TO BE HANDED OVER TO CIVIL
AUTHORITIES.[12]

The signal was an indication of how seriously Japanese subversion was now being taken. It was not just occurring on the
front line. Operations Collar and Trousers had failed to pick
up all the Japanese agents and, in the southern state of Johore,
the 8th Australian Division, which had yet to see any action,
was already reporting that fifth-columnists were marking
strategic crossroads with a combination of lamps and cloth
strips.

By late December, the police were reporting centres of subversive activity in the Perak river and Kangsar areas of western
Malaya and warning in particular of the activities of an Indian
group calling itself the Red Flag Society. The RAF even flew
night-flights over Singapore Island hoping that fifth-columnists
would believe it was a Japanese air raid and put on lights. 'Night
reconnaissance over Singapore Island had object induce fifth
columnists disclose position of lights and flares noted during
air raid warnings,' explained a signal from Air Officer Commanding, Far East, to the Air Ministry.[13]

The orders to 'liquidate' subversives were often carried out
to the letter. Seven Malays handed over to the police after being
caught laying signs to indicate gun positions at Alor Star airfield
were ordered to be 'obtained from police immediately and all
of them disposed of as expeditiously as possible'.[14]

There were also a number of summary executions of suspected fifth-columnists. Some were genuine cases, like that of a
Tamil, a known Japanese agent who held power of attorney for
Japanese property in Malaya and had been in contact with other
known subversives. He was shot dead while trying to escape.
But with many the justification for the killing was extremely
dubious. The Argyll & Sutherland Highlanders are believed

to have executed several suspected fifth-columnists with little in the way of firm proof against them.

Such behaviour would have done nothing to persuade those Indian soldiers who did have doubts that they were on the right side. In one incident, north of the Slim river, a company of Punjabi troops, led by a young British lieutenant, came across two Malays in the jungle. The lieutenant ordered them to be questioned by a Malay-speaking member of his company, but when he was not satisfied with their replies, he pulled out his revolver and shot them both through the head, much to the consternation and horror of his jemadar, who was far from convinced that they had been guilty of anything other than being in the wrong place at the wrong time. The young officer was to die before the Battle for Slim river, but his treatment of the Malays surely had an effect on some of the watching Indian troops.

But when Patrick Heenan arrived in Malaya, in October 1940, such matters were a long way off and his treatment of the Indian troops and the local Malay and Chinese population as equals meant that he had no problems setting up a network of pro-Japanese contacts across northern Malaya.

CHAPTER 11

MOLE IN MALAYA

Patrick was transferred out of the 2/16th Punjabis on 18th March 1941 after he had made a number of unauthorised trips into Thailand. Colonel Moore had decided that he was 'too hot to handle' but, in an extraordinarily naive move, his suspicious behaviour was apparently ignored. Patrick was made a GSO III (Int), a Grade Three Intelligence staff officer, and posted to a newly formed secret unit which liaised on intelligence matters between the Army and the RAF.

Malayan High Command had decided to set up two Air Intelligence Liaison Sections and had begun to draft in officers and train them for their new role. But the two sections, 301 AIL Section, based in Singapore, and 300 AIL Section, at Alor Star in the north, were not formed until 1st May 1941, so Patrick spent some of the time between 18th March and 22nd June, when he arrived at his new unit, training at Seletar airfield with No. 100 Squadron RAF.[1,2] 'An Irishman called Heinan [sic] came to Seletar about six months before the war, as a captain in the Army, to attend an Air Ground Liaison Course,' wrote Pilot Officer Basil Gotto in his personal diary.[3] He recalls playing squash with Patrick.

The man appointed to take command of 300 AIL Section was Major James Cable France, a Territorial Officer in the Royal Artillery who had arrived in Malaya early in 1941. France was a Yorkshireman. Born at Dewsbury in 1912, he was rather small, fair-haired and freckled. He threw himself enthusiastically into anything he did and he was extremely popular with his men. 'Major France was the best officer I ever served with,' says former Private Jack 'Bladder' Wells, one of the unit's dispatch riders and the only known survivor of 300 Section. 'He was something out of this world.'[4]

'Jimmy' France had always wanted to fly. He had taken lessons in England and had even asked his commanding officer in the Territorial Army for permission to transfer to the RAF, but this was refused. So when he was stationed at Butterworth Naval Base in early 1941 and saw a notice inviting applications for an appointment as 'Air Intelligence Liaison Officer, General Staff Officer Grade II (AILO GSO II)', he decided this was the job for him. Here was his chance to become involved with aircraft, albeit indirectly and, after a genial night in the mess, he asked his commanding officer's permission to put his name forward. 'By all means apply,' said the colonel. 'But you haven't got a hope of getting in – you are, after all, only a Territorial.'[5]

But the colonel reckoned without France's infectious enthusiasm. Something in the small, intense Territorial Army officer impressed the selection board and France took command of his new unit on its formation, following a brief period of training with No. 21 Squadron, RAF, at Sembawang airfield, near the Naval Base in Singapore. The announcement of France's appointment in Army orders caused great amusement since it ended with the words: 'As from the date of Major France's appointment as GSO II AILO the word 'intelligence' will henceforth be dropped and his title will be ALO Commanding No. 300 Air Liaison Section, Malaya.' (The word 'intelligence' was being dropped in an effort to play down the secret aspects of the unit although in practice the original title was still occasionally used.)

The headquarters of 300 Air Liaison Section was set up at Alor Star airfield, the home of No. 62 Squadron, RAF, although from time to time officers and men from the unit were attached to the nearby Sungei Patani and Butterworth airfields. Two-thirds of the twenty-four airfields on the Malayan peninsula had no operational presence prior to the war, and of the eight that did possess it, only four had operational air squadrons: Alor Star and Sungei Patani in the north-west, and Kota Bharu and Kuantan in the east.[6] All three north-western airfields were very similar, each having one concrete runway. Butterworth, despite having no operational aircraft, was larger than the other two. Alor Star, where 300 Air Liaison was based, also had two grass runways, which formed an isosceles triangle with the longer concrete runway.* There were three hangars at Alor Star which were used for aircraft maintenance. Serviceable aircraft were parked in the protection of U-shaped pens, and there was 'a control tower of sorts'.

All the mess and accommodation buildings were made of wood and had palm-leaf roofs. They stood on brick piles to keep out the white ants. 'Accommodation for the NCOs and men was excellent, though we had to travel to the East Surreys' camp at Jitra to see a film,' says Corporal Fred Jackson, who was an ambulance driver attached to No. 62 Squadron.[7] The officers' accommodation was made up of long mess blocks, each holding about twenty officers, every one of whom had his own room.[8] Major France had a senior officer's bungalow to himself.[9]

In addition to the Indian State Forces from the 1st Bahawalpurs guarding the camps, there were a number of locally enlisted police, mostly Sikhs, known as *Jagas*. On mobilisation, these were joined by elements of the locally-raised Defence Volunteers. The arguments over airfield defence between the Army and the RAF caused tensions even at a local level. A Joint Defence meeting at Alor Star in mid-1941 decided that an army request for trees to be cut down to give defending troops a clear field of fire would 'interfere with camouflage schemes especially where natural camouflage exists'. In October of that year a similar meeting was told that 'at least one battalion was necessary for the defence of the aerodrome and not one company of infantry'.[10]

There were few anti-aircraft guns defending the north-western airfields. Sungei Patani was the only one with any completed anti-aircraft gun emplacements when war broke out, and these were only four 40mm Bofors guns. Alor Star had some 3-inch naval guns dating back to the First World War and a battery of light guns. Only five airfields, all of them in and around Singapore, had radar defences, so detection of enemy aircraft

* See Appendix 2.

relied heavily on air patrols and a not very efficient local Observer Corps.

The Air Liaison section had four officers: France himself; his second-in-command, Captain Harry Gilbert Landray of the Royal Garhwal Rifles, who arrived on 20th June 1941; Captain Cadbury-Jones of the Royal Artillery; and Patrick Heenan. There were two senior NCOs, one of whom was Sergeant Vincent of the Loyal Regiment, and around sixteen other ranks. These included France's driver, Private Jock Grove – who was a member of one of the two Scottish regiments based in Malaya at the time, the Argyll & Sutherland Highlanders and the Gordon Highlanders – as well as 'Bladder' Wells and the other dispatch rider, or 'Don-R' as they were called, Private A. H. 'Fred' Cox, who, like Wells, came from the East Surrey Regiment. Cox and Wells had been regular soldiers together since the mid-1930s and were inseparable.[11]

The unit's role is not recorded in any open government files. Elizabeth Leetham, France's daughter, says her father 'kept very quiet about this after the war, because it was under wraps'. But by piecing together various bits of information in the official files and the testimony of 'Bladder' Wells, it is possible to build up a picture of a unit capable of providing Patrick with a mass of information that would have been useful to the Japanese. France and his officers helped plan the perimeter defences of the north-western airfields at Alor Star, Sungei Patani and Butterworth, and probably those in the north-east as well, since there was no equivalent section based in that area. They also took part in the preparation and implementation of the air defence scheme for Penang. As the unit's name suggests, they also liaised on intelligence matters between the Army and the RAF, one of its most important tasks being the collection and collation of pictures taken on aerial reconnaissance missions, some of which were flown over Thailand until protests from the Bangkok government brought them to an end. Wells says the unit had a special piece of optical equipment with which to study the photographs. The unit was also actively involved in airfield defence exercises and its officers lectured on Army–RAF liaison and helped plan conferences and exercises designed to improve cooperation between the two services.

The following summary of an exercise practising aerial sorties against an enemy force, which was written by Patrick Heenan, is held in the Public Records Office at Kew. Patrick appears to have acted as umpire for the friendly aircraft. The exercise involved two imaginary sides 'Malaya', the friendly forces, and the 'Slits', the enemy. The 'Malaya' forces included troops from 5/14th Punjabis (40th Pathans) and 3/16th Punjabis together with three aircraft from No. 21 Squadron Royal Australian Air Force. The 'Slits' forces included troops from 1/8th Punjabis and three other aircraft from 21 Squadron RAAF, with Harry Landray as umpire for the 'Slits' aircraft.[12] In an operation similar to 'KROHCOL' – the proposed Allied advance into Thailand in the event of a Japanese attack – a column of 'Malaya' troops, codenamed 'STOKOL' after Lieutenant-Colonel Stokes, the CO of the 5/14th Punjabis who was in charge of the column, were to advance north along the road from Arau to Jitra, in the face of a large enemy force moving south. The Australian aircraft, watched by Patrick Heenan, were to provide air support.

Summary of events during exercise 23-6-41 to 25-6-41

'Malaya'

1. 'Malaya' air force – 3 Wirraway aircraft. 21 Sqd., R.A.A.F.
2. Pilots – F/Lt D. B. Hudson. F/Lt P. A. Wright. F/O Shepherd.
3. *Events on 23-6-41.*
   Five sorties took place.
   Sorties 'A' and 'B' were imaginary, the pilots' reports being made up by the chief umpire and passed to 'STOKOL' commander. The tasks of sorties 'C' 'D' and 'E' were to report enemy movement in:
   (a) KAKI BUKIT, BUKIT KETRI, KANGAR area, where the 3/16 Punjab Regiment was deployed. No enemy seen was reported.
   (b) BAN SADAO–CHANGLUM road area. Great enemy movement was reported and the presence of two enemy battalions was established.
   (c) ARAU–KODIANG–JITRA road and railway area. No enemy movement seen. 'E' flight (F/Lt P. A. Wright) lost its way and violated Thai territory. A court of enquiry was held on this incident next day.

Immediately on return of this sortie I (Capt. P. S. V. Heenan, A.I.L.O.) went up with the same pilot as observer and completed the task.

The 3/16 P.R. were seen on the KODIANG–JITRA road, embussed in about 30 trucks, en route to new positions North of Jitra. This was reported to 'STOKOL' commander. No sign of enemy activity was seen although this was an ideal bombing target.

4. *Events on 24-6-41.*

Four sorties took place.

Tasks were to report enemy movement in CHANGLUM–KODI-ANG–JITRA area. Great enemy activity was reported, all in a South-ward direction. Further tasks were to report any sign of enemy outflanking movement East or West of the JITRA–KEPALA BATAS road. Though such a move did occur, resulting in the capture of KEPALA BATAS aerodrome, the thick plantation East of the road screened the attacking force, 1/8 Punjab Regiment, from observation from the air. Pilots reported no enemy seen.

5. *Events on 25-6-41.*

No sorties went up. Scheme ended at approx 0900 hrs.

Special Points.

1. On 23-6-41 a bombing attack was carried out by 62 Squadron R.A.F. on enemy concentrations North of a line running East and West through point 103965. Reports indicate that this was partially suc-cessful.

2. On 23-6-41 'STOKOL' was not given a Call Sign. It was thus very difficult to locate from the air.

3. On 23-6-41 the Wireless Tender of 'STOKOL' was situated in rubber trees. This caused interference and in future the aerial at least should be well clear of trees.

Alor Star.   P. S. V. Heenan. Capt.
3-7-41.   300 A.I.L.O. Section.

His new job gave Patrick far more opportunity to move around than he had had with the 2/16th Punjabis and he visited a number of airfields, lecturing on Army–RAF liaison.[13] 'Recently we have had attached to us a Captain Heenan of the 11th Division as our liaison officer between the 11th Division and the RAF,' wrote an RAAF officer in a letter to his wife, one of a collection published later in Australia in *Great was the Fall*. 'He has been giving us a series of lectures on Army–Air Force cooperation as experienced during this war. This chappie is to live in our mess, so that will be of added interest.'[14]

Living in the same mess as Patrick was certainly interesting.

The other officers called him 'Tom', possibly because of his womanising which continued apace. 'We knew Heenan had a girlfriend but never who she was,' says Major France in his memoirs. In fact, he had a number of different girlfriends across Malaya. 'Bladder' Wells recalls that 'Heenan had a girlfriend, Chinese or Malay, in one of the *kampongs* close to Alor Star'; while Pilot Officer A. D. Elson-Smith, the author of *Great was the Fall*, who spent a night out on the town with Patrick in Penang, was far from impressed with the women he knew there. 'Captain Heenan visits us still,' he wrote. 'He is liaison officer too for Alor Star RAF 'drome, some 18 miles away. I have been out with him once, but I did not like the ladies we met, White Russians. No my cheri! I'm fussy. Still he is good company in the mess.'[15]

But the most important of Patrick's many girlfriends was a woman he met in the Cameron Highlands, a hill station east of Ipoh, a picturesque resort area that was extremely popular with officers seeking rest and recuperation. The long road up to the Cameron Highlands climbed from the small town of Tapah towards a 6,000-foot peak called Gunong Batu Brinchang. The resort area was on four different levels with a small shopping bazaar at each level. The highest level was at Tanah Rata where there were a number of hotels and holiday homes. There was also a golf course and many other amenities. The main attractions, apart from golf, were tennis, riding and walking, and there were magnificent views over untamed jungle interspersed with beautiful tea estates. The weather up there was perfect, warm but not too warm during the day and cold enough at night sometimes to sit around log fires. As a bonus, there were no mosquitoes.

Prior to 1939 the Camerons was a rather staid place, even in 'the season' – a place to take the family, where the only illicit pleasure was an over-indulgence in alcohol, a common occurrence among expatriate colonial communities. But with the influx of reinforcements for the British and Indian Armies, those visiting the area had begun to adopt a more relaxed, even debauched, attitude. Young officers flooded there at weekends or on local leave, looking for respite from the lowland heat and for female company. They found a warm welcome among the grass widows and their daughters, and from some of the young women at the Tanglin school, a school for European girls on the second level run by a Miss Anne Griffith-Jones. 'How attractive were so many of Miss Griff's girls,' says Dorothy 'Tommy' Hawkings, who ran a kindergarten attached to the school. 'The news spread throughout South-east Asia, and many war-weary, tired and dispirited groups of men were renewed with vitality and hope in the company of such charming girls.'[16]

It was hardly surprising that Patrick should have been drawn to the Cameron Highlands, spending some of his local leave there and, in all probability, the occasional long weekend. It was here that he met 'Pinka' Robertson. She ran the only riding school in the Cameron Highlands, which was attached to the Tanglin Girls School. She was a good-looking, twenty-nine-year-old half-Norwegian and, in the words of a woman friend, had 'a big bosom and lovely grey eyes'. 'Pinka' was a nickname. She had been born Gyda Jean Robertson at Walton-on-Thames on 28th October 1911. Her mother, Gyda Thorkildsen, from Arendal in Norway, had married Robert Macfarlan Robertson in January 1911. The family had moved to Malaya where Robertson managed a rubber plantation between Seremban and Port Dickson.

In her early twenties Pinka had gained a reputation among the men at Seremban's Sungei Ujong Club, one of the country's top clubs, of being 'argumentative, pig-headed and entirely unseduceable'. But by 1941, when she and Patrick began their affair, she appears to have changed her attitude. One female friend says she had become 'man-hungry', not in the sense of being promiscuous, but because, in the words of someone else who remembers her, 'she was looking very hard for a husband'. Perhaps in Patrick she saw a man who might be a match for her; they both had a reputation for liking an argument. Whatever her reasons, she was not the first woman to fall under his spell. Normally, Patrick openly discussed his sexual experiences with his fellow officers but, in Pinka's case, as with the woman in Japan, he was reticent.

Nevertheless, she appears to have met at least one of his fellow officers, possibly during a visit to Patrick at Butterworth or perhaps Penang, where there were a number of hotels in which they could have stayed during those pre-war months. For within days of escaping from Singapore to Java in early February 1942, she had married Flight Lieutenant R. D. I. Scott, the officer who had been left in charge of Butterworth aerodrome after it was evacuated by the squadrons based there on 9th December 1941. Either this rather hasty marriage was made to a man she had known only a few days or she had met Scott previously in which case she was almost certainly introduced to him by Patrick, whose popularity with the ladies still contrasted sharply with his reputation among those with whom he worked. 'On one occasion, he made a derogatory remark about me in the Mess, when I was not present,' says Dr Nowell Peach who, as a young RAFVR Flight Lieutenant, was a medical officer with No. 62 Squadron. 'I was told that our CO, Squadron Leader Bertie Keegan, had hotly defended me and almost come to blows with him. This bears out his unpopularity among us.'[17] Patrick also made frequent visits to the officers' mess of the 2/16th Punjabis who were stationed close to Alor Star. 'He was a large good-looking fellow, but a thoroughly objectionable character,' says Alan Elliott, the only surviving officer from the 16th Punjabis who served in Malaya.[18]

Nor was he any more popular among the other ranks. 'Heenan was a horrible man,' says 'Bladder' Wells. 'I reckon we had the best officer in the army in Major France, and in Captain Heenan, the worst. Major France used to loan some of us one of the unit's vehicles [the section had Alvis and Ford V8 staff cars, and an open lorry] providing we could wangle some petrol off the RAF boys, and we used to drive into Butterworth. Heenan didn't like this, and several times tried to stop us but was overruled by the Major. We sometimes got joy-rides on the Blenheims, and Heenan tried to stop those as well.'[19] Fred Jackson also recalls how he and his fellow drivers disliked

Patrick, who was 'contemptuous' towards the other ranks. Some of them did think he must be a spy, Jackson says, but he cannot now remember why.

But if Patrick appeared to have lost his affinity with the other ranks, he was as close as ever to the Indian troops and is thought to have controlled the subversive elements in the area from Butterworth to Penang and up to the Thai border – the Chinese or Malay girlfriend at Alor Star could have been one of his agents. He had contact with Captain A. D. Jahangir and other future members of the Indian National Army in the 1st Baha-walpurs who were guarding the north-western airfields, and possibly also with similar elements in the 1st Hyderabads who were to kill their commanding officer, Colonel Hendricks, at Kota Bharu. Patrick is also known to have made a number of trips into Thailand, where he met a white planter, and to have maintained contact with the mysterious 'Dutchman'.[20]

'He made three or four visits to plantations near the Thai border in the state of Perlis which was just north of us in Alor Star, Kedah,' said Fred Cox. 'I drove him each time, and each time the trip was to have been for reconnaissance, but I was always ordered to stay in the staff car, whilst he went into a bungalow, and each time I discovered the occupant was a Dutchman. He made light of the visits, I was told it was not necessary to mention it to anyone, but on the second visit I told Jimmy [France] who told me to let him know of any other facts which came to my attention.'[21]

Patrick seems to have made little effort to disguise his espionage activities, yet his behaviour was beginning to arouse suspicions among the other officers and the men. 'At Alor Star, we had Captain Heenan as our Squadron Air Intelligence Liaison Officer,' says Squadron Leader D. A. Thomas, who at the time was a Flight Sergeant with No. 62 Squadron. 'We were the only squadron there and I ran the hockey team. Captain Heenan played regularly for us; the team was composed mainly of NCOs and Captain Heenan became unusually friendly with us, always asking questions, obviously gleaning information.[22]

'For quite a time, Warrant Officer Swindlehurst had been

Heenan's source of information where serviceability and avail-
ability of the squadron's aircraft was concerned. WO Swindlehurst had at his disposal a small Singer van and Captain Heenan
would say to him: "Swin, take me round the airfield and get
me up-to-date with the serviceability of the aircraft, I need it
for a briefing," or he would give some other reason and, quite
naturally as Heenan was the AILO, Swindlehurst would oblige.'

Another innocent source of information was Flight Sergeant
Ron Wardrop (now Squadron Leader R. E. Wardrop). He was
the Armourer Sergeant of Flight 'A' of 62 Squadron, and Patrick
Heenan asked him for details of the RAF's SCI (Smoke Curtain
Installation) equipment. This was a device for laying smoke-
screens, and Patrick wanted to know all about it, Wardrop says,
'the purpose for which the SCI was used, which planes could
carry it, weapon loads, etc. Later, of course, I knew exactly
why he wanted the information.'

About six months before the Japanese invasion, £40,000 was
allegedly discovered in Patrick's Malayan bank account. It was
an extraordinarily large sum of money – worth around £1.25
million at today's values – certainly too large to be just his own
reward from the Japanese.[23] It may have been the pay-chest for
a network of Japanese agents across northern Malaya. 'Heenan
was under suspicion from then on,' says Dr A. W. Frankland,
who as a young Royal Army Medical Corps captain was later
assigned to visit him in prison. 'He could not explain why this
vast sum of money had suddenly appeared in his bank account.
He said: "Oh, it was a gambling debt that had been repaid".'[24]

But the very size of the sum of money raises doubts about
the story. Why would the Japanese, with a wide network of
agents of their own nationality across Malaya, trust a non-
Japanese with such a large sum? There is nothing in Major
France's half-finished memoirs to indicate that he knew anything about the money, although he surely ought to have been
told, and none of the other police and service officers involved
in the case has any knowledge of it. It is perfectly possible that
the £40,000 existed, but on the other hand it could have been
just another of the stories that were to emerge about 'the Officer

Traitor' in the vacuum of information created by the secrecy surrounding the affair.

One allegation levelled against Patrick, however, was almost certainly untrue. As his story spread among the PoWs held by the Japanese, it became part of the mythology of 'the Heenan affair' that, during his time with the 2/16th Punjabis, he had been implicated in a corruption scandal involving faulty pill-boxes constructed in Penang. When the pill-boxes were tested, they were found to have been made of a second-rate material that could not withstand bullets. Patrick was supposed to have been in charge of awarding the contract for the pill-boxes and had been taking backhanders. But it is extremely unlikely that an infantry officer would have been involved in the construction of pill-boxes, normally the responsibility of the Royal Engineers, and a former senior civil servant in Singapore says the case bears a remarkable resemblance to one involving another officer.

This was Captain Robert Charles Loveday, RE, Surveyor Singapore District, who was responsible for the erection of military defences and installations. In the summer of 1940, Loveday's fellow officers became suspicious and recorded a conversation between him and the Chinese representative of a big European contractor. Subsequent investigations showed that Loveday had conspired with a number of contractors, both British and Chinese, to organise what that same former civil servant describes as 'a ring, whereby one would agree to tender for a particular job and quote the lowest price, but including a hidden additional amount, and having been awarded the job would collect his money and divide the hidden amount between his co-conspirators and, of course, the good captain.'

The work carried out on defence projects by the contractors was 'found to be significantly inferior, and with regard to a string of machine-gun posts in Singapore and south Johore, these were positively dangerous, structurally unsound,' the former civil servant says. Loveday was questioned by police and his married quarter was searched but this revealed nothing. Meanwhile the Chinese whose conversation with Loveday had been recorded was pulled in by the police and 'sweated'. Eventually the full story emerged and a decision was taken to use the Chinese as a Crown witness against Loveday who was sentenced by a court-martial to two years in civilian prison and cashiered.

'While the case was under way, and publicity attached to it, a common topic in Singapore was Mrs Loveday's appearance here and there with her knitting-bag (always a knitting-bag!) full of money, because none was found on him,' the former civil servant says. Loveday's share was estimated at around £25,000, the rough equivalent of £800,000 now. Soon after the trial, Mrs Loveday left Singapore with another man, and presumably her knitting-bag full of Captain Loveday's cash. The former civil servant says he never heard of any similar case in Penang, so this seems to have been the story to which Heenan's name became erroneously linked.

Even though Major France may not have known about the money allegedly found in Patrick's bank account, he was already beginning to have his own suspicions. 'I was now getting worried about the behaviour of my Photographic Captain GIII – Tom Heenan. I discovered that, during my absences, he had done two outrageous things: firstly, he had taken a party of my troops on "ground exercises" and on these he had taken photographs of all the junctions and crossroads from Alor Star to and into Thailand, whilst the signposts were still in position. These would, of course, have been removed in the event of war. I found out also that he had been sent to me by the Hyderabads [France presumably means the Punjabis] because he had been doing similar excursions into Thailand when with them and he was "too hot to handle". They should have told the truth to the General Staff. They claim he was sent because he was a specialist photographer. He certainly was, as time would surely tell! Whilst I was away he had gone to the Station Commander and persuaded him that he had my permission to see my documents – highly secret and kept in the Commander's safe.'[25]

The way in which the 2/16th had palmed off their problem officer on to a unit where his work would involve everyday contact with highly classified material is a damning indictment

of the strange standards prevalent at the time. Patrick's trips into
Thailand ought at least to have triggered someone's suspicions,
particularly when combined with the fact that he had suddenly
returned from a long spell in Tokyo with a new-found interest
in all things Japanese and a previously undiscovered talent as
an expert photographer.

Ramsey Tainsh had warned his superiors in India that Patrick
'should not be put in any key place as he was a deeply hurt
man'. But this warning was ignored. It was apparently incon-
ceivable that a British officer could be a spy. And despite the
mounting evidence against Heenan – including, if the story is
true, his unconvincing reason for having suddenly acquired a
large sum of money – even France found difficulty in persuading
anyone that he was a security risk. In a note in the margin of
the major's memoirs, his daughter has written: 'How soon my
father suspected Heenan, but no-one seemed to care much.'

This attitude was typical of the general complacency in
Malaya towards the Japanese, encouraged by the false image
of 'Fortress Singapore'. It was a favourite saying at the time
that Japan was, after all, 3,000 miles away – few people stopped
to note that Britain was 6,000 miles away – and Tojo, that
ridiculous little cartoon character with round spectacles and
slant-eyes, could not possibly pose a threat to the British. But
in Patrick Heenan's case the attitude of the military authorities
who placed him in such a critical position seems to have been
bordering on madness. As Dr Frankland says: 'If he was under
suspicion, and I was told he was, why was he given this
extremely important job as Air Liaison Officer? That seems
almost criminally stupid.'

The Air Liaison Section could scarcely have been bettered
as a platform from which to obtain useful intelligence for the
Japanese. In his own role, Patrick had access to virtually any
information about the northern airfields, the aircraft based there
and, of course, their defences that he wished to see. He had
even been involved in formulating the plans for the Allied aerial
response to any invasion. He would also have had access to
details of the Air Recognition Strips, which allowed pilots to

identify friendly forces on the ground, and to the daily changing Air Recognition Codes used by the pilots to identify friendly aircraft – the predecessors of the modern-day IFF (Identification Friend or Foe) systems. During the initial landings at Kota Bharu, several air crews reported that Japanese warships were signalling to them using the correct Air Recognition Code of the day – 'K'.[26]

Knowing everything Patrick had told them about the airfields, the Japanese aircraft were able to attack the Allied aircraft with virtual impunity. 'They had absolute air supremacy and all day long their bombers, old types of dive-bombers, biplanes mostly, were up and down our lines attacking any movements they could see,' wrote Pilot Officer Basil Gotto. 'Our fighters up country were having no success and were continually being caught having just landed, and in fact lost an enormous amount of aircraft on the ground.'[27]

Patrick's photographic 'excursions' would have provided a host of information useful to the Japanese as they began the invasion of Malaya. There was only one main arterial road running from Singora, where the main Japanese force was to land, down the west of Malaya, and the Japanese would have needed no help in navigating that route. But the network of minor roads between Alor Star and the Thai border, many of them nothing more than cart tracks, were also put to good use by the advancing Japanese. It could well have been these roads, where they led and the locations of any bridges or culverts, that interested Patrick's controllers.

France's reference to 'highly secret' documents suggests that Patrick may even have been in a position to provide the Japanese with virtually everything they needed. In his role as Air Liaison Officer and a Grade II Staff Officer, France would almost certainly have been privy to parts of 'Operation Matador', the planned British response to a Japanese attack, and the Allied battle-order for the defence of Jitra. If these were the 'highly secret' documents kept in the Squadron Commander's safe, then Patrick would have been able to tell the Japanese the exact strengths, equipment, locations and plans of the waiting Allied troops. There were several reports of dead Japanese officers being found with maps and documents detailing most of the British defences in the north. At least some of this information would have come from Patrick, who would also, from his own observations, have been able to provide them with details of morale among the front-line troops.[28]

But even if the best information Patrick was able to supply concerned the northern airfields and the British and Australian air strengths, it was to have a quite devastating effect, ensuring the advancing Japanese forces total air superiority from the very start of the campaign. Through a combination of extraordinary incompetence on the part of Patrick's superiors and sheer good luck, the Japanese had contrived to place a mole at the heart of the Allies' northern air defences.

Three weeks before the enemy landings, Captain Landray was killed in a flying accident. He was performing a loop-the-loop in a private aircraft when it crashed, killing outright both him and his passenger, Second-Lieutenant B. C. Snell of the 6th Rajput Rifles. It was a bad blow for France, who was one of Landray's closest friends. The two men and Squadron Leader A. S. K. 'Pongo' Scarf of No. 62 Squadron at Alor Star, who won the first VC of the Malaya campaign, were all 'bosom buddies', according to 'Bladder' Wells.[29] But if it was a personal tragedy for France, it was a major tragedy for the Allied cause, for Patrick Heenan was appointed to replace Landray as second-in-command of the section, allowing him even greater access to the secret information held in its files.

CHAPTER 12

THE BALLOON GOES UP

When Squadron Leader the Rev. Harper, who as plain Donald Harper had worked with Patrick at Steel Brothers, arrived at Alor Star a few weeks before the Japanese invasion, he was surprised to discover his former colleague already there. With the worrying prospect of war looming large, it was good to have a fellow rugby player to train with. The strenuous activity helped relieve the tension that was beginning to affect the British airmen and soldiers waiting impatiently in northern Malaya, many of them already in their preliminary combat positions. 'You could feel it in the air at times,' says 'Bladder' Wells. 'You could reach out and touch it. You couldn't help worrying about things. It kept me awake.'[1]

Only a blind optimist or a fool, and there were still a few around in the higher echelons of both the civilian and military administrations, doubted that the Japanese would attack. The only questions remaining were where, when, and what would the Allies do in response. As warnings came that Japanese naval units based in Indochina were on the move, a string of code-words emanated from HQ Malaya Command: '*Awake*', the warning of an increase in international tension; '*Albert*', the order for the Air Observer scheme to be brought into force; and '*Seaview*', the order for troops to move forward into preliminary positions.

These were followed rapidly by further orders: '*Oilcan*', the mobilisation of the Federated Malay States Force Volunteers; '*Seaview 2*', the move to the second degree of readiness; and '*Spring east*', the laying of shrapnel and anti-tank mines. Finally, on Saturday 6th December 1941, came '*Raffles*', the ominous order to move to the first degree of readiness.

It was scarcely surprising that Wells and many of the other Allied troops and airmen waiting in northern Malaya had very little sleep during those last few nights of peace. Sleeping in the heat of the Malay night was always a fitful process in those days before air-conditioning, and with the rapid increase in tension it became well-nigh impossible.

For France, and for Patrick Heenan, it was a particularly worrying time. Both men were playing an increasingly danger-ous game. France was by now convinced that his second-in-command was a spy, but reluctant to act until he had proof. Patrick was equally suspicious, certain that he had already been discovered, but now left with no choice other than to stay in place and hope that the Japanese would arrive before the British had enough evidence to arrest him.

He was living on a knife-edge and taking desperate measures to keep any evidence from France. About two weeks before the Japanese landings he approached Dr Nowell Peach, the Medi-cal Officer of No. 62 Squadron. 'He sought my advice, or cooperation, in regard to the development of film,' Dr Peach recalls. 'He knew that I was interested in birds and had taken some photographs in the vicinity of the camp. On second thoughts, he may have tried to "plant" photographic material on me! But fortunately I was unable, or disinclined, to help him. Had I done so, I might well have been implicated in his subsequent activities.'[2] Patrick, an expert photographer, hardly needed Peach's advice on the development of the film; but what he did need was a safe place to hide it.

A few days before the invasion Major France's suspicions were confirmed when the Station Commander, Wing Com-mander R. G. Forbes, told him that Patrick had lied to him in an attempt to have a second look at the highly classified docu-ments held in Forbes's safe. 'The CO [Forbes] told me that Heenan had again, during my absence in Penang, tried to obtain my "Most Secret" papers, which were in his safe, on the pretext that he had my permission to see them to make notes for a lecture I was to give. I also discovered that he had again been over the frontier into Thailand to take photographs.'

France still felt that he needed more evidence against Patrick, so he worked out a plan to get him out of his room in the mess in order to search it. 'I fixed it the next day for a couple of other officers to borrow my Alvis and take him with them to the Alor Star club for a drink. In his absence, we searched his room and found a small Bible full of underlined sentences and an obvious code. Next we found a portable typewriter and in the base-board, which was a file drawer, copies of "sitrep", situation reports, that started "Dear Mum". The rest was a report of our aircraft positions, strengths, and a part of our aerodrome showing bomb dump, fuel stores, etc., all marked with a cross.' France resolved to go to divisional HQ in Penang the next day, Monday 8th December, to inform Major-General Murray-Lyon, GOC 11th Indian Division.[3] 'As things turned out, I had to wait an extra day.'

Given the evidence against Patrick that France now had, it is difficult to understand why the traitor was not immediately arrested. There was surely no need to wait for Murray-Lyon to order his detention, and even if it was felt that this was vital before such serious charges could be brought against a fellow officer, there could have been a more strenuous effort made to get in touch with the divisional commander. Murray-Lyon was a well-liked man, known for his approachability, and it should not have been a problem. Possibly it was felt necessary to catch Patrick in the act, but at this stage every extra moment of freedom was a bonus for him, providing valuable breathing space in which he could keep the Japanese informed of British movements.

There is one other possible reason why France may have waited. He would certainly have discussed the matter with the station commander, Wing Commander Forbes, and the other senior officer with troops on the base, Lieutenant-Colonel H. E. Tyrrell, the CO of the 1st Bahawalpurs, the Indian States Force unit defending the north-western airfields. Tyrrell came from the same parent unit as Patrick, the 2/16th Punjabis. The news that a fellow officer of 'The Regiment' was a spy would have been almost too awful to bear. In the circumstances, it would not be at all surprising if Tyrrell – appalled by the potential damage to the regiment's good name – urged caution, more time to be sure that the suspicions were justified, and France, as a Territorial Army major, not a Regular, would have felt duty-bound to defer to the colonel's judgement.

The news of the Japanese landings at Kota Bharu reached Alor Star in the early hours of Monday 8th December. 'We were woken up just after four,' says 'Bladder' Wells. 'A guy came in and said the balloon had gone up. We all knew what that meant. We had been expecting it for days. So, anyhow, we went over to the office. Some of the lads were already there, we were all sort of half asleep, and at the same time a bit scared, if you know what I mean. We started doing our work and what-have-you. Jimmy France was doing his phoning up and everything else.'

The news of the landings at Kota Bharu was soon followed by further signals announcing others at Singora and Patani in Thailand. The Blenheims of 62 Squadron at Alor Star, and 27 Squadron at Sungei Patani, were ordered to take off at first light to attack the Japanese ships at Kota Bharu. Dawn in the tropics close to the equator comes at around 0600 hours every morning with only a minute or two variation, but that morning it seemed to take forever. 'We were expecting the Japs,' says Wells. 'It was the longest wait of my life.'

As dawn broke eleven Blenheim bombers of 62 Squadron took off and headed east. An hour later, and thirty miles to the south, nine Blenheims of 27 Squadron and a flight of Buffalo fighters from 21 Squadron took off to join them. By the time 62 Squadron's Blenheims arrived at their target, the Hudson bombers from Kota Bharu airfield had already played havoc with the Japanese ships and there was nothing left to attack. So they diverted north-west towards the Japanese landing force at Patani. Under fire from Japanese fighters and heavy ack-ack, they attempted a hit-and-run raid on Patani airfield. But their bombs dropped short of the target and they headed back for base. Meanwhile, the Blenheims of 27 Squadron arrived at Kota Bharu amid such torrential monsoon rain that they were forced to head back to Sungei Patani without dropping their bomb loads.

Back at Alor Star, the men of 300 Section and 62 Squadron were surprised that they hadn't yet come under attack. The Japanese had raided Sungei Patani airfield at 0730 that morning but Alor Star was so far unscathed. 'Jimmy France ordered some of us outside to keep our eyes open for aeroplanes,' says Wells. 'Heenan dished out the orders and sent me out to the back of the huts.' Meanwhile, Patrick himself kept going off somewhere. 'He was always disappearing,' says Wells. 'We knew he was carrying on with a Malay or Chinese girl in the area, although no-one ever saw her. Perhaps he went off to see her. Perhaps she was in on this thing with him.'

Wells saw the Blenheims return around 1000 hours to refuel. Shortly afterwards, Patrick reappeared and came over to speak to him. 'He told me: "They've bombed Singapore, they've hit several 'dromes to the south." This must have been between ten and twelve o'clock midday and I said to him: "Well, look sir, why is it that we haven't been hit yet? I mean we are right up in the front line." And he said: "Oh they will do, they will do."

'You know, he was taking it so casually. Anyhow, we were standing there and we didn't chat a great deal because nobody liked him. He was one of those sort of blokes. So we stood there and after a while, well, I can remember this sure enough, though it meant nothing at the time, but I thought about it afterwards, what did he keep looking at his blinking watch for? He was looking at the sky, he was expecting them! He knew exactly when the blighters were coming!

'The way he was doing it, see. I remember saying to him, "Why it's queer, we still haven't . . ." "We will be," he said. "Don't you worry. They'll be over soon." And those were his very words. Suddenly, we heard them coming. There was a formation of twenty-seven bombers, and I can tell you how many they dropped. They dropped five bombs each. We knew all this afterwards. Heenan and I sprinted for the nearest trench, about 130 yards away. But I beat him and he landed on top of me.'

Dr Nowell Peach was in the station medical centre when he

heard the Japanese aircraft coming over. 'I seem to remember, vaguely, that Heenan had gone missing from the camp before the Japs struck and that there was a rumour that telephone wires had been cut, probably by him,' Peach says.[4]

'At about 11 am, I was in my Sick Quarters, when I heard the humming of a flight of aircraft and, on stepping outside, saw a wave of twenty-seven bombers approaching from the south-west at about 10,000 feet. I trained my binoculars on them and, to my surprise and horror, saw the Japanese markings – from the direction of their approach, I had expected them to be ours. I rushed back into Sick Quarters and raised the alarm. (Fortunately none of the bed-patients was very ill.)

'We all ran to the back door, where we were temporarily jammed in the confusion, and out into the slit trench. Once inside, we looked up and saw the attacking planes, in close formation over the airfield. At that moment, the first bombs exploded and within seconds several went off within a few yards of our retreat, throwing earth across the trench. It was one of their customary "pattern bombings". One bomb landed on our dispensary and I can still recall the smell of the explosive mixed with pharmaceutical preparations.'

At least seven, possibly eight men died during that first raid on Alor Star, and a number of others were injured. As Wells and Heenan climbed out of their trench, they saw a Flight Lieutenant lying dead nearby with a huge shrapnel wound in his groin. But in many ways the worst effect was the damage to the aircraft. Nine of the eleven Blenheims sitting on the ground for refuelling had been damaged, four of them seriously. Several buildings had been damaged or set on fire. The attack would have been far worse but the Japanese had only dropped light fragmentation and anti-personnel bombs – they planned to use the airfields themselves and wanted to avoid too much damage to the runways.

But it was the timing of the attack that was most critical. The Japanese had bombed Sungei Patani at 0730 in the morning but had ignored the neighbouring Alor Star airfield until 1100, despite the fact that it was further north and nearer to their lines. The weather was clear over north-western Malaya that morning, so there seemed to have been no reason to ignore Alor Star, unless they knew that 62 Squadron's Blenheims were not there. Although nine of 27 Squadron's Blenheims had also left for Kota Bharu by the time of the 0730 Japanese raid, there were three more still on the ground together with about half of 21 Squadron's Buffaloes. The Japanese bombers that attacked Alor Star at 1100 had launched a second raid on Sungei Patani half an hour earlier, by which time the Blenheims involved in the aborted raid against Kota Bharu had also returned to refuel.

'Our fighters up-country were not having any success, and were continually being caught having just landed, and, in fact, lost an enormous number of aircraft on the ground,' as Pilot Officer Gotto had written in his diary. And he added: 'Incidentally, I believe some of this can be blamed on an Irishman called Heinan [sic].'

Gotto was not alone in his belief. A number of the men who were there at the time said afterwards that it was as if the Japanese knew exactly when and what to take out. One army officer recalled: 'The coincidence of Jap raids with the take-off or landing of our aeroplanes was becoming too regular to be mere luck.'

Patrick's continual disappearances, possibly even the native girlfriend herself, were a cover to allow him to contact the Japanese. 'It's strange,' Wells remembers remarking to the section Senior NCO, Sergeant Vincent. 'Every time we make a move, Captain Heenan seems to push off somewhere.'

The Japanese had known it was not worth attacking Alor Star until their man on the ground told them the Blenheims had returned. Once he had tipped them off that the aircraft were back and refuelling, Patrick knew they were coming. 'Don't you worry,' he had told Wells, looking at his watch. 'They'll be over soon.' In the words of the only member of 300 Air Liaison Section known to be still alive: 'He was expecting them! He knew exactly when the blighters were coming!'

Further heavy raids on Sungei Patani and Alor Star that day led Air Vice-Marshal C. W. H. Pulford, AOC Far East, to order the evacuation of both airfields. Those aircraft at Alor Star that could be made serviceable were to fly south to Butterworth the next morning. The raids on Sungei Patani had been so devastatingly effective that only four Blenheims and four Buffaloes were left and they flew to Butterworth late on Monday afternoon. The ground staff at Sungei Patani left in a panic after false rumours, allegedly spread by the Bahawalpurs defending the base, that the Japanese ground forces were approaching.

Monday 8th December had been a terrible day for the men at Alor Star, many of whom were witnessing the carnage of war for the first time. There were raging fires to put out, battles against time to repair aircraft, the injured to be ferried to hospital and, most dispiriting of all, the dead to be buried. Perhaps it was the general chaos that prevented France doing anything more positive about Patrick. The strange decision not to arrest him earlier had already caused immense damage. By the end of the day, the RAF presence in the north of the country had been virtually destroyed. Aircraft, fuel and ammunition dumps, operations rooms and communications facilities had been attacked with a surprisingly high degree of precision. Patrick had done his job well. But he was far from finished yet.

Flight Sergeant David Thomas had been stuck in Kota Bharu on a Blenheim that had broken down. He had finished repairing the aircraft on Sunday night, but by Monday morning with hell breaking loose all around, the Blenheim could not get permission to take off because the Hudsons of No. 1 Squadron were busy bombing the Japanese troop transport vessels.

'About 1700 hours that day, a general order was given to evacuate Kota Bharu, and so we took off for Alor Star,' he says. 'We were attacked by Jap fighters but got away with it. As we approached Alor Star, we could see that it had been bombed by the Japs; some of the buildings were still smouldering. On the approach, the flaps would not lower and so a flapless landing had to be made – 90 to 100 mph, fast in those days! Unknown to us, the starboard tyre had been holed by a bullet or two, so on touch-down that tyre flew off its rim. We careered along the runway; after a few hundred yards, the aircraft left the runway, got on to the grass and skidded through a large arc to the right and came to a stop. Fortunately, we didn't hit anything.

'The Officers' Mess was one of the buildings that had been bombed so the officers now shared the Sergeants' Mess with us. As soon as I got into the Mess, Captain Heenan literally pounced on me and asked me questions about Kota Bharu – "What was it like there during the day? Were there any Hudsons serviceable when you left? How many times did the Jap fighters strafe the place? How was the order given to evacuate the airfield?" – and so on. He was a smooth character when he wanted information. After dinner that evening, it was: "Oh, Tommy, one other thing," and so he went on. Little did I know his reason for wanting to know the information that I gave him.'

That night most of the people at Alor Star were kept busy preparing for the evacuation. Warrant Officer Swindlehurst, in effect the station's chief engineer, organised his men into shifts to repair as many aircraft as possible. They worked so hard that, by morning, seven Blenheims were able to fly south to Butterworth. Wing Commander Forbes was organising a stay-behind party under Squadron Leader Keegan to keep the airfield operational as an advanced bomb-loading and refuelling base. Others were kept busy loading trucks with equipment and stores.

Major France had very little sleep that night, but not because of the preparations for the move to Butterworth. He was certain that Patrick now knew he suspected him. He was worried at what the traitor might do in a last desperate effort to prevent anyone exposing him as a Japanese agent. 'I was convinced that Heenan knew I had seen through him, and rightly as it transpired,' France says. 'Before I went to bed, I placed linen threads across the verandah of my "cabin", and across the doorway attached to my shooting seat, hung about a foot from the floor. About 4 am, it dropped on to me, and woke me up in time to hear footfalls and then someone running along the balcony and into the night. I wasn't quick enough to see who it was, unfortunately, but I got dressed and did not sleep again that night, partly because I believe that Heenan had come to kill me, and partly because I could hear gunfire in the distance to the north.'[5]

This bizarre incident, and France's apparently sincere belief that a fellow officer was out to kill him, makes it all the more strange that he did not order Patrick's arrest. But next day, Heenan still remained free and the two men acted as if nothing had happened.

It was early that morning, as the convoy was preparing to travel the journey by road to Butterworth, that France was quite literally handed the piece of evidence that would provide him with irrefutable proof that Patrick was a traitor:

'Before we set off from Alor Star, [Harper] asked me to take in my car his beautiful field communion set,' France writes in his memoirs. 'I wrapped it up and put it on the back seat. When we reached Butterworth, I assembled my transport under the palm trees and then to my utter amazement saw, in the back of one of my own trucks, the padre's communion set. I was sure it was still in my car, wrapped in my coat. I ran back to my Ford, and sure enough there it was, still wrapped in my coat. Two? I knew the padre had only one.'[6]

Patrick was busy organising machine-gun positions overlooking the beach, so France had the opportunity to examine the second communion set. 'I collected the mystery case and took it into my mobile recce office. It was a perfect copy, to the last detail, of the padre's field communion case externally, but inside, behold a complete two-way radio receiver and transmitter. Another small suitcase I found with it held batteries.'

France told his driver to put the two cases back in the truck exactly where they had been found. 'Then the two of us, from a hidden position, waited and watched. Before very long, Heenan arrived, picked up the cases and dashed off into his tent.'

The fake communion set had been a clever ploy. They were issued to all RAF padres, so it would have been easy to hide in the station chapel and what better cover for a practising Catholic than frequent visits for prayer and meditation? Patrick could have slipped in and out of the chapel at Alor Star almost with impunity. If he was carrying the 'communion set' around 'for the padre', it is unlikely that anyone would search it. Times have changed, but in those days, tampering with religious property would have been regarded as something akin to sacrilege for both British and Indian troops.

How Patrick came by the set is a mystery. He could of course have stolen it and adapted it to his own purposes. But before Harper's arrival there had been no padre at Alor Star to steal it from. France described the fake set as 'a perfect copy' and the radio fitted snugly inside. The Japanese, even before the war, were well known for their expertise in making copies of just about anything, and it is perfectly possible that the 'communion set' and the radio it contained were custom-made for the job. It could not have been a copy of Harper's set, he had not been at Alor Star long enough. But Patrick had three-months notice that he was being posted to an air base, giving the Japanese ample time to prepare the fake communion set.

France now knew that he could wait no longer, something had to be done before the spy did any further damage. 'I had to make an immediate decision. I sent my driver first of all to make sure Heenan was in our "office" truck, and then to get the radio from his tent and hide it in my car. I went to the Wing Commander's Ops Room and told him my story and we agreed to try again to contact the General at Penang Fortress. He was out but when I said it was vital, I was told to report to his HQ at 8am the next morning.'

By now it was late afternoon. France sent for Patrick intending to tell him that he would have to man the office in the morning. 'He was nowhere to be found. We searched everywhere – no Heenan. I therefore sent a number of patrols along the coast each way and into the swampy area to our north.' Having discovered the radio was missing and, knowing that the game was finally up, Patrick had got heavily drunk, perhaps to calm his nerves, before putting on civilian clothes and trying to make a run for it. Heading north, he got no further than the swamp before he saw one of the patrols sent out by France. The patrol was ordered not to attempt to arrest him. 'I instructed them to watch him, and eventually he made his way back to his tent,' France says.

Throughout the day, the Japanese had made several attacks on Butterworth. 'We all had to run into the sea and stand in water up to our chins as there was no cover on the beach,' Fred Cox said. In the most effective of the raids, all the remaining Blenheims bar one were damaged on the ground as they waited to take off for an attack on Singora airfield. Only 'Pongo' Scarf's Blenheim remained unscathed, but he pressed on to Singora alone, dropping his bombs on target under heavy anti-aircraft fire and attacks from Japanese fighter aircraft. Despite being wounded in the back, Scarf managed to steer his crippled air-craft to Alor Star airfield where it crash-landed. He died later in hospital but his crew were saved. Scarf received a posthumous VC, the first of the campaign, for his gallantry.[7]

How much Patrick managed to tell the Japanese when he first rushed to his tent with the communion set is impossible to say, but even after the radio had been hidden in France's car, he still had another set on which to contact them and the timing of the raid that took out most of the Blenheims, just as they were waiting to take off, indicates the likelihood that Patrick was responsible. 'It was discovered that Captain Heenan had been absent each time we had been in a heavy raid,' Fred Cox said. 'This was because he was a traitor, for he carried a portable wireless, which we all thought was a small typewriter, but he was seen in a small native hut in Butterworth typing without any paper in the machine.'[8]

When France arrived at Divisional Headquarters in Penang on Wednesday morning, he was immediately ushered in to see Murray-Lyon. 'I told him my story and he said: "We were sure someone was passing information on our every move. Arrest him at once. No! On second thoughts, I will phone the military police and send a detachment to arrest him." I then heard him give the orders for the arrest over the phone. He congratulated me, and said a report would be sent to Singapore.'

France rushed back to Butterworth and arranged for his driver, Jock Grove, and an Air Force officer to help in Patrick's arrest. 'Major France made arrangements for Jock to pick Heenan up,' says 'Bladder' Wells. 'As Heenan was walking up the road, a Flight Lieutenant who must have been in on it called out, "Where are you going, Patrick?" Heenan replied: "I'm just going up the road, not very far." The Flight Lieutenant climbed into the car and said: "Come on, I'll give you a lift" and off they drove.

'An hour later, Jock Grove was back. He was all shaken and white and he told us this: he had driven the car north to the police station and stopped outside. "There were suddenly policemen everywhere," said Jock. "All armed with Tommy guns, and they arrested Heenan and took him away. God it was scary! I thought they were going to shoot us all."'

One of the arresting officers was Chief Inspector 'Sandy' Minns of the Straits Settlements Police Force. The arrest took place between 1100 and noon. His men, half of them civilian police and half RAF police, were so nervous that Minns was worried he might end up getting shot himself. 'I remember I was going to be shot because I was in the line of fire from the windows and a sergeant who was outside the windows,' Minns said. But Patrick made no attempt to resist arrest and Minns ordered them not to shoot. He then took Patrick to Penang police station where he was charged.⁹ Nigel Morris, the police officer in charge of the Penang station, remembers seeing him brought in. 'The prison was under my office and I saw this well set-up officer called Heenan brought in under arrest. It was a military matter, so I didn't have much to do with it.'

The other officers at Butterworth were stunned by the news of Heenan's arrest. 'When I reported at 7 o'clock a further shock awaited me,' wrote Pilot Officer A. D. Elson-Smith in a letter home. 'I have told you in past letters of a Captain Heenan who has been a liaison officer for the 11th Division to the RAF stations of Alor Star, Sungei Patani and Butterworth. Well my dear, here's the key to the cause of the walloping that we have had in the north up to date. He was arrested this afternoon at 2 o'clock pm by Major Francis [sic] of Military Intelligence as a spy.

'There is no question of the authenticity of this arrest; since they have got the dope which proves his guilt beyond doubt. Just realise this b— has been living with us in our mess for four months, drinking and playing cards and joining in our general living condition. He has had access to our operational rooms together with a full and concise knowledge of our administration, in every form pertaining to our strength, possible strength and in short the guts of everything.'[10]

As they struggled to come to terms with the fact that an 'officer and a gentleman' had been willing to bring Japanese bombs down on his own comrades, the feeling of betrayal among Patrick's fellow officers was intense. 'This simplifies the whys and wherefores of this dreadful debacle and to what extent his activities have sold us out southwards we have yet to experience,' Elson-Smith wrote. 'No words of mine, or of anyone else for that matter, can express the feelings we have towards this man who though clever has sold us out so uniquely.

'Of course his fate is sealed, yet the damage he has done cannot be estimated since, according to his own statements, when he joined us, he had completed fifteen years in the Army, serving in all parts of India. This man evidently controlled all the subversive elements in the northern area from the Prai River to Penang and the Thailand border. Well, my dear, whatever I might have thought of the natives, I never gave thought to such a climax as this. No doubt the authentic information leading to his arrest will be made public one day, but you can take it from me, it was by the little things and careless indifference to our apparent stupidity that he was finally caught, and thanks to Major Francis [sic] who is certainly a credit to our military intelligence.'[11]

Patrick's arrest sparked a major investigation. Seven Malays had been rounded up on spying charges following the evacuation of Alor Star the previous day, Tuesday 9th December. The incident was taken seriously enough for Headquarters Malaya Command to become involved and for summary justice to be meted out. 'Seven Malays arrested at Alor Star on 9/12 are still in custody,' the War Diary of the General Staff at Singapore records in a note of a conversation between a duty intelligence officer and a staff officer at III Indian Corps. 'Corps Cmd has directed that they be obtained from police immediately and all of them be disposed of as expeditiously as possible.'[12]

It is not clear if any of these people were members of a network run by Patrick but it seems highly likely that they were. The day after Patrick's detention, Thursday 11th December, a Malay foreman was also picked up. 'A Malay overseer at Alor Star aerodrome was arrested this a.m. in possession of plans of the aerodrome – Jap propaganda and signalling apparatus. Police handing over to the military.'[13] The network was being folded by British intelligence but the damage had already been done.

As Elson-Smith wrote his letter home, other officers were coming in at frequent intervals with reports detailing their contacts with Heenan and what they might have told him. Captain Jahangir and Squadron Leader the Rev. Harper were among a number of Patrick's known contacts questioned. Harper remembers being under suspicion 'because of my earlier association with Patrick at Steel Brothers'. He was also implicated in the affair by Patrick's use of the fake field communion set, but at the time was not even aware of its existence.[14]

There are a number of other confirmations of the arrest in documents held in the PRO and in the personal papers of the officers concerned at the Imperial War Museum. In one of the latter, General Murray-Lyon lists the following entry for 11th December 1941: 'Capt Heenan ALO (arrested by RAF) sent under arrest to III Indian Corps for investigation.'

In his journal of the campaign pencilled in Changi PoW camp on the blank pages of an Army Manual, Major Cyril Wild wrote under the date, 10th December 1941: 'Heenan ALO arrested.'[15] Colonel A. M. L. Harrison, a Gurkha officer, referring to the action which won Squadron Leader 'Pongo' Scarf a posthumous VC, wrote: 'A day or two after this incident at Butterworth, a British officer of the AIL Section was caught writing a letter to his "Mother" in which he detailed certain RAF timings; further search of his quarters revealed other compromising documents.

He was arrested.'[16] Pilot Officer Basil Gotto records in his unpublished diary: 'He [Heenan] was with the Air Force in Alor Star when the war started doing liaison work, and later retired with them to Sungei Patani and Butterworth. At the latter place, he was arrested as a spy. Wireless sets and all appropriate trimmings were found in his kit.'

Rumours of the arrest spread throughout the Allied forces, diminishing still further their rock-bottom morale, consequent on the speed of the Japanese advance. As the Allied commanders clamped a blackout on all news of the affair the confused reports of what had happened only added to the bewilderment of their troops.

There was one officer traitor, no, there were two! He was Irish, or British. No, definitely Australian. The Japanese spy had been in the RAF, the British Army, the Australian Imperial Forces. He had been court-martialled, shot, hanged, sent home for trial. No-one seemed to know for sure what had happened, even some of those closest to the events.

The only certainty was that the Japanese advance down the peninsula had become virtually unstoppable. The Allied air forces had been wiped out within the space of thirty-six hours and two of the Royal Navy's finest ships had been sent to the bottom of the ocean. After the sinking of the *Prince of Wales*, 'I began to consider the possibility of losing Malaya,' wrote Major Freddie Spencer Chapman. 'But even then I felt certain that it would be possible to hold the island fortress of Singapore.'[17] Without air cover, the Allies were to spend the next two months in an ignominious retreat down the Malay peninsula, most of them believing, like Spencer Chapman, that once they reached the 'impregnable' Fortress Singapore, the tide would at last turn.

CHAPTER 13

THE FALL

Private David Gibson was just twenty-one when he arrived in Malaya in early 1941 to join his battalion, the 2nd Argyll & Sutherland Highlanders. Within a few months, he had volunteered for the provost company attached to III Indian Corps HQ at Kuala Lumpur and had become a member of the Line of Communication Police. The main role of the 'L of Cs' was policing headquarters and controlling military traffic. They were supposed to wear green forage caps in the same way as the Military Police wear red caps, but there were none available in Malaya so the only signs of distinction were the MPs' armbands.

Gibson was promoted to lance-corporal – there were no privates in the 'L of Cs' – and posted to Penang. On Wednesday 10th December 1941, he was ordered to go to the civilian jail in Georgetown, Penang Island, to where Patrick Heenan was being brought under heavy guard. The prison comprised a set of cages built around a central courtyard, Gibson says. 'Heenan was put into one of the cages. He was very restless, stalking around like a caged animal. As the day wore on, he kept charging up and down, waving his passport at me. Why would he have done that? I thought he was trying to con me to let him out.'[1]

It is strange that Patrick had his passport with him. Members of the British forces did not normally need them since they travelled on special papers while on duty in the Empire. So Patrick would have had no need of his passport unless he planned to head north for Thailand. Even so it is surprising that it was not taken away from him with his other personal possessions when he was first arrested.

Gibson was in the prison with Patrick again on the following day, Thursday 11th December, when the Japanese launched their first major air raid on Penang. Several hundred people, mainly Chinese, were killed and hundreds more injured as the aircraft rained bombs and incendiaries down on the city. There was considerable damage to buildings and so many fires that the emergency services were unable to cope.

The prison was in the centre of the city and Gibson, who had never been in an air-raid before, admits he was scared, but not so scared as Patrick appeared to be. 'Heenan was highly perturbed, far more scared, I think, than I was,' he recalls. This sudden onset of fear on Patrick's part is also difficult to understand. He had gone through Japanese raids at both Alor Star and Butterworth in the past forty-eight hours and shown no sign of being particularly worried. Nor did he lack courage. Few cowards enter the boxing ring and he had proven himself under fire on the North-West Frontier. Perhaps the agitation was not fear but just pent-up adrenalin caused by the thought that the bombs might damage the building and give him a chance to escape.

Heenan was to be taken to Singapore for court-martial and Gibson was chosen to escort him down, along with a captain in the Gordon Highlanders.[2] Under heavy guard, Patrick was sent back across the harbour to the mainland on the afternoon of Thursday 11th December and put on a train at Butterworth railway station bound for Singapore.

Patrick was handcuffed to Gibson who had been left in no uncertainty over how to react should the prisoner attempt to escape. 'I was told: "This guy is not to get away. If he tries, shoot him",' Gibson says. The handcuffs never came off throughout the entire journey and Heenan and Gibson even went to the toilet together.

Gibson cannot remember anything of his prisoner's demeanour on the long hot journey down the peninsula. He believes Patrick must have exchanged some words with the escorting officer but cannot recall anything that was said. But he does remember that 'Heenan did not try to escape'.

Late on Friday 12th December, the train reached Singapore, where military policemen under Lieutenant-Colonel Brian K.

Castor, Deputy Provost Marshal, took charge of the prisoner. Castor's daughter says her father often spoke about a spy. While she cannot now remember the spy's name she does recall there was 'a lady of mixed nationality' somehow involved.[3] Gibson believes Patrick was taken to Changi Jail but is not sure. He himself returned to Butterworth and then Penang, taking part in the military evacuation of the island on Tuesday 16th December. He was captured by the Japanese at the fall of Singapore.

A court of inquiry into the Heenan affair was held at Taiping, a town about forty-five miles south of Penang, a few days after Patrick arrived in Singapore. The precise date is unknown but it must have been some time between Saturday 13th December and Wednesday 17th since the town was evacuated in the face of the Japanese onslaught on the following Thursday and Friday. The task of the hearing was to collect oral and written evidence in preparation for the court-martial itself and Major France and his driver, Jock Grove, were almost certainly present since their evidence was crucial. They can be located in Taiping around this time, along with other evacuees from Butterworth, since Major France's memoirs record that 300 AIL Section became involved in the evacuation of civilians from the town. Wing Commander Forbes and Lieutenant-Colonel Tyrrell would also have been potential witnesses and at least one member of 62 Squadron gave evidence.

Flight-Sergeant (now Squadron Leader) David Thomas recalls that Warrant Officer Swindlehurst returned from the inquiry visibly shaken by the experience. 'From Butterworth, we retreated to Taiping,' he says. 'We formed a Sergeants' Mess and one day there, I noticed that WO Swindlehurst had not been around all day. He turned up in the evening looking very bitter and upset. I remember asking him where he had been and his reply was: "You know that so-and-so Heenan? He is a Jap spy and today I had to give evidence; to think that I have been giving him information on our aircraft grieves me. Anyway he is to be shot." Swindlehurst was visibly shaken and then told us of how he used to take Heenan around the airfield at Alor

Star in his Singer van. Heenan was the subject of conversation for weeks.'[4]

Meanwhile, the exhibits of evidence against Patrick and his personal luggage were collected together and put on a train to Singapore. The statements of witnesses were sent to HQ Malaya Command in Singapore on Saturday 20th December. France was required to go there in person but, possibly as a result of his involvement in the evacuation of Taiping on Friday 19th December, was unable to get there until Christmas Eve.

The Deputy Assistant Attorney-General had ordered that France report to Singapore to discuss the Heenan affair and he travelled down overnight on Christmas Eve, leaving Kuala Lumpur at 2000 hours and arriving in Singapore on Christmas Day with orders to return on a train leaving the same day.

He was going to be too busy even to be allowed to spend Christmas evening in Singapore. But when he arrived there, he was staggered to hear that one of Patrick's female friends had got there before him and had made off with the exhibits to be used in evidence at the court-martial.

'When I went to GHQ, I was to hear an amazing story concerning Captain Heenan after his arrest,' Major France recalled in his memoirs. 'He was taken to Changi on Singapore Island and a few days later all his luggage and the evidence against him was put on a train to Singapore in the guard's van to be collected by Col Castor [Lt-Col. Brian K. Castor].

'When Heenan's luggage arrived at the Central Station [in Singapore], a beautiful woman in a huge Cadillac came on to the platform and said she had been ordered to collect this baggage. The station staff took it to her car and she drove off with it. Just after she had gone Colonel Castor and his MPs arrived at the station only to be told the lady's story and find the vital evidence gone! The car and lady were soon spotted and detained. She turned out to be half-Swedish and had been head of a riding school in the Cameron Highlands. We knew Heenan had a girlfriend but never who she was. She too was jailed to be tried later.'[5]

Only one woman fits all the details supplied by Major France.

There was only one riding school in the Cameron Highlands and that was run by Pinka Robertson. She was half-Norwegian, not half-Swedish, but that would have been an easy mistake for a non-Scandinavian to make. And one of the staff of the Tanglin School, to which the riding school was linked, says she did drive a large American car. Pinka is not remembered by those who knew her as being particularly beautiful, but she is described as having 'very pretty eyes and a big bosom'.[6]

Pinka's reasons for attempting to make off with the evidence can only be guessed. There is no evidence at all that she was a 'Mata Hari' who was directly involved in his spying activities. It is perfectly possible that she was blinded by her love for him and her determination to find a husband. Despite France's note that she was 'jailed to be tried later', there is no record of any court appearance and she was able to leave Singapore for Java in early February 1942, so the authorities clearly had little or no evidence of her involvement in Patrick's treachery. Perhaps they accepted an explanation that she did not know she was committing an offence when she picked up Patrick's possessions from the station.

But a number of questions remain unanswered. How did she know what train they would be on? Who told her to pick them up and what reasons did they give her for doing so? And if Major France's report is correct, why did she tell the station staff that she 'had been ordered to collect this baggage'?

Within days of Pinka's arrival in Java, she had married Flight Lieutenant R. D. I. Scott who had also escaped. Perhaps she was still desperate for a husband, but it is equally possible that this was an attempt to gain respectability by distancing herself from Patrick and losing the name under which she had been arrested. Certainly the marriage did not work out and she divorced her husband in 1945. The year after that she was in Worthing, in Sussex, where she is known to have associated with several surviving Malayan government officials who were recuperating from their experiences in Japanese prisoner-of-war camps. She subsequently returned to Malaya where she lived until returning to England in the mid-1960s. She died on the

Isle of Wight in 1992. If her visit to Worthing was spent checking that she was safe to return to Malaya, she was probably
wasting her time. The former government officials are unlikely
to have known anything about the Heenan affair or her role in
it. Harry Miller, who was a journalist on the *Straits Times* when
Heenan was arrested and therefore in a good position to learn
most of what went on, knew nothing about it.

But rumours of 'the officer traitor' did circulate among the
servicemen stationed in Singapore. 'A lot of people in the place
knew that an officer was being brought down under escort,'
says Dr A. W. Frankland. 'How it got around I don't know, but
it was common gossip that he was going to be court-martialled.
People knew that he had gone into the prison and were very
interested as to what was going to happen. With a war on,
would the court-martial ever happen and if an officer is going
to be court-martialled and he hasn't been released it must be a
very serious thing to be court-martialled for. Even on the island,
it was common parlance that he was a spy.'[7]

The court-martial did go ahead, beginning on Friday 2nd
January 1942. On New Year's Eve, Major France received 'an
urgent order to leave on the next train to Singapore Fortress
and report there as soon as possible. I travelled through the
night and went straight to GHQ where I was greeted by
the GSO1, Brigadier Blackburn, who took me to the office of
the Deputy Assistant Adjutant-General. I was cross-examined
all day about what became known as "the Heenan Affair", and
I was briefed for the forthcoming court-martial. It was to start
the very next day.

'For the next two or three days, I attended Heenan's court-
martial as a key witness. He was found guilty of treason and
espionage and condemned to be shot. It was a terrible experience as he had been a brother officer, but I felt relieved, if a
little shattered, when it was over. I was then ordered to return
immediately to my Air Liaison Section who were still in KL.
Before I left, I heard that Heenan in Changi Jail had asked for
a Catholic priest to make a confession, and this wish had been
granted him. His execution was held up by what I suppose was

red tape. Details of the trial had to be sent to London for confirmation of the sentence which took some considerable time. It was, however, confirmed in the end.'[8]

While he was in Singapore, France was called to a meeting by Air Vice-Marshal C. W. H. Pulford at which they discussed the Heenan affair. Lieutenant-Colonel G. Qasim Gilani, the most senior Indian officer in the 1st Bahawalpurs, the Indian States Force battalion defending Alor Star, Sungei Patani and Butterworth, told a British officer of the Indian Army after the war that Captain A. D. Jahangir, his fellow Bahawalpur officer, had been implicated in the case. It had been suggested at Patrick's court-martial that Jahangir, who along with Qasim Gilani joined the Indian National Army, was among a number of Bahawalpur officers who provided Heenan with information on various aspects of airfield defences, but these allegations were not proven to the satisfaction of the court. Jahangir went on to become the General Secretary of the Indian Independence League in Singapore during the Japanese occupation.

The hearing almost certainly took the form of a 'field court-martial' which has special powers under conditions of war. There were probably five officers sitting on it as judges, and the most junior would have had to be at least a captain of some years seniority. There would have been a legal adviser from the Army's Attorney-General's Department and there would have been officers conducting the prosecution and defence. The findings and sentence of a court-martial have no effect until confirmed by the military commander – the convening officer or his superior. Everything is subject to review by the military authorities. There is an appeal procedure, but in time of war this may be overridden by military commanders in the interests of discipline. This applies in particular to the death sentence, but would not have been relevant to Patrick's case since the entire matter was being kept secret.

Patrick was imprisoned at Tanglin Barracks in Singapore in a small prison block where Japanese prisoners-of-war were held. Dr Frankland, then a captain in the RAMC, was responsible for their welfare. He has a vague memory of an officer in the

Military Police being in charge but 'my main dealings were with a sergeant. I used to see him quite a lot. There was a sergeant and six other men. The prison was available for all the prisoners-of-war. I can't remember, in a court of law I couldn't swear, but there were four, maybe five, Japanese prisoners that we caught in the whole of that campaign. We had great difficulty keeping them alive. They wanted to commit *hara-kiri*.

'There was an officer and I knew he was Irish, and he was attached to an Indian Army Regiment but I was told I mustn't discuss him with any of my fellow officers at all. I just had to see that he was all right. The very first time I saw him, I told him: "I'm a doctor. If you have any medical problems, report them to me but I will be coming to visit you as, if you like to use the word, a prisoner's friend. So if you've any questions or there is anything that you can't get from the military police or the people looking after you, I might be able to help you." He sometimes said he had nothing to do all day and he could read, that's all. So I did, I think twice, take him books, what-ever was in the mess, *Reader's Digest* or that sort of light reading.'

Although he had been told not to discuss Patrick with any-body, one officer did approach Dr Frankland, trying to find out information about the prisoner he was visiting. 'One of the officers in the mess described himself as the most senior major east of Suez. He was so lazy, so stupid and so inefficient. I always said he shouldn't be wearing the King's uniform because he was, to my way of thinking, anti-British. One day, he came up to me and said: "You're seeing an officer in the prison, aren't you? Do you know his name?" And I said: "I'm not allowed to tell you what his name is. I'm not allowed to tell you anything about him."

'He said: "I wonder if you can do something for me. I have a worry about a certain cousin of mine. If I showed you a photograph, could you pick out this man, do you think?" I replied: "Show me it and I can say whether I recognise anyone." So he brought a photograph to me. It was of an old boys' "do", I suppose, and I said there's the man I'm looking after. I've never seen a man go white so suddenly! I said: "If that's your cousin, was he by any chance at Cheltenham?" and he said: "Yes, why?" I said: "Well he's wearing an Old Cheltonian tie." Here was this officer. He'd gone so pale.'

Dr Frankland did not discuss the charges against him with Patrick – 'We didn't discuss anything at all' – and he cannot at this distance recall what he looked like. But he does remember one incident where Patrick yet again appeared to be afraid. 'The air-raid alarm went when I got inside the prison. So I said, and I was seeing Heenan at the time, I said: "Let's go and see what's happening. We can go up on top of the roof" – because it was fairly high up, I remember that – "and we can see where they are bombing. Will it be Keppel Harbour, the naval base, or one of the aerodromes? It won't be us." He said: "Well, it might be, it might be, it might be. They may not be accurate," and so on. I looked up and here was this man frightened! I'm not a brave person, but I've been in various bits of this and that, but I would be the last person to describe myself as brave. We got him up the top and I don't know if you could see but you could hear the Japanese planes. We sent up our aircraft and we saw three of them shot down by planes that you couldn't see. He said: "Oh, we must go down, we must go down, we must go down." I have never been in the presence of someone who was so frightened, and unnecessarily frightened, I thought. And I think you could say, from that moment onwards, I really despised him.'

So there was a second incident of Patrick apparently showing fear in the face of what for him was 'friendly fire'. This episode and the similar one in Penang appear to be totally out of character. Patrick had been in far more dangerous situations and shown no fear. Perhaps he wanted to be at ground level in case a bomb hit the barracks, giving him the opportunity to escape among the confusion. There is no way of telling.

By Sunday 8th February, the Japanese were on the island. By the next day, all the Japanese infantry engaged in the initial assault on the north-west coast were ashore and consolidating their positions while the Australians had fallen back in disorder to Tengah airport. Dr Frankland did not see Patrick again after that.

Some time over the next few days, between Tuesday the 10th and Thursday the 12th, Patrick was interrogated by a Special Branch officer in the Straits Settlements Police. This officer says: 'In February 1942, say about the 10th or even later (almost total confusion everywhere but still trying to cope with own specific duties plus helping out with the results of bombing, helping people get away by ship, etc. etc.) a military escort of some kind, can't recall whether Army or RAF, brings to my office Captain P. S. V. Heenan, "believed to have been signalling to enemy aircraft at Sungei Patani in northern Malaya". No document of any kind support accusation, no details, no indication of accusers' identities, nothing. Escort unable to enlighten me on anything whatsoever, except to say he had instructions to hand the captain over to the civil police.

'I probably consulted my chief, at any rate proceeded to question Heenan, being unable to ask him anything but "is this true?", or words to that effect. And naturally, he replied: "of course not", or: "I don't know what you're talking about." In short, he said nothing of any use to me, and whatever further conversations we had, I got nowhere. (It's always helpful, shall we say, to base even the simplest questioning on even the smallest scrap of evidence, or solid accusation. I had neither, and it was useless trying to find anyone who could provide it.) Heenan had no difficulty, I was obviously wasting my breath, he just sat there and barely troubled to show any emotion, either of an innocent person falsely accused, or a guilty one in danger of being exposed. I admit I was not too satisfied myself, having been handed this hopeless job, even allowing for existing conditions, but what to do? Incidentally Heenan, in uniform, was an impressive figure, well set up, and on the face of it a typically smart British officer – though probably a bit travel-stained.

'We were operating under Defence Regulations. Half an hour of this was more than enough, so I exercised my authority under the Regulations, signed a warrant of detention, and sent Heenan under escort to Outram Road Jail.'[9]

Given that Patrick had already been court-martialled, this is a quite extraordinary story, and the only way it makes any sense at all is in the context of the chaotic conditions that existed in Singapore during those last few days before the capitulation. Perhaps the papers relating to Patrick had already been lost or destroyed. Certainly all the military officers involved in the case would have had other matters on their minds at the time – even non-infantry officers were being used in the front line. But it still seems strange that someone, somewhere, had not taken the trouble to brief the Special Branch officer or even the escort.

It is not clear if the guard who escorted Patrick was part of the original contingent of military police guarding him at Tanglin Barracks, but he is known to have been taken to Outram Road Jail. Commandant Maurice Lenormand, a Vichy French officer arrested by the British and incarcerated in Outram Road gaol wrote in an article in the Japanese newspaper *Syonan Shimbun* dated 2nd April 1942 that 'a captain of the New Zealand Army, whose name was Heenan' was also held there. And by Friday 13th February, 'Black Friday', Patrick was back in the care of the same military policemen.

No-one who was in Singapore at the time ever thinks of that day as anything other than 'Black Friday'. It was the day on which the last flicker of hope for the defenders of the city was snuffed out – the mood of despair only increased by the departure early on the previous day of the last convoy of large escort ships.

The news that the final convoy was to leave the beleaguered city had quickly spread throughout Singapore. Passes were issued to people authorised to join the ships, the *Empire Star*, the *Gorgon*, and their escorting warships, HMS *Durban* and HMS *Kedah*.[10] Such passes were issued to the last batch of nurses on the island, to RAF personnel, and to other officers with specialised talents. This latter group included Major Angus Rose of the Argyll & Sutherland Highlanders, now an accepted expert in jungle warfare, who sailed on the *Durban*.

On the night of Thursday 12th February, a group of Australian deserters stormed the gangway of the *Empire Star*, shooting and killing a British officer who tried to stop them.[11] The incident was far from being the only case of unauthorised evacuation. A story that went the rounds of the Malayan Navy Volunteer Reserve after the war, said that Commander R. Bailey, the man in charge of auxiliary vessels under Rear Admiral Spooner, sailed from the colony without permission on 10th or 11th February on a vessel called the *Bulan*. Admiral Spooner sent a message ordering Bailey to be held at Batavia pending his own arrival. It is perhaps lucky for Bailey that the admiral died en route, but he did not get away completely scot-free. An officer who knew the story and came across Bailey in Colombo later in the war punched him in the face.

So Black Friday dawned with the knowledge that most of the troops and civilians still remaining on the island were there to stay. Water was in short supply. Large areas of the city were in ruins. The hospitals, many of them makeshift, and the first-aid stations were filled to overflowing with the dead and dying. There was widespread looting and the dockside murder of the officer was far from being the only one. Deserters from the front line and soldiers unable to find their units again, many of them drunk, roamed the streets. Wavell's report, made in the summer of 1942, blaming the Australian troops for the fall of Singapore is full of eyewitness reports of drunken Australians.

None of this would have surprised the Japanese. ULTRA intercepts of Japanese intelligence reports sent from Singapore to Tokyo revealed that, as early as March 1940, Japanese agents had identified the behaviour of the Australian soldiers as an Allied weakness. British intelligence analysts spoke of 'frequent reports sent to Japan on the misbehaviour of Australian troops in Singapore. They make themselves unpopular with the local inhabitants by drunkenness, rows, welshing on restaurants and molesting women troops.' The Japanese files no longer contain any reference to Australian misbehaviour, largely due to the fact that at the end of the war they were all confiscated by the Americans, who only returned them after weeding out any information which might be damaging to the Allies.

But the Australians' indiscipline is deeply ingrained on the memories of many of those who were in Singapore on Black Friday. Australian troops shot the secretary of the Union Jack forces club in Singapore 'because he would not supply liquor', one of the statements pinned to the back of the Wavell report claimed. 'The Rex Hotel was smashed up for the same reason and Australians were looting while the Japs were invading the island. Towards the end, Australians stormed evacuee ships with Tommy-guns and a week before the surrender, many were to be seen clearing out in rowing boats and sailing ships.' One British staff officer wrote to his father telling him that 'the general behaviour and attitude of the AIF on Singapore island certainly reflects nothing but discredit on its commander. Some people seem to think that the mere fact of being an Australian gives one a free hand to behave like a hooligan.'

Another letter intercepted by the censors and appended to the Wavell report said: 'Yes. It's true – thousands upon thousands just came pouring into Singapore. Before they went into action – and mark you they were the last to be put in – they were soon lying all over the streets of Singapore dead drunk. It really was a disgusting performance. I have never seen men such absolute cowards and so thoroughly frightened. What fine soldiers. If America wants Australia, let her have it and good riddance to a damned rotten crowd.'

One of the eyewitness reports came from Vice-Admiral Sir John Hayes who, at the time, was a young naval lieutenant. He still recalls the horror of the events vividly. 'The streets were full of debauched, drunken Australian soldiers, deserters from their units, breaking their way into any hotel they could find. They invaded one of the last liners to leave, the *Empire Star*, which was trying to embark women and children evacuees. One officer was trying to quell them and they shot him. They were like a crowd of present-day football hooligans, rioting for the sake of it, crazed with ill-discipline and looted alcohol, a shabby advertisement for their nation.'

Singapore was quite literally black that day. A shroud of black smoke from burning rubber in the godowns on the harbour hung over everything. Orders had been given that no stocks were to be left for the Japanese. The acrid smoke from the rubber mixed with that blowing in from the burning oil installations on Pulau Bukom and the other refinery islands to the south, raining black soot down upon the island.

Overlaid on this was the noise of the artillery barrages from both the British and the Japanese and the sound of Japanese bombs exploding during the by now almost incessant air attacks. No-one in Singapore knew it then, but with his supplies running out and facing an enemy still with three times the number of men he had, General Yamashita, the Japanese commander, was becoming desperate, throwing everything into the final onslaught on 'the impregnable fortress'.[12]

'Everyone aged ten years that day,' says one survivor. 'It was a day of utter hell. This particular day we had the Japanese at their most ferocious and all anyone could do was to keep a shred of sanity and try to help where it could do some good, among the fires and rubble. There were parts of the city we hardly recognised and it was at this time that we got some idea of what had been happening in Europe for the last couple of years. For several days past, our troops had been struggling back from the northern parts of Singapore, exhausted and demoralised, without leaders, many of them in a kind of permanent shock, they wandered about the city, sitting in their dozens on the steps of buildings. All organisation seemed to have collapsed. These soldiers had been thrown into a war in conditions that they knew nothing about, against an enemy they had never seen before and whom they could not distinguish from the local inhabitants.'[13]

'Black Friday' was the day when the recriminations began to flow among the Allied generals. During a meeting held at 1400 hours on Friday the 13th, General Heath 'did not see any use in continuing the struggle'. The Australian General Gordon Bennett agreed. But General Percival said there were other things to consider. 'I have my honour to consider and there is also the question of what posterity will think of us if we surrender this large army and valuable fortress.' General Heath replied scathingly: 'You need not bother about your honour. You lost that a long time ago in the north.'[14,15]

For days, people had been preparing for the worst, if still hoping for the best. Anything that might have been of use to the Japanese was being destroyed. Not just the rubber and oil. Boats ferried bag after bag of important documents out into the straits, where they were weighted and sent to the bottom of the sea. With the reports of the Christmas Day atrocities committed by drunken Japanese at the fall of Hong Kong still fresh in people's minds, and in order to stop the alarming wave of drunkenness, stocks of alcohol were being destroyed.[16]

'Black Friday' was also the day on which someone decided that something had to be done about Patrick Heenan. Perhaps someone in authority passed the word that he was to be 'disposed of as expeditiously as possible', the words used to describe the fate of the seven Malays picked up at Alor Star the day before Patrick was arrested. Certainly, there were a number of rumours that he had been shot.

The only ones who would have known for sure were the military policemen assigned to guard him. Even Dr Frankland, Patrick's 'prisoner's friend', did not know what had become of Patrick until some three months after the fall of Singapore when the MP sergeant joined him as a prisoner of the Japanese.

'I eventually ended up in Changi,' Dr Frankland recalls. 'And one day, just by chance, who should I run into but my friend the MP sergeant. He greeted me with great glee. "I thought you were getting your PoWs to Java or Sumatra," I said. "No. I didn't get as far as that," he replied. "Well I'm more interested in someone else," I said and he replied: "I thought you might be."

'I don't know who he was or whether he is still alive, but I have a vague idea that he did talk about his officer who decided that something must be done about this man [Heenan], who by this time, Friday the 13th, had changed from this very gloomy, morose, frightened officer who knew what might be happening, and he had got absolutely impossible, saying: "Well, you'll be in the bag soon, you'll be in prison or you'll be shot or some-thing." He was quite infuriating.

'They decided they were going to carry out summary justice on this impossible man who was getting so cocky, he obviously was a spy. There was no doubt from his behaviour and every-thing else. So they decided to cast lots in some way. I had an idea that the officer had come up to him and decided that sum-mary justice must take place. They did have a pack of cards and it was decided that as everyone, according to the sergeant, wanted to have the "privilege and pleasure and honour" they would draw cards, and the sergeant won with a queen. So it was he who had the pleasure.'

In the late afternoon of 'Black Friday', Patrick Heenan was taken down to the harbour. It would have been a short journey from wherever he had been kept in those last few days. What went through his mind as he travelled through the devastation surrounding the dockside can only be guessed at. He must have known, deep down, that this might be a one-way trip although, perhaps, he was hoping that he was to be shipped out to Java. He had only to survive a little longer and he would be safe in the hands of his Japanese friends.

The sun was just going down on Black Friday as they stood Patrick Heenan on the edge of the harbour facing out to sea. 'He was told to look at the setting sun because it was the last time he would see it,' Dr Frankland says. In those last few moments, would he have been able to see the sun through the pall of black smoke that hung in the sky? The sergeant raised his pistol, put it to the back of Patrick's head and pulled the trigger. 'There was a revolver shot, he was given a push and went into a watery grave.'

CHAPTER 14

THE AFTERMATH

Five hours after Patrick Heenan met his death, at exactly 2300 hours on Friday 13th February 1942, the Royal Navy's *Motor Launch 310* left Singapore in an attempt to escape from the island. There were 27 passengers on board and a seventeen man crew under the command of Lieutenant J. Bull, RNZVR. Two of the passengers were very senior officers, Rear Admiral E. J. Spooner, Rear Admiral, Malaya (RAMY), and Air Vice-Marshal C. W. H. Pulford, Air Officer Commanding, Far East. There were five other naval officers, one other RAF officer and one army officer – Lieutenant Ian Stonor of the Argyll & Sutherland Highlanders. Stonor was ADC to General Percival who had ordered him to leave.[1] The other men on board were a Chinese cook, nineteen naval ratings, six Marines, two RAF other ranks and eight Army other ranks, including five military policemen led by a sergeant.

The people being evacuated on the ships sailing out of Singapore during those last few days were officers and men with specialised abilities, those who were not needed for the continued defence of the island, including a number of RAF personnel, and those who might be at danger from the Japanese, including the last batch of nurses and one of the Japanese interpreters, Lieutenant Michael Ringer, an Intelligence Officer with a prison sentence hanging over his head in Japan.

Given the general state of anarchy, with deserters everywhere, and drunkenness, looting and killing rife, military policemen would not normally have fallen into the category of those whose qualifications were no longer required. Provost troops had always been in short supply – on 1st April 1936, there were only twenty Corps of Military Police NCOs and other ranks in the whole of Malaya – and a party of sixty reinforcements had been sent with the 18th British Division in January 1942. Yet despite this the party of five Military Police, led by a sergeant, was placed on board a VIP launch escaping from the island, a decision that must have been taken at a senior level. They were not present as armed bodyguards for the senior officers, Stonor says. Anyway, there was already on board the launch a body of Marines which was well-armed with a three-pounder gun and a stock of small arms.

But if they were the sergeant and his men who had 'executed' Patrick Heenan, there would have been a very good reason to get them off the island. The victorious Japanese must have made some effort to find their spy, as an article by the Vichy-French officer Lenormand early on in the Occupation in *Syonan Shimbun*, the official Japanese version of the *Straits Times*, recorded that Captain Patrick Heenan had been shot by the British.[2]

There are other factors, apart from the ranks and the very presence of MPs on the launch at a time when they were desperately needed in Singapore, which support the theory that these were the men who sent Patrick to his 'watery grave'.

Almost from the start of its voyage, *ML310* was plagued by misfortune. The launch's steering gear broke down in the Singapore Strait and she ran aground on a small reef. During an attempt to survey the damage below the *310*'s water-line, Lieutenant Richard Pool, RN, had his hand severely crushed. Early next morning the tide refloated the craft and they set off again, reaching an island where they hid from enemy reconnaissance aircraft until dusk. As night fell, they set course for the Tuju Islands, about 150 miles south of Singapore. They reached the islands the following morning and hid up again.

But Pool's hand was badly inflamed and it was decided to run for the town of Muntok, Banka Island, where there was known to be a doctor. Admiral Spooner took the decision to risk a daylight passage but *ML310* was sighted by a Japanese squadron of three cruisers and two destroyers off Tjebia Island. One of the cruisers opened fire while another sent up a seaplane. It dropped four bombs which narrowly missed *ML310*. With the two destroyers closing in, the launch made a run for Tjebia but went aground again. A boarding party from one of the destroyers then wrecked *310*'s engine and – unaware of the presence of Spooner and Pulford, who had decided to conceal their ranks – left the escapees marooned on the island.

Over the next ten weeks, fifteen of the original party were to die on the island in addition to three escapees who arrived later. They fell mainly to a deadly strain of cerebral malaria and included Spooner and Pulford. Two others went missing and three managed to reach Java in a small native boat. Twenty-three survivors, including the five MPs, were eventually rounded up by the Japanese and taken back to Singapore. They arrived back on 23rd May 1942, just over three months after they left, and having been questioned by the *Kempetai*, were sent to Changi Jail. The timing coincides with Dr Frankland's renewed acquaintance with the MP sergeant in Changi prison. He is positive that it was 'about three months later'. Additional circumstantial evidence is provided by the sergeant's response to one of Dr Frankland's first remarks. 'I thought you were getting your PoWs to Java or Sumatra,' he said, to which the sergeant replied: 'No. I didn't get as far as that,' precisely what he might have said had he been on the *ML310*.

The names of the five MPs on board the launch were published in a complete crew and passenger list given in *Course for Disaster*, written by Richard Pool, the Royal Navy lieutenant whose hand was crushed.[3] They were: Sergeant Wright, Lance-Corporal Shrimpton, Lance-Corporal Turner, Lance-Corporal Schief and Lance-Corporal Stride. Shrimpton died within days of arriving back in Singapore, the others all survived their PoW experiences, but Reginald Stride was a special case. He was not involved with guarding Heenan, in fact he was ordered to join *ML310* because 'he was married and was very young'. He barely knew Sergeant Wright and the other MPs; but he says they could have been involved in guarding Heenan.

So was Sergeant Wright the man who executed Patrick Heenan? Dr Frankland remembers the sergeant as being in his mid-thirties with 'an earthy, broad country accent' and Reginald George Edward Wright would certainly fit that description. He was born in East Dereham, Norfolk, in 1905, and according to his son Cecil, always spoke with a broad Norfolk accent. After a period in the reserve, he was called up to join the Royal Norfolks in 1938. He was with the regiment at the evacuation of Dunkirk but later transferred to the Corps of Military Police and was posted to Singapore with the 18th Division in January 1942, when he was thirty-seven years old. Cecil Wright says his father never spoke of his experiences at the fall of Singapore and since he died at East Dereham in 1973 there is no way of confirming his involvement. Even if he had been alive and was the sergeant in question, it would be surprising if he were willing to admit responsibility.

Dr Frankland believed that the MP sergeant had been ordered to carry out the execution. 'I had an idea that the officer had come up to him and decided that summary justice must take place.' Did 'the officer' make the decision to dispose of the prisoner, perhaps because Patrick Heenan's attitude was becoming unbearable, or did he receive instructions to do so from above? There is evidence to suggest the latter. If the MPs were indeed the five men on board the *ML310*, they must have been given their places on the orders of someone in high authority, but by whom?

The sergeant told Dr Frankland that Heenan had been taken to 'the harbour' to be shot. There were two in Singapore, Keppel Harbour and the Inner Harbour. Keppel Harbour was ringed with a high-security perimeter fence, and on the night in question all the gates were guarded by military and civilian police trying to control the crowds, deserters among them, who were still trying to get places aboard the few remaining evacuee vessels. Furthermore, a great deal of cargo burning was still going on in the dockside godowns in an attempt to prevent commodities falling into Japanese hands. Keppel Harbour would have been a busy place that evening, and certainly no place to carry out a secret execution. The authorities had gone to great lengths to keep the Heenan affair under wraps; they would not have wanted the shooting to take place in a well frequented area.

It seems likely, therefore, that Patrick Heenan was disposed of in the Inner Harbour. This was where small vessels usually berthed. On that night it would have been busy too, but not as busy as Keppel Harbour. Part of the Inner Harbour was called Telok Ayer basin, and it was here, from early that afternoon, that *ML310* had been berthed waiting for its VIP passengers. It was tied up alongside the 'end of the basin'.

From information supplied by Squadron Leader T. C. Carter, it seems that Air Vice-Marshal Pulford boarded the launch during the evening of the 13th.[4] This was within an hour or two of Patrick Heenan's being shot after being taken to the harbour from Outram Road Jail, which was less than a mile away from the basin.

Pulford was well aware of the Heenan affair, he had told Major France that he would be awarded the DSO 'for apprehending Tom Heenan and evacuating Taiping before it fell', so it could have been Pulford who issued the instruction that resulted in Patrick's death. If it was, then everything seems to tie in. Pulford gives the order, Heenan is brought down to the Inner Harbour quayside and shot, and then the Military Police are ordered aboard the nearby *ML310* to get them away from any chance of Japanese reprisals. Pulford was the type of man who would have thought of the possible consequences if the MPs had been left behind. He was well-liked, and had a deep interest in the welfare of his men. He was only there himself at that late hour because he had refused to leave until he was reasonably sure that the last of his own men were away – his few remaining aircraft had flown to Dutch East Indies bases some days before. He was particularly concerned over the fate of the RAF technicians who had been busily destroying the island's radar installations to prevent any of the highly secret equipment falling into Japanese hands.

But if Heenan's sentence had been confirmed, as Major France said it had, why had he not been shot by a properly constituted firing squad?

The final stage of the court-martial process is known as promulgation, when the offence, the sentence and its confirmation are read out before the offender. In the case of a field court-martial involving the death sentence, promulgation is usually carried out immediately prior to the execution itself.[5] It seems that in Patrick Heenan's case, promulgation failed to take place, in which event part of the legal process required by King's Regulations was omitted.

There are a number of possible reasons why the death sentence was not carried out in the manner laid down in the regulations. Following the court-martial, in early January 1942, the military authorities had many other things on their minds, which would have no doubt led to some delays in the correct judicial process. There was also the question of whose responsibility it was to confirm the sentence. Patrick was a member of the Indian Army not the British Army and this may have involved difficulties of precedent. Was it solely an Indian Army matter, or did the decision rest with General Percival, who was in the British Army, or someone senior to him outside Singapore?

The possibility of an appeal would have produced further problems. If an appeal was allowed, to whom was it to be made? There was no precedent for what to do in a case of treason by a British officer of the Indian Army. Patrick held the King's Commission, but was the King to sign the death warrant, or was it in this case the responsibility of the Governor-General of India? All of these technicalities might have created difficulties for the Adjutant-General's office, holding up the confirmation process.

It is even possible that Major France was wrong in believing that the sentence had been confirmed. He may have heard that Patrick had been shot and made the not unreasonable assumption that this had occurred in full accordance with King's Regulations.

One other reason for 'holding fire' is suggested by Elson-Smith, the author of *Great was the Fall*, when he expounded on the possible extent of Patrick's treachery. 'Of course his fate is sealed,' he said. 'Yet the damage he has done cannot be estimated.' Patrick had served 'in all parts of India', he added.[6] The authorities would surely have wanted to interrogate Patrick to find out how much he had told the Japanese about the military situation in India but the intelligence officers responsible for such work would have been busy with the attempts to hold back the Japanese advance. This might explain the curious decision to ask the Special Branch officer to interrogate Patrick, when he knew nothing of the case and had no files on it.

The official files may be missing but the wealth of eyewitness testimony, particularly that of Major France, Pilot Officer Elson-Smith, Chief Inspector Minns and Dr Frankland, leaves little doubt that 'the officer traitor' was indeed Patrick Heenan. And there are many others who served with him who are willing to confirm this in private but are reluctant to talk publicly about what they regard as a shameful and dishonourable affair.

The memoirs of France, the letters of Elson-Smith, the testimony of Minns and the private papers of General Murray-Lyon, Colonel Wild and Colonel Harrison all confirm Patrick's arrest. 'There is no question of the authenticity of this arrest,' said Elson-Smith, 'since they have got the dope which proves his guilt beyond doubt.' As to his subsequent handling by the authorities, his imprisonment, his court-martial and his 'execution', France, Frankland and David Gibson, Patrick's escort on the train to Singapore, all provide valuable evidence.

But what was Patrick's precise role in the Japanese victory? Elson-Smith said he 'evidently controlled all the subversive elements in the northern area from the Prai River to Penang and the Thailand border'. This is perhaps the flimsiest of the allegations against him. But it was made by a man who was there and is supported both by the arrest of a number of Malays at Alor Star around the same time as Patrick, including the native foreman at the airfield discovered with 'plans of the aerodrome, Jap propaganda and signalling apparatus', and by Patrick's close association with a number of Indian officers, including Captain Jahangir, who later held a senior position in the Japanese-backed Indian National Army and was implicated in the Heenan affair by the prosecution at Patrick's court-martial. None of this is substantive proof, but *boryaku* – or subversion – particularly of the Indian Army, was a key part of the Japanese strategy and the main role of Major Fujiwara's Bangkok-based *F-Kikan* organisation. It is unlikely that they would not have made use of Patrick's close links with Indian officers to help them in this.

As to the precise extent of his espionage activities and how much information he gave away, this will almost certainly never be known. Even those men who arrested him, interrogated him and subsequently sentenced him to death, probably never knew for sure. But as an intelligence staff officer he would have had extensive access to a large amount of secret information. He also made a number of secret trips to the Thai border to photograph possible routes into Malaya and to meet a mysterious 'Dutchman', taking care to tell his driver that it was 'not necessary to mention this to anyone'. Major France records how Patrick lied to gain access to his 'Most Secret' papers held in the station commander's safe. The contents of these documents can only be the subject of speculation but for the Japanese they would surely have been merely the icing on the cake.

For since Patrick's job gave him access to all the Allies' plans for the air defence of northern Malaya, it must be assumed that these were passed on in full to the Japanese. Certainly this would explain their remarkable success in destroying the Allied aircraft so quickly, many of them on the ground. The results of this treachery can be seen in the Allies' lack of air superiority throughout the campaign. This alone was to have 'disastrous consequences', says the official history. 'As a means of defence and as support of land operations in the forward areas, the British air effort had almost ceased to exist within twenty-four hours of the opening of hostilities'. It was to be one of the most influential factors in the Allies' defeat.

'The Heenan Affair' has remained a well-kept secret until now. The Allies imposed an information blackout on the subject and Patrick's fellow officers in the Indian Army refused to discuss him at all. In what might constitute a part of this unofficial cover-up, Heenan's name appears only once in the official regimental history of the 16th Punjab Regiment, on the list of officers who served in Malaya, in italics to indicate that he was on detached assignment.[7] The fact that this is the only time his name appears is strange because he was the Heavyweight Boxing Champion of India in 1936 and, while much lesser sporting achievements by members of the regiment during the same period are recorded, this one is not mentioned at all. The omission is all the more remarkable given that one of the co-authors of the regimental history went to Cheltenham College with Heenan and served alongside him on the North-West Frontier.

There may be one other piece of evidence of a cover-up. The War Graves Commission records the following entry against Heenan's name: 'Died 15th February 1944. No known grave.' In fact, Heenan died two years and two days before the date recorded by the War Graves Commission. The incorrect date could of course be a genuine error – there were many such inaccuracies among the details collected from ex-PoWs after the war. But one thing is certain. If Heenan had survived the fall of Singapore, he would have had no need to die a prisoner. As far as the Japanese were concerned, he had done his job and done it well.

The two cover-ups, official and unofficial, had some strange consequences that were probably never envisaged by those former officers of the Indian Army who took part in the unofficial one. The name of Captain P. S. V. Heenan is carved in stone on column 263 at Kranji War Cemetery in Singapore among a list of those of his regiment who died in Singapore. It does not belong among the names of the honoured dead. It is also on a war memorial at Cheltenham College. In the school's main dining-hall, the name P. S. V. Heenan is cut into the marble surface of one of the slabs containing the names of the many 'old boys' who died and brought honour to both their school and country over the years. It does not belong there either.

Patrick's mother Annie appears not to have known about her son's treachery. After the war, Major Peter Adams was second-in-command of the 2/8th Punjab Regiment in India. 'I was sent on a course at the Senior Tactical Administrative School at Dehra Dun. My wife and I were invited to a cocktail party by our instructor and his wife. During the party, after a

...lng Post, Wednesday, Sept. 18, 1946

MR. WAL
SECRET L
TO PRES

U.S. DISCL

REFERRED FOR PIQUANCY

ATHS.—
/-. IN
line 5/6.
ourt Page
-. THE
E.C.4.
.1.

at Sunny-
to Con-
Hall, Mil-
3BOTT. a

at Redhill
RY (née
iter.
to May
Ridgeway.

at Stoke
ION and
a son.
t Cedar
t, wife
Peter)
e Her-
les, to
ANLEY
d).
ueen
née

MARRIAGES (continued)

SWABEY—CHESTER-MASTER.—On Sept 17, 1946, quietly, in Hove, MAURICE, only son of the late Captain F. SWABEY and of Mrs. Swabey, of St. Lucia, West Indies, to BETTY, widow of Pilot Officer J P CHESTER-MASTER, and younger daughter of the late Mr. J R Hargreaves and of Mrs. Hargreaves, of 14, Rochester-close, Hove.

WHITAKER—MILLINGTON.—On Sept. 16, 1946, at Epsom, J. H. WHITAKER, M.D., to MARGARET MARY MILLINGTON.

ON ACTIVE SERVICE

HEATON.—On Sept. 13, 1946, as the result of a motor accident whilst serving with the Royal Armoured Corps in Italy, NORMAN ANTHONY (Tony), very dearly beloved and most loving son of Mrs. V. C. Humfrey, of High Ridges, Botley, nr. Chesham, Bucks, aged 19.

HEENAN.—Previously reported missing, now officially presumed died in Singapore on or about Feb. 15, 1942, Capt. PATRICK STANLEY VAUGHAN HEENAN, 2/16 Punjabis, A.I.L.O., attd. Imperial Forces, Malaya, only son of Mrs. B. J Carroll, 46, Manor-rd., Cheam, Surrey. No letters, please.

IN MEMORIAM

" THEIR NAME LIVETH FOR EVERMORE "

CARMICHAEL, L.A.C. IAN ROSS, R.A.F.—In loving remembrance of our beloved Ross, lost at sea when Japanese p.o.w. transport was sunk off Sumatra, Sept. 18, 1944.—Mother and Sheila.

FROM OUR OWN CO
NEW YOF

The mystery of
Truman apparent
his Secretary of C
Wallace, to plea(
a reorientation
foreign policy is tc
explained by a rem
ment which was p
to-night.

This is a confid
several thousand v
to the President a
gested, at the (
Cabinet meeting
like Mr. Wallace
views.

Mr. Wallace's
Truman, which
July 23, was mad
the Departmen
Washington
when it v

Extract from *The Daily Telegraph and Morning Post* 18th September 1946 few cocktails, my hostess, having heard I had been a PoW of the Japanese, came up to me and said: "Did you know Pat Heenan?" I immediately answered: "Do you mean the chap who was shot as a traitor?" She had been a friend of Heenan and she knew his mother. She knew nothing about Heenan's death and she said Heenan's mother knew nothing about it either.'[8]

If Annie had known, she would surely not have drawn attention to it by placing the following advertisement in *The Daily Telegraph and Morning Post* of Wednesday 18th September 1946 under the heading: 'ON ACTIVE SERVICE'.

HEENAN. – Previously reported missing, now officially presumed died in Singapore on or about Feb. 15, 1942, Capt PATRICK STANLEY VAUGHAN HEENAN, 2/16th Punjabis, A.I.L.O., attd. Imperial Forces, Malaya, only son of Mrs. B. J. Carroll, 46, Manor-rd., Cheam, Surrey. No letters, please.

Despite the request for no letters, Annie Carroll did receive at least one piece of correspondence. It came from a man who knew some of the details behind her son's death. The message was scribbled on the back of an unsigned postcard with no return address. It told Annie that her son died on Friday 13th February 1942. It did not say why, but it ended with the words: 'He has no grave other than a watery one'.

APPENDIXES

APPENDIX 1

MALAYA COMMAND, 1941–42

Composition (after the arrival of all reinforcements) of British Empire Ground Forces engaged in the Malayan Campaign, 1941–1942.

British Infantry Battalions

2nd	Argyll & Sutherland Highlanders
2nd	East Surrey Regiment
2nd	Gordon Highlanders
1st	Leicestershire Regiment
2nd	Loyal Regiment
1st	Manchesters (Machine-gun Battalion)
5th	Bedfordshire & Hertfordshire Regiment
1st	Cambridgeshire Regiment
2nd	Cambridgeshire Regiment
4th	Royal Norfolk Regiment
5th	Royal Norfolk Regiment
6th	Royal Norfolk Regiment
1/5th	Sherwood Foresters
4th	Suffolk Regiment
5th	Suffolk Regiment
9th	Royal Norfolk Fusiliers (Machine-gun Battalion)

Indian Infantry Battalions

2/10th Baluch Regiment
2/17th Dogra Regiment
3/17th Dogra Regiment
2/12th Frontier Force Regiment
1/13th Frontier Force Rifles
2/1st Gurkha Rifles
2/2nd Gurkha Rifles
2/9th Gurkha Rifles
4/19th Hyderabad Regiment
2/9th Jat Regiment
4/9th Jat Regiment
6/1st Punjab Regiment
5/2nd Punjab Regiment
1/8th Punjab Regiment
7/8th Punjab Regiment
1/14th Punjab Regiment
5/14th Punjab Regiment

6/14th Punjab Regiment
2/15th Punjab Regiment (stationed in Borneo)
2/16th Punjab Regiment
3/16th Punjab Regiment
2/18th Royal Garhwal Rifles
5/18th Royal Garhwal Rifles
7/6th   Rajputana Rifles
5/11th Sikh Regiment

Indian State Forces Infantry Battalions

Jind	1st Hyderabad
Kapurthala	1st Mysore
1st Bahawalpur	

Malay Infantry Battalions

1st Malay	2nd Malay

Australian Infantry Battalions

2/18th	2/29th
2/19th	2/30th
2/20th	2/4th (Machine-gun Battalion)
2/26th	

New Zealand

24th Pioneer Construction Unit

Artillery Units

80th Anti-Tank Regiment	(48x2 pounder guns)
85th Anti-Tank Regiment	(48x2 pounder guns)
5th Field Regiment	(16x4.5 Howitzers)
22nd Mountain Artillery Regiment	(16x3.7 Howitzers)
88th Field Regiment	(24x25 pounder guns)
118 Field Regiment	(24x25 pounder guns)
122 Field Regiment	(16x4.5 Howitzers)
135 Field Regiment	(24x25 pounder guns)
137 Field Regiment	(24x25 pounder guns)
148 Field Regiment	(24x25 pounder guns)
155 Field Regiment	(16x4.5 & 25 pounder guns)
1st H.K. & Singapore⎤	
2nd H.K. & Singapore⎬	(anti-aircraft guns)
3rd H.K. & Singapore⎦	

Many other corps and units were represented in Malaya Command. These included Royal Engineers, Royal Corps of Signals, Royal Army Service Corps, Royal Indian Army Service Corps, Royal Ordnance Corps, Corps of Military Police (granted the prefix Royal at a later date), Royal Army Medical Corps, and Motor Transport Companies. (Some of the latter of the Australian Imperial Force conducted themselves brilliantly in support of the 11th Indian Division from the start of the campaign.) Royal Marines from the *Prince of Wales* and *Repulse* later joined the decimated Argylls to form a unit known as the 'Plymouth Argylls'.

Local Defence Forces

Federated Malay States Volunteer Forces (FMSVF)
  1st (Perak) Battalion
  2nd (Selangor) Battalion
  3rd (Negri Sembilan) Battalion
  4th (Pahang) Battalion
  Armoured Car Squadron
  Light Artillery Battery

Unfederated Malay States Volunteer Forces (UMSVF)
  Northern States supplied one weak battalion.

FMS Police Force

Negri Sembilan Local Defence Corps
Pahang Local Defence Corps
Perak Local Defence Corps
Selangor Local Defence Corps

Johore State Forces
  Johore Volunteer Engineers
  Johore Volunteer Force
  Johore Local Defence Corps

Other State Forces
  Kedah Volunteer Force
  Kelantan Volunteer Force
  Perak River Platoon
  Sultan Idris Company

Sarawak Rangers
Sarawak State Forces ⎰Volunteers
                 ⎰Armed Police
                 ⎱Coastal Marine Service

Straits Settlements Volunteer Forces (SSVF)
  1st Singapore Volunteer Corps
  2nd Singapore Volunteer Corps
  3rd Penang & Province Wellesley Volunteer Corps
  4th Malacca Volunteer Corps
  Singapore Royal Artillery Volunteers
  Singapore Royal Engineer Volunteers
  Straits Settlements Armoured Car Company

Miscellaneous Units
  Chinese Labour Corps
  Dalforce (Irregular Force led by Lt-Col. J. D. Dalley)
  Local Defence Corps Singapore
  Malacca Local Defence Corps
  Malayan Volunteer Air Force – formerly SSVAF
  Observer Corps
  Overseas Chinese Anti-Japanese Army (KMT Faction)

Overseas Chinese Guard Force
Penang Local Defence Corps
Singapore Civil Defence
Special Technical Corps
Straits Settlements Police Force
Voluntary Aid Detachment

Hong Kong

2nd Royal Scots
Royal Rifles of Canada
Winnipeg Grenadiers
5/7th Rajput Regiment
2/14th Punjab Regiment
1st Middlesex (Machine-gun Battalion)

APPENDIX 2

RAF, ALOR STAR

Squadron Leader David Thomas, who served at Alor Star in 1941, drew from memory a diagram of the airfield (redrawn, overleaf). He writes: 'The attached sketch shows how I remember RAF, Alor Star. I visited there in 1989. The airfield is now a joint MAS (Malaysian Air Services) and RMAF (Royal Malaysian Air Force) base and is known as Kepala Batas Airfield. The only building I recognised which was there in 1941 was the bulk aircraft fuel installation, Item No. 22.'

The key to his sketch is as follows:

1	River (Surgi) Kedah
2	Elephant Hill (hazard, particularly when night-flying!)
3	Village (Kampong) of Kepala Batas
4	Guard room
5	Officers' Mess
6	Sick quarters
7	Station headquarters
8	Operations
9	Squadron offices
10	Sergeants' Mess
11	Airmen's accommodation
12	Station workshops
13	Airmen's and corporals' Mess
14	NAAFI
15	MT yard
16	Main stores
17	Station armoury
18	Bomb dump
19	Hangars (3 off)
20	Bowser sheds (Refueller trailer garages)
21	The Watch Office (Duty pilot and airmen of the Watch. Also parking area for fire tender and ambulance)
22	Bulk fuel installation
23	Government Rest House
24	Metalled runway
25	Two grass runways (only used for take-off and landing of light aircraft. Also used as a dispersal area)
26	Perimeter wire.

NOTES
1. Area between Items Nos. 21 and 22 used as sports fields.
2. In 1939, when I landed at Alor Star on my way to Singapore from

Cranfield, all that was there was Item No. 24, then a grass strip. We spent the night in the Government Rest House (Item 23). The staff were proud to display the signature of Amy Johnson in their visitors' book. She had night-stopped there on her solo journey to Australia flying a DM Tiger Moth in the early 1930s. The Rest House is now on the other side of the road, nearer to Alor Star.

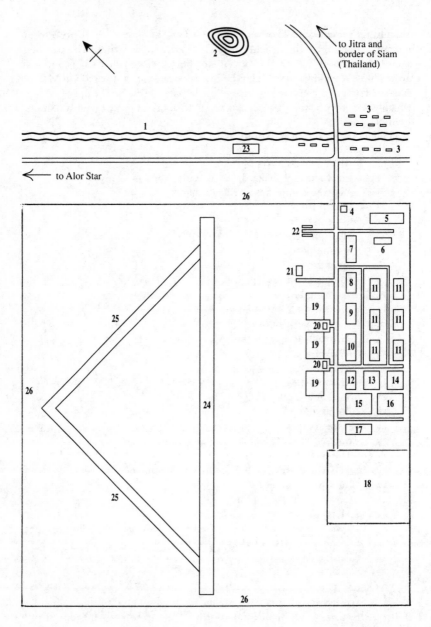

NOTES

INTRODUCTION (*pages 1–4*)

1. Letters received from Ministry of Defence, Foreign and Commonwealth Office (as successor to Colonial Office), and India Office Library and Records.

2. Various references in files in the Public Records Office (PRO), Kew, including WO172/33 and WO172/18.

3. An RAAF officer, *Great Was the Fall*, Perth, Australia, 1945. This officer was the late Flight Lieutenant A. D. Elson-Smith, RAAF.

4. Peter Calvocoressi and Guy Wint, *Total War*, Vol. 2, London, 1972 and 1989.

5. Raymond Callahan, *The Worst Disaster*, Newark, 1977.

6. Kenneth Attiwill, *The Singapore Story*, London, 1959.

I: PRELUDE TO WAR (*pages 5–20*)

1. In a furious letter to the Chiefs of Staff, dated 19th January 1942, Churchill expressed his anger at the discovery that Singapore was not the Island Fortress he and many others had believed it to be. 'I must confess to being staggered by Wavell's telegram of the 16th and other telegrams on the same subject,' he wrote. 'It never occurred to me for a moment, nor to Sir John Dill, with whom I discussed the matter on the outward voyage [to Washington Conference], that the gorge of the fortress of Singapore, with its splendid moat half a mile to a mile wide, was not entirely fortified against an attack from the northward. What is the use of having an island for a fortress if it is not to be made into a citadel? To construct a line of detached works with searchlights and cross-fire combined with immense wiring and obstruction of the swamp areas; and to provide the proper ammunition to enable the fortress guns to dominate enemy batteries in Johore, was an elementary peace-time provision which it is incredible did not exist in a fortress which has been twenty years building . . . I warn you this will be one of the greatest scandals that could possibly be exposed.' Winston S. Churchill, *The Second World War*, Volume IV, *The Hinge of Fate*, Cassell, 1951.

2. Masanobu Tsuji, *Singapore, The Japanese Version*, Constable, London, 1962.

3. The 'Purple' cipher was similar to Germany's 'Enigma' machine but operated on a series of electrical switches rather than wheels. After the United States entered the war, the British classification 'MOST SECRET' was changed to 'TOP SECRET' to bring it into line with American practice.

4. Despatch No. 55260 (MI2) 0210, 2/12/41. (MI3 was the department of military intelligence responsible for Western Europe. MI2 covered the rest of

the world and was therefore responsible for Malaya and Singapore.) Brooke-Popham's reply was No. K386/6 dated 1453 hours, 4/12/41.

5. Brigadier W. St J. Carpendale, 'Report on Operations of 11th Indian Division in Kedah and Perak', 1941. (This was written after Carpendale was superseded in command of 28th Indian Brigade in December 1941.)

6. Aircraft figures 1) 'Royal Australian Air Force, 1939–1942', Douglas Gillison, Australian War Memorial, Canberra, 1962; 2) 'The Fight Awaits – Royal Air Force 1942', Denis Richards and Hilary Saunders, HMSO, 1975; 3) 'Clipped Wings – The Collapse of British Air Defence Malaya 1941–1942', Philip Rivers, 1990.

7. Air Chief Marshal Sir Robert Brooke-Popham. Despatch dated 28th May 1942: 'Operations in the Far East, from Oct 17 1940–Dec 27 1941'.

8. It is easy to criticise Brooke-Popham's indecision fifty years on. However, General Sir Alan Brooke (later Field Marshal Lord Alanbrooke), the then Chief of the Imperial General Staff, wrote in his diary on 6th December 1941: 'It is not possible to tell whether they [the Japanese] were going to Bangkok, to the Kra peninsula, or whether they were just cruising around as a bluff.' As CIGS, Brooke was, in theory at least, the top military strategist in the British military establishment.

9. The full text can be found in FO371/28193 in PRO.

2: THE BATTLE FOR MALAYA (*pages 21–47*)

1. Letters to Peter Elphick in 1992 from Capt. R. B. Monteath, 3/17th Dogras.

2. Personal War Diary of Lt-Col. Charles Wylie, 2/1st Gurkhas, who has generously permitted Peter Elphick to copy his work.

3. WO172/156, War Diary of Signal Section, Singapore Fortress, PRO, Kew.

4. WO172/221, War Diary CSO Royal Signals. PRO, Kew.

5. 'Survival Was For Me', Duncan Wilson, Wigham, 1991.

6. ibid.

7. 'The Second World War', (omnibus volume) *Winston S. Churchill*, Penguin, London 1989.

8. *Shenton of Singapore*, Brian Montgomery, Leo Cooper, London, 1984. (Brian Montgomery was the brother of Field Marshal Viscount Montgomery of Alamein, and related to Lady Thomas.)

'British Civilians and the Japanese War in Malaya and Singapore', Joseph Kennedy, London, 1987.

9. L/WS/1/952. India Office Library and Records, London. There appears to be no trace of this signal in Colonial Office Records. Could the copy in the Indian records be a 'rogue' copy which somehow escaped a cover-up attempt?

10. War Diary of Lt-Col. Charles Wylie, op. cit.

11. George Chippington, *Singapore – The Inexcusable Betrayal*, Hanley Swan, 1992.

12. F. Spencer Chapman, *The Jungle is Neutral*, Cape, 1949.

13. WO106/255OB. WO106/2591, XC20386. PRO, Kew. 12.

14. Unpublished papers of Lt-Gen. Sir Lewis Heath. Imperial War Museum, London. Archive Box No. 1441.

15. Letters to Peter Elphick in 1992 from Sqn Ldr J. A. Stephen.

3: THE PLANTER TURNED NAVAL OFFICER (*pages 48–66*)

1. Letter to Peter Elphick, dated July 1992, from Emile Ryan, ex-Straits Settlements Police, who took part in this officer's arrest with Inspector Sandy Minns.

2. Dr O. Elliott Fisher, late of the Malayan Medical Service, in a letter dated 1st December 1992 to Peter Elphick confirms Windsor's knowledge of chemistry in the following anecdote. 'In 1946 I was stationed at the hospital at Kuantan,' he writes. 'There I met C. J. Windsor. One day a Chinaman was brought in. He was very seriously ill – hadn't been able to pass a motion for a long time. When I examined him I managed to pull out a small piece of rubber from his rectum, and found out that during the Japanese occupation years he had regularly drunk liquid latex because he was so hungry. This had built up over a period and solidified, thus causing the problem. I didn't know what to do, and asked Windsor for advice. Without any hesitation he told me to try liquid paraffin as that was a solvent for latex. Anyway, I pumped a lot of liquid paraffin into the Chinese, and very soon I managed to pull out a fist-sized ball of rubber! Windsor had saved his life.'

3. Windsor probably changed his name in Malaya or Singapore. There are no records in Britain of any deed poll or any other of the methods he might have used to change his name.

4. Information received in telephone conversations between J. B. Masefield, an ex-Senior Officer of the Malayan Police, and Peter Elphick. Jack Masefield is a nephew of the late Poet Laureate, John Masefield.

5. Letters and telephone conversations between Peter Elphick and Guy Madoc, CBE, KPM, CPM, between August 1992 and January 1993.

6. Sheikh Hussin bin Sheikh Ali of the Malayan Navy Reserve was a crew member of the *Kelana* when it was sunk in December 1941. He was wounded during the Japanese air attack. He met Mrs Edna Windsor when he was hospitalised in Singapore. Sheikh Hussin reported that, when the Windsors were unable to get places aboard an official evacuation ship, Windsor bought a small auxiliary sailing craft. Together with another MRNVR lieutenant, and Sheikh Hussin, and a Ceylonese cook, the Windsors sailed it to Pekan Baru in Sumatra just before Singapore fell on 15th December 1942. From there a Dutch Army vehicle took them to Padang on Sumatra's west coast. Sheikh Hussin was taken off by HMS *Tenedos* and transferred to HMAS *Hobart* which took him to Colombo. He does not record whether the Windsors travelled to Colombo the same way.

Dato H. F. Biles gives a variant of this story. He says that Mrs Windsor did get on an evacuation ship at Singapore and it took her to Colombo. For Windsor himself, Dato Biles gives the same escape story as Sheikh Hussin. The Windsors eventually met up in Colombo from where they went on to South Africa.

7. Vice-Admiral Sir John Hayes, *Face the Music*, Pentland Press Ltd., Bishop Auckland, 1992.

8. War Diaries, HQ Singapore, and GS Ops. WO172/15 and WO172/18 respectively. PRO, London.

9. Pilot Officer Basil Gotto was a member of 36 Squadron at Kuantan aerodrome at the time, but he did not take part in the attack. (His plane was out of commission.) He spoke to the pilots involved when they returned from the sortie. In his unpublished diary, '100 Squadron versus Imperial Japan' he writes, 'Incidentally, the attack "36" were on was against some ships reported off Beserah, north of Kuantan, but it turned out to be a false alarm.'

10. War Diary, HQ Singapore. WO172/15. PRO, London.

11. Woodburn Kirby, *The War Against Japan*, Volume 1: *The Loss of Singapore*, HMSO, London, 1957. The sinking of the three Italian battleships by 21 torpedo bombers of the British Fleet Air Arm in November 1940 had taken place at the port of Taranto. The US fleet lost at Pearl Harbor, three days before the loss of Force Z, had also been in port.

12. The *Repulse* and the *Prince of Wales* were not the Royal Navy's first losses in the war against Japan. The first Navy ship to be lost was HMS *Peterel* sunk in the river off Shanghai in the early morning of 8th December 1941, two days earlier than the two capital ships.

13. Vice-Admiral Sir John Hayes, op. cit.

14. War Diary of HQ 22nd Indian Brigade. WO172/142. PRO, Kew.

15. Papers of Lt-Gen. Sir Lewis Heath at Imperial War Museum, London.

16. War Diary of HQ 22nd Indian Brigade. WO172/142. PRO, Kew.

17. War Diary of 5/11th Sikhs. WO172/127. PRO, Kew. Includes additional material written after the war by Lt-Col. J. H. D. Parkin, DSO, the officer commanding the battalion during the campaign.

18. The question arises why, if there was some form of Japanese landing at Kuantan, it is not referred to in the Japanese version of the campaign written by Colonel Masonobu Tsuji, the Japanese Chief of Operations and Planning Staff. Tsuji was boastful of the Japanese achievements, not without cause. If there had been such a landing, he would certainly have known about it. It may not have achieved its original aim, but since, if it did take place, it was indirectly responsible for the loss of Force Z, why did he not mention it? *Singapore, 1941–1942*, Masonobu Tsuji, Oxford, 1988.

19. Correspondence from the customs officer to Peter Elphick in 1992. This officer, who does not wish to be named, served after the war broke out on the intelligence staff of Brigadier H. B. Taylor, OC 22nd Australian Brigade at Johore.

20. Correspondence and telephone conversations with Guy Madoc, CBE, KPM, CPM. (The Sultan of Pahang had a high regard for Windsor. In the 1950s he appointed both Mr and Mrs Windsor to the State Council, a rare honour for Europeans.)

4: HUMBLE ORIGINS (*pages 67–75*)

1. Alys Lowth, *Emerald Hours in New Zealand*, Wellington, 1907.

2. Rt Hon. Leslie Robert Menzies, *A Gold Seeker's Odyssey*, London, 1937.

3. Annie certainly did not have a husband prior to 1910. The only other registered marriage of an Ann Stanley in New Zealand at that time is of a different woman. Registrar-General's Office, Lower Hutt, New Zealand.

4. 'Asylum' and 'Thacker' Almanacs, various editions.

5. 'Imperial Gazeteer of India', Vol. XX, Oxford, 1908.

6. Maurice Collis, *Trials in Burma*, London, 1953.

7. George Orwell, *Burmese Days*, Penguin edition, 1989.

5: 'WE HAVE NOT SECURED A SCHOLAR' (*pages 76–91*)

1. Most of the information about Patrick Heenan's time at Sevenoaks School has kindly been supplied by members of the present school staff, by the past headmaster, B. Scraggs, and by 'old Sennockian' Allan Pearce.

2. a. Information kindly supplied by Cheltenham College.
  b. Details about Cheltenham College from *Then and Now*, published by the Cheltonian Society, 1991.

3. Henry Hardy was Cheltenham's first designated 'Headmaster'.

4. Dill, previously CIGS, died on a mission to Washington in 1944 and is buried in Arlington Military Cemetery, which is also the last resting place of Maj.-Gen. Orde Wingate, of Chindit fame, who was killed in an air crash in Burma in 1944 (his body was recovered by the Americans). Other famous military Cheltonians are Sir John Bagot Glubb, 'Glubb Pasha', the renowned commander of the Arab Legion; and Lt-Col. H. C. McNeile who, as 'Sapper', created Bulldog Drummond.

5. Information supplied by Major Peter Adams.

6. Cheltenham College had seven internal boarding houses, each housing about sixty boys. Privately run boarding houses were much smaller, housing around fifteen boys.

7. Information received from two contemporaries of Patrick Heenan who prefer not to be named, and from F. D. G. O'Dwyer.

8. Further evidence of Patrick's difficulty in making friends and fitting in is provided by the fact that even F. D. G. O'Dwyer, who captained the boxing and rugby teams of which Patrick was a member, has only a few memories of him 'as a strange boy'. The same applies to two other members of that Cheltenham First XV, J. M. Bryce-Smith and T. A. Higson, although all three recall each other very well indeed.

9. Information from Patrick Heenan's Application for a Commission in the Supplementary Reserve of Officers. India Office Library and Records, London.

10. The authors' thanks to Cheltenham College staff for the translation.

11. Last Will and Testament of B. J. Carroll. Principal Registry of the Family Division, London.

12. Information from Sutton Central Library.

6: GOING BACK OUT EAST (*pages 92–104*)

1. H. W. Braund, *Calling to Mind*, a history of Steel Brothers, Oxford, 1975.

2. Forestry conservation was regarded as very important even then in pre-

war Burma. There was very strict legislation regarding forestry: every teak tree, for example, was the property of the government and could not be felled without a licence. Areas from which mature trees had been extracted could not be worked again for thirty years.

3. Rev. Donald Morrison Harper, correspondence and telephone conversations with Peter Elphick during 1992.

4. Letters to Peter Elphick, written in 1992 by an Indian Army officer who wishes to remain anonymous.

5. Major S. T. A. Longley, 16th Punjab Regiment. Letter to Peter Elphick, June 1992.

6. a) Metropolitan Police Museum; b) City of London Police Records Office.

7. Kensington Public Library. This entire terrace was pulled down when the Cromwell Road, on the main route into London from Heathrow Airport, was widened in the early 1970s.

8. Section 62 of the Supplementary Reserve Regulations stated, in the circumlocutory style beloved by civil servants, that 'Permanent commissions as 2nd lieutenants in certain sections of the British Army, and in the Indian Army, may be granted to officers of the Supplementary Reserve who fulfil the qualifications laid down in the Regulations under which Commissions in the Regular Army may be obtained by officers of the Supplementary Reserve'. *Regulations for Officers of the Supplementary Reserve of Officers*, HMSO, 1939.

9. Ibid.

10. Major Peter Adams in correspondence with Peter Elphick during 1992. Adams fought in Malaya in the 1/8th Punjab Regiment. He was captured by the Japanese and retired from the Indian Army with the rank of major.

11. Brigadier J. D. King-Martin, CBE, DSO, MC. Correspondence and conversation with Peter Elphick in December 1992.

12. G. T. A. Douglas in correspondence and conversation with Peter Elphick, November–December 1992. Gawain Douglas was seconded to the RAF during the Second World War and won the DFC in Burma.

13. Nigel Hamilton, *Monty: The Making of a General*, Volume I, 1887–1942, Hamish Hamilton, 1981.

14. Edmund Iremonger, *Amongst Those Present*, New Horizon, 1983.

15. a. John Masters, *Bugles and a Tiger*, London, 1956.
   b. Edmund Iremonger, op. cit.

16. Major Alisdair Ramsey Tainsh, MBE, 16th Punjab Regiment. Correspondence and conversations with Peter Elphick during 1992.

7: ODD MAN OUT *(pages 105–118)*

1. Since it was the intention on mobilisation to bring the strength of each regiment up to ten battalions, the training battalion, based at the regimental depot, was always designated the 10th Battalion.

2. Lawford and Catto, *Solah Punjab – the History of the 16th Punjab Regiment*. Gale and Polden, 1967.

3. Once a week the entire battalion would go off on a route march. Eight

or ten miles at first, building up to twenty, and all carried out at the rate of two minutes a furlong (sixteen minutes a mile). After a few weeks of this, even the newest recruits were marching like clockwork and neither watch nor furlong markers were required.

4. Information in letters received in 1992 from an Indian Army Officer who wishes to remain anonymous.

5. John Masters, op. cit.

6. The Indian Other Ranks and their British equivalents were: Sepoy (Private), Lance-Naik (Lance-Corporal), Naik (Corporal), Havildar (Sergeant), Quartermaster-Havildar (Quartermaster-Sergeant), Havildar-Major (Regimental Sergeant-Major).

7. Information from Major Alisdair Ramsey Tainsh.

8. This was almost certainly a copy of the so-called 'Tanaka Memorial' of 1929, which purported to lay out the Japanese plans for overseas expansion.

9. Information received from an Indian Army Officer who wishes to remain anonymous.

10. The Viceroy's Commissioned Officer ranks of Risaldar-Major, Risaldar, Subadar-Major, Subadar and Jemadar had no precise British equivalent. They exercised power similar to that of a captain or a lieutenant but the most junior British officer outranked them. Jemadars wore one pip like a British Army second-lieutenant, Subadars, or in the Cavalry, Risaldars, wore two pips like a British full lieutenant and Subadar-Majors, or in the Cavalry, Risaldar-Majors, of whom there was only one in each battalion, wore a crown, like a major. VCOs were never saluted by British Other Ranks.

11. The diary of Colonel Cyril Wild. Imperial War Museum. One of these interpreters was Lieutenant Michael Ringer of the 17th Dogra Regiment, who had lived in Japan working for his family firm. He had been arrested in 1940 along with a number of other Britons, including his brother Vanya and the Reuters Correspondent in Tokyo, Melville Cox, in one of the periodical series of tit-for-tat detentions sparked by the British deportations of Japanese nationals from Singapore. Cox later fell to his death from the window of a police station where he was being interrogated (see Chapter 9). Ringer was tried in Tokyo, found guilty and sentenced to imprisonment but was immediately deported. In February 1942, he was serving as an Intelligence Officer on the staff in Malaya, and although all the interpreters volunteered to stay behind at the capitulation, it was thought prudent to get him away because of the sentence still hanging over his head in Japan. He left Singapore on the very last night before the capitulation. Vanya Ringer, who was also deported from Japan, joined the Indian Army and served as a lieutenant in the 5/14th Punjab Regiment until his death at the Battle for Slim river.

12. John Masters, op. cit.

13. Correspondence from: a) Colonel Sato Kikuji, Chief, Intelligence Department, Ground Staff Office, Defence Agency, Tokyo; b) Military History Department, National Institute for Defence Studies, Tokyo.

14. There were a number of Indians with anti-British sentiments living in Japan. One of these was Rash Behari Ghose, the exiled Indian nationalist described by the Foreign Office files of the time as the 'No. 1 enemy of British in India'. He had fled India for Japan in 1912 after throwing a bomb at the then Viceroy, Baron Hardinge of Penshurst, who was sitting in a howdah on

top of an elephant at the time and was severely wounded. Rash Behari Ghose had been officially exiled after the attack and married a Japanese woman who ran an Indian restaurant in Tokyo and played host to many Indian dissidents, including A. M. Sahay, a prominent Indian leader, who travelled the country making anti-British speeches.

Heenan may also have been introduced to Thomas Baty, a Briton who had been a legal adviser to the Japanese Foreign Ministry for more than twenty years and who had strong pro-Japanese views. He was to write anti-British and anti-American articles for Japanese publications throughout the war, but never returned to Britain and was never tried. He died in Japan in 1954.

15. Major Alisdair Ramsey Tainsh. Letters to Peter Elphick, and information from his book *Food Policies and Health*, Longman, 1948.

8: ON THE NORTH-WEST FRONTIER (*pages 119–131*)

1. Information from Major Alisdair Ramsey Tainsh in letters to Peter Elphick. (At this date there were no Military Police units in India. The police referred to were probably Garrison or Regimental Police.)

2. Information from an Indian Army Officer who wishes to remain anonymous.

3. Information from Major S. T. A. Longley in a letter to Peter Elphick.

4. The main camp followers were: bhisti, water-carrier; dhobi-wallah, washerman; khidmutgar, table servant; mehta, sweeper; and syce, groom.

5. Information from a 'fellow officer', who wishes to remain anonymous, contained in letters to Peter Elphick written in 1992.

9: 'A HOTBED FOR JAPANESE SPIES' (*pages 132–157*)

1. Force Emu, aptly named since it was sent in response to Australian demands, consisted of the 2nd Battalion, Argyll & Sutherland Highlanders (who, due in no small part to their jungle training, were to prove one of the most effective fighting units in Malaya), the 4/19th Hyderabad Regiment, and the 5/14th Punjab Regiment.

2. All the ships in that convoy survived the war with the exception of the *Hector* which was sunk in Colombo Harbour by Japanese carrier-based aircraft on 5th April 1942. HMS *Danae* became the Free Polish Navy Ship *Conrad* from 4th October 1944 to 28th September 1946.

3. Information received in 1992 from Captain Alan Elliott, now the only surviving officer to have fought with the 16th Punjab Regiment in Malaya.

4. Lawford and Catto, op. cit.

5. WO208/4567, 'Far East Black List of Enemy Agents'. FECB Singapore Intelligence Summary. 'Retained in Department'.

6. Letters to Peter Elphick written in 1992 by Harry Miller, former editor of the *Straits Times* of Singapore.

7. FO371/22173/532. PRO, Kew.

8. WO208/1915. FECB Report No. 5401, November 1941. PRO.

9. III Corps HQ, on the 27th December 1941, reported that a photograph album seized from an interned Japanese photographer in the Cameron Highlands, contained numerous photos of signposted areas in that area.

10. In WO208/1530. No. 088236. PRO, Kew.

In that same file, item No. 089275 contains the following summary by Allied intelligence analysts of another intercepted message sent from Singapore to Tokyo on 19th March 1940. It shows the way Japanese agents were briefed to report on every aspect of the Allied troops from well before the war.

It is also the earliest record yet found which mentions the behaviour of Australian troops.

'A MOST SECRET source remarks on the frequent reports sent to Japan on the misbehaviour of Australian soldiers in Singapore. They make themselves unpopular with the local inhabitants by drunkenness, rows, welshing on restaurants and molesting women troops. It is not, however, considered that in the present precarious state of Malayan–Japanese relations these incidents should be used for propaganda by the Japanese, except secretly. Care should be taken in preparing broadcasts and other propaganda, the effect of which is small, not to over-criticise the British authorities and other residents in Asia.'

11. WO172/125. War Diary of 22nd Indian Infantry Brigade, Signals Section. PRO, Kew. Australian troops later radio-located a transmitter in the grounds of the palace of the Sultan of Johore. The British military adopted a hands-off approach to this report.

12. Sir Shenton Thomas, Governor of the Straits Settlements, had sent the following encoded message to the Secretary of State for the colonies on 2nd June 1941:

MOST SECRET

NO. 266   GOVERNMENT HOUSE

C-IN-C FAR EAST AND C-IN-C CHINA REPRESENT THAT WE ARE RUNNING SERIOUS RISK BY ALLOWING JAPANESE SHIPS TO LOAD IRON ORE ETC. OFF THE COAST OF MALAYA BY NIGHT. THEY POINT OUT THAT IT WOULD BE EASY FOR ANOTHER JAPANESE SHIP CARRYING LANDING PARTY TO MAKE CONTACT AT NIGHT WITH THE VESSEL LOADING ORE AND TO TRANSFER PARTY TO LIGHTERS, WHICH WOULD BE TOWED TO THE SHORE AND BY SURPRISE LANDING ESTABLISH COVERING POSITION WHICH THEY MIGHT BE ABLE TO HOLD PENDING ARRIVAL OF LARGER FORCES. COMMANDERS-IN-CHIEF ADVISE THEREFORE THAT FROM SUNSET TO SUNRISE ALL TUGS AND LIGHTERS SHOULD BE REQUIRED TO LIE INSIDE HARBOUR MOUTHS ON THE EAST COAST AND ALSO ON THE WEST COAST OF JOHORE.

The message then goes on to detail what restrictions should be imposed on the Japanese ships, before ending with the words:

I CONSIDER THAT THESE PROPOSALS SHOULD BE ACCEPTED. IT IS CERTAIN THAT IN SIMILAR CIRCUMSTANCES THE JAPANESE WOULD NOT HESITATE TO ADOPT THESE AGAINST US. C-IN-C CHINA IS TELEGRAPHING ADMIRALTY.

13. Angus Rose, *Who Dies Fighting*, Cape, 1944.

14. Despatched 0605 on 2nd December 1941, No. 55259.

15. Unpublished papers of Lt-Gen. Sir Lewis Heath in the Imperial War Museum.

16. FO371/24715. PRO, Kew.

17. Richard J. Aldrich, *Conspiracy or Confusion? Churchill, Roosevelt and Pearl Harbor*, Journal of Intelligence and National Security, Vol. 7, No. 3, 1992, pp. 335–46.

18. Colonel Hayley-Bell's team were not the only ones whose accurate predictions were ignored. J. N. Becker, a British businessman based in Thailand, warned the British government in September 1941 that Thailand was planning to side with Japan in any forthcoming war. He was later attached to British Intelligence. After the war, when he tried to return to the Far East, he was at first prevented from obtaining a passport by the British, for reasons unknown. In August 1948, he was shot dead in his office in Singapore by a Chinese. The Singapore police reported that his murder had no political significance even though Becker had again made an accurate prediction, claiming to have knowledge of the Communist plot to seize power in Malaya.

19. FO371/22174. PRO, Kew.

20. FO371/22173/532. PRO, Kew.

21. Full details can be found in FO371/24740 and FO 391/653/23. PRO, Kew. See also Shinozaki Mamoru, *Syonan, My Story*, Singapore, 1975.

22. Masanobu Tsuji, *Singapore, 1941–1942*, Oxford, 1988. Colonel Kunitake was to return to Malaya as a senior officer on the staff of the Japanese commander, Lieutenant-General Tomoyuki Yamashita, known by the Japanese as 'the Tiger of Malaya'.

23. Shinozaki, op. cit. Details of the Cox case can be found in FO/371/2470. PRO, Kew.

24. John W. M. Chapman, 'Tricycle Recycled: Collaboration among the Secret Intelligence Services of the Axis States, 1940–1941', Journal of Intelligence and National Security, Vol. 7, No. 3, 1992.

25. WO208/1925. FECB Report No. 5401, November 1941. PRO, Kew.

26. CO426/50503. PRO.

27. *The Automedon Story*. The Blue Funnel cargo liner, *Automedon*, under the command of Captain W. B. Ewen, was on a voyage from Liverpool, via Durban, to Singapore, Hong Kong and Shanghai, when she was intercepted by *Atlantis*, which, under 5,000 yards away, dropped her guise, cleared for action and fired a warning shot over *Automedon*. Captain Ewen ordered a radio message sent out, but only 'RRR Automedon 0416N' was transmitted before the bridge and radio-room were demolished by shellfire. ('RRR' was the code for raider interception.) Captain Ewen and all the other officers on the bridge were killed. The sole survivor among the bridge party was the helmsman, Stanley Hugill, who afterwards stated: 'Three volleys hit us within three minutes and it was all over'. One of the ship's gunners made for the after-gun, but was killed as more shells tore into the stern section. When a party from *Atlantis* boarded the vessel, they found it in a complete shambles. Some ship's papers had been destroyed, but not those in the ship's safe. Because the ships were lying in a relatively busy shipping lane, the captain of the *Atlantis*, Kapitän zur See Rogge allowed three hours only for the transfer of the remaining crew of the *Automedon* (31 British, 56 Chinese, and 3 passengers) to *Atlantis*, together with the papers found in the safe, 120 mailbags from the hold, a stock of food, and some 550 cases of Scotch whisky and two million cigarettes which the ship was carrying as part of her cargo. As well as the top-secret mail, the Germans gained possession of a copy of

the secret Admiralty Sailing Instructions, the Official Merchant Navy Code Book, and deciphering tables Nos. 7, 8, and 9. In the mail-bags, there were Cabinet papers, details of minefields, new fleet cipher tables, and a number of coded secret service documents. The ship was too badly damaged to put a prize crew on board, so she was scuttled at 1500 hours, with time bombs. (Stanley Hugill, together with other survivors was later transferred to a tanker and spent the rest of the war in a German PoW camp. He died in 1992, aged eighty-five.)

The *Automedon* was the raider's thirteenth victim in a successful twenty-month voyage during which she sank a total of 22 Allied vessels amounting to 150,000 tons, in addition to acting as a U-boat supply ship. The *Atlantis* – she was originally the Hansa Line's *Goldenfels* – was capable of 18 knots. Kapitän Rogge was one of the old-style German naval officers and tended to model himself on the legendary Kapitän Muller of the *Emden* from the First World War. He treated his prisoners as well as could be expected under the circumstances. It was not his fault when, on 9th June 1940, the *Tirranna*, one of his prize ships, was sunk off Bordeaux by the British submarine HMS *Tuna*. She had a prize crew and 293 prisoners-of-war on board, and 87 lives were lost including some of the prisoners. The *Atlantis* met her own end under the guns of HMS *Devonshire* on 22nd November 1941. All but seven of her crew were saved.

The British failed to learn from the *Automedon* incident. On 10th May 1942, the British steamer *Nankin* was captured by the German raider *Thor* in the Indian Ocean. She was on a voyage from Australia to Ceylon, and in her cargo were mail-bags carrying more secret documents. The *Thor* was to sink after an explosion when lying alongside the replenishment tanker *Uckermark* in Yokohama harbour on 30th November 1942. During her two-year career as a raider she had destroyed 152,443 tons of Allied shipping.

28. WO208/1529, Malayan Campaign and Fall of Singapore. Extracts of report from Lieutenant-Colonel H. C. Phillips, RA, formerly GSO I (Ops) Malayan Command.

29. Unpublished papers of Colonel Cyril Wild in the Imperial War Museum.

30. Information contained in letters, written in 1992, to Peter Elphick from Emile Ryan, Singapore, a retired police officer in Malaya and Singapore.

31. *Syonan Shimbun*, p. 4, Singapore, 2nd April 1942.

32. Letondu ran his chicken farm in West Johore. It is not known what he was suspected of. Madame Letondu was committed to Outram Road Prison, and her two children were placed in the care of the Salvation Army. Madame Letondu and the children were repatriated back to Europe after the war on a returning troopship. It is not known what happened to Letondu himself.

33. See Chapter 3.

34. Two such agents arrived in Haiphong in Indochina aboard the Japanese freighter *Bangkok Maru* in November 1940. It is thought that they afterwards infiltrated into Malaya.

10: SUBVERSION (*pages 158–169*)

1. An encoded message from Army Headquarters Singapore to the Australian Government on 23rd December 1941 gives the following troop strengths for Malaya Command on 5th December, three days prior to the Japanese invasion.

Regular Forces:	British	19,391
	Australian	15,279
	Indian	37,191
	Asiatics	4,482
Volunteer Forces:	British	2,430
	Indian	727
	Asiatics	7,395
	Total	86,895
Stationed in Borneo:	British	56
	Indian	994

The Indians made up 49 per cent of the total; the British, 25 per cent; the Australians, 20 per cent; and Asiatics, six per cent.

2. The Japanese were not the only Axis power to support the Indian nationalists. Subhas Chandra Bose, described by Gandhi as a 'patriot of patriots', escaped from India to Germany in 1940 and with German funding raised a force of Indian volunteers to fight against the Allied powers. After the fall of Singapore, he arrived in Penang after a three-month voyage from Germany by U-boat. He then flew to Tokyo and set up an independent Indian government-in-exile with the INA as its military arm.

3. Fujiwara Iwaichi, *F-Kikan - Japanese Army Intelligence Operations in SE Asia during World War II*, Hong Kong, 1983. One of Fujiwara's contacts, a leading Indian nationalist called Pritam Singh, told him that the Indian Independence League cells were actively involved in attempts to win over the many Indian soldiers in northern Malaya who were sympathetic to the League's aims.

4. From the papers of Lieutenant-Colonel E. L. Sawyer, MBE, in the Imperial War Museum. 88/33/1. Sawyer was awarded the MBE after the war for his work on the INA, which he carried out at great risk to his life. His notes, now stored in the Imperial War Museum, are dilapidated and stained after years of keeping them hidden from his captors.

One of the Indian officers he names in the list was a member of an Indian firing squad ordered by the Japanese to execute two British and two Australian PoWs in September 1942.

5. Mahmood Khan Durrani, *The 6th Column*, London, 1955.

6. Papers of Lt-Col. E. L. Sawyer MBE. Op. cit. See Note 4.

7. War Diary of the 1st Bahawalpurs, WO 172/211 in PRO.

8. Ibid.

9. See K. K. Ghosh, *The Indian National Army*, Meenakshi, India, 1969; and Shahnawaz Khan, *My Memories of the INA and its NETAJI*, Delhi, 1946.

10. Unpublished papers of Colonel Cyril Wild in Imperial War Museum.

While imprisoned in Changi prisoner-of-war camp after the capitulation, Wild compiled a day-by-day, unit-by-unit journal of the campaign pencilled on the blank pages of an army manual.

11. Report on sequence of events at Penang by Major-General D. M. Murray-Lyon, WO 106/2552 in PRO.

12. War Diary of HQ III Indian Corps, WO 172/33 in PRO.

13. 'Operational and Intelligence Summaries', WO 106/2557 in PRO.

14. War Diary of HQ 15th Indian Brigade, WO 172/117 in PRO.

11: MOLE IN MALAYA (pages 170–185)

1. AIR 28/1 in PRO.

2. The confirming order from HQ 11th Indian Division for Heenan's move was numbered A/119 and dated 20th May 1941.

3. '100 Squadron versus Imperial Japan'. Unpublished personal war diary of Pilot Officer Basil Gotto, RAFVR.

4. Interview with Private Jack Wells, former member of 300 AILO Section, carried out by Peter Elphick. Wells has changed his surname to Cayless, his stepfather's name, but he will be referred to throughout in this book by the name he was known in Malaya: 'Bladder' Wells. The East Surrey Regiment, Jack's parent unit, traditionally used the nickname 'Bladder' for anyone called Wells.

5. This quotation and others come from Major France's uncompleted memoirs by kind permission of his daughter, Mrs Elizabeth Leetham.

6. The operational squadrons were No. 62 Squadron, Alor Star, equipped with Blenheim bombers; No. 27 Squadron, Sungei Patani, Blenheims; No. 21 Squadron, Sungei Patani, Buffalo fighters; No. 1 Squadron, Kota Bharu, Hudson bombers; half of No. 36 Squadron, Kota Bharu, Vildebeeste torpedo bombers; No. 8 Squadron, Kuantan, Hudson bombers; No. 60 Squadron, Kuantan, Blenheim bombers; and the other half of No. 36 Squadron, Kuantan, Vildebeeste torpedo-bombers.

7. Corporal Fred Jackson, a member of 62 Squadron at Alor Star in 1941. Correspondence with Peter Elphick.

8. Flight Lieutenant Nowell Peach, Medical Officer of No. 62 Squadron at Alor Star in 1941. Correspondence with Peter Elphick.

9. At Sungei Patani the quarters had been built in nearby rubber plantations which acted as a depressant on the occupants. The demoralising effect of camps set in long monotonous lines of trees with the rubber deadening all sound is frequently mentioned in accounts of the campaign.

10. AIR 28/1 in PRO.

11. After the war Cox and Wells joined the Slough Fire Brigade together but they lost touch with each other in the mid-1970s when Cox moved north. He died in 1990.

12. AIR 28/1 in PRO.

13. There were two series of lectures on cooperation with the Army held at Alor Star between 18th August 1941 and 20th August 1941 and between 9th September 1941 and 11th September 1941. (AIR 28/1 in PRO.)

14. From *Great was the Fall*, op. cit.

15. Ibid. Many White Russians were dispersed throughout the Far East after the Russian Revolution. Those who did not manage to bring any money or valuables with them were often forced to take on menial tasks. Some of the women and their female offspring became prostitutes and bar girls. Peter Elphick recalls seeing such women – 'probably their offspring!' he says – in Shanghai in 1957 and in Hong Kong in the early 1960s.

16. From an unpublished manuscript, 'Front Line Daughter', by Dorothy 'Tommy' Lucy, née Hawkings.

17. Dr Nowell Peach. Interviews and correspondence with Peter Elphick.

18. Information to Peter Elphick from Captain Alan Elliott.

19. Private Jack 'Bladder' Wells, interview with Peter Elphick.

20. One file in the Public Records Office at Kew, closed for another twenty-five years, deals with the possibility of a Lower Perak plantation manager's cooperating with the Japanese from November 1941 until January 1942. The author of the report is E. G. S. Hall. This would not have been the planter over the border in Thailand who was visited by Heenan, but he was probably known to him. Lower Perak is in Malaya, near Ipoh, and not far from the Cameron Highlands. At least one other Perak planter at the time was considered a security risk because he had a Japanese wife. He was a Scandinavian, possibly a Norwegian, called O. W. Grut.

21. Letter from Private Fred Cox, former member of 300 AILO Section, to Mrs Elizabeth Leetham.

22. Squadron Leader D. A. Thomas, correspondence and conversations with Peter Elphick, 1992.

23. Data supplied by the Central Statistical Office.

24. Dr Alfred W. Frankland, ex-Captain RAMC, Singapore 1941–42. Interview with Michael Smith and Peter Elphick, 1992.

25. From Major France's uncompleted memoirs.

26. Douglas Gillison, *Royal Australian Air Force, 1939–1942*, Canberra, 1962; Dato Michael Wrigglesworth, *The Japanese Invasion of Kelantan in 1941*, Kuala Lumpur, 1991.

27. From the unpublished war diary of Basil Gotto.

28. Given Heenan's presumed importance to the Japanese, it might be considered surprising that he is not mentioned by Colonel Masanobu Tsuji, the 25th Army's Chief of Operations and Planning Staff, in his book on the victory, *Singapore, The Japanese Version*, Constable, London, 1962. But the number of people who knew about Heenan would have been kept to the minimum as a standard procedure to protect the source under the 'need to know' principle and Tsuji would not have needed to know where the information was coming from, merely what its intelligence value was estimated to be and how to apply it.

29. Private Jack 'Bladder' Wells, interview, cit.

12: THE BALLOON GOES UP (*pages 186–201*)

1. Private Jack 'Bladder' Wells. From recorded interview with Peter Elphick in November 1992.

2. Information in letters from Dr Nowell Peach to Peter Elphick, 1992.

3. From the uncompleted memoirs of Major James France. They go on to describe the General concerned as General Sir Lewis Heath, GOC III Indian Corps, but France was writing forty years after the event and in fact it was Murray-Lyon, who was in Penang, whom he had contacted. Heath was at his HQ in Kuala Lumpur.

4. Letters from Dr Nowell Peach.

5. From the uncompleted memoirs of Major France.

6. Rev. Harper, who had volunteered to stay behind at Alor Star, acting as a cipher clerk in addition to his other duties, does not remember the incident. But he still has the RAF issue communion set to which France referred. Inside the now rather battered, black leather-covered box is a blue velvet interior specially fitted to hold silver-plated communion utensils, a cup, a wafer dish, wine bottles and a tray. On the front of the box under the metal fastening is an imprinted crown and the letters A.M. for Air Ministry.

7. Although Scarf's VC was the first of the campaign, it was not gazetted until after the war, on 21st June 1946.

8. Letter from Private Fred Cox, former member of 300 AILO Section, to Mrs Elizabeth Leetham.

9. Information received by Captain Philip Rivers from ex-Superintendent Sandy Minns, Straits Settlements Police, in the early 1980s. Written information received by Peter Elphick from Sandy Minns via his son Mike Minns. Sandy Minns himself died in Australia early in 1992.

10. From Great was the Fall, op. cit.

11. Elson-Smith's story has a number of minor errors in it, as might be expected in a letter written so soon after the event. The Major Francis referred to is, of course, Major France. He was not the arresting officer. It was in fact Minns whose account of the time of the arrest, between 1100 and 1200, is therefore more likely to be accurate. Elson-Smith also refers to Heenan's having been in the army for fifteen years when he had only served six years.

12. War Diary of General Staff, Singapore, WO 172/18 in PRO.

13. Ibid.

14. Rev. Harper did not find out about the 'fake' communion set until told by one of the authors, Peter Elphick, during the interview which provided the information used in this book.

15. Diary of Colonel Cyril Wild, written at Changi in 1942.

16. Draft papers of Colonel A. M. L. Harrison among the papers of General Percival in the Imperial War Museum.

17. F. Spencer Chapman, op. cit.

13: THE FALL (*pages 202–217*)

1. David Gibson, formerly of the Argyll & Sutherland Highlanders. Correspondence and various interviews with Peter Elphick.

2. Gibson cannot remember the name of the captain, but it is an intriguing possibility that he might have been Captain Ivan Lyon, one of the few Gordon Highlanders captains in Malaya at the time where he had been posted to 'special duties'. He escaped from Singapore and was later to gain fame as the leader of Operation Jaywick which blew up thousands of tons of Japanese

shipping in Singapore Harbour. He was to lose his life in an attempt to repeat that feat in Operation Rimau.

3. Castor, who was Secretary of Essex County Cricket Club before the war, weighed more than seventeen stone before he was captured by the Japanese. He came out of Changi Prison weighing only nine stone and having lost an inch in height. After the war, he resumed his old post with Essex before becoming Secretary of Surrey County Cricket Club. He died on 2nd October 1979.

4. Letter from Squadron Leader David Thomas to Peter Elphick. Thomas has another strange tale to tell of a later event that perhaps provides further proof of other 'white men' in the area working in support of the Japanese. 'I was driving one of our 15 cwt trucks south, retreating once more towards Kuala Lumpur, when we stopped to stretch our legs. We were not near any village and yet soon after we stopped a chap appeared as if from nowhere. He was a civilian, was white, and wore shorts and shirt. He came over to us and asked where the Japs were. I gave a guess and said: "About ten miles up the road," and pointed north. Then without looking at anyone in particular, he replied: "Stout fellows." He turned and as quickly as he appeared he walked between the trees and was gone. We looked at one another and said: "Who in the world would be referring to the Japs as stout fellows?" [Thomas is certain that the man meant the Japs and not his group.] I thought he was a Brit but he could have been a Swede or a Swiss national working in a local tin mine or on a rubber plantation. He could have been a friend of Heenan!'

Former RAF Sergeant Stan Ford also recalls a strange encounter with white men who were apparent supporters of the Japanese during the evacuation of the northern airfields. Ford, at the time a Leading Aircraftsman, had been attached to RAF Butterworth's HQ section and on the morning of 11th December, the day after Heenan's arrest, he was in a party of three – with Corporal 'Butch' Lewis and LAC Henry – left behind with orders to lay charges to blow up the airfield.

'The charges were 250-lb. bombs and gelignite,' he says. 'We started the job about 7.30 in the morning, and it was about ten o'clock when suddenly there were two men standing behind us. One, a big man, was in civvies, while the other was a Company Sergeant Major with New Zealand flashes on his shoulders. The CSM asked us what we were doing, so the Corporal told him. The CSM then introduced the big guy in civvies as a Colonel. The Colonel then ordered us to stop laying the charges. Well, we did, for even the CSM was senior to us. We were glad to leave anyway, for we didn't much like being left behind. The Colonel was very friendly towards the CSM but very authoritative towards us.

'It was a 250-mile drive to Kuala Lumpur where our officers were now stationed at the Majestic Hotel. We were questioned by Flight Lieutenant Scott about the incident and he then phoned HQ Singapore, and then put each of us on the phone to give our version of the events, and we were asked to swear that it was the truth we had reported. I don't remember the name of the officer at HQ. He did say that the Colonel and CSM would be shot when caught.'

When Ford read in a PoW magazine of the search for information on the

Heenan Affair, he telephoned Peter Elphick and asked for a description of Heenan. Ford was immediately struck by the physical resemblance between Heenan and 'the Colonel', and thought they might be one and the same person. It could not have been Heenan since Butterworth was evacuated after his arrest and Ford is absolutely certain of the date, having heard the day before of the sinking of the *Prince of Wales* and *Repulse*. The New Zealand flashes are also strange – Ford is again certain – since there were few New Zealanders involved in the Malayan campaign. The CSM may have been a member of the New Zealand No. 24 Construction Unit, a group of about two hundred who had been involved in airfield construction.

5. The uncompleted memoirs of Major James France.

6. Two other women with later connections to the Japanese were also suggested as the possible lady accomplice: Doris van der Straaten, who during the occupation was the mistress of Colonel Koda of the *Kempetai*; and Mrs Sue Pearson, who later broadcast pro-Japanese propaganda on a radio station based at Surabaya in Java and became known as 'Surabaya Sue'. Neither matched the description given by Major France.

7. Information from Dr A. W. Frankland to Michael Smith and Peter Elphick, 1992.

8. France in his memoirs recalls that when he was summoned by Air Vice-Marshal Pulford, he was told that he was to be awarded the DSO 'for apprehending Tom Heenan and evacuating Taiping before it fell to the Japanese'. The award was subject to confirmation, 'but owing to the fall of Singapore . . . [it] never got into the London Gazette. Many other decorations of officers and men suffered the same fate.'

9. Information received from a former senior officer in the Straits Settlements Police who wishes to remain anonymous.

10. Captain Selwyn Capon of the cargo liner *Empire Star* was awarded the CBE for his part in the evacuation of Singapore. (He had been awarded the OBE in the First World War.) The *Empire Star* was torpedoed and sunk in the North Atlantic on 26th October 1942. Captain Capon, who was fifty-two, was among those who were lost.

11. Some of these deserters were later killed in an air attack on that ship while they were manning a Bofors gun. When the ship arrived at Batavia, the rest were taken ashore under guard by sailors and Marines from HMS *Durban*. A Captain Percy Bulbrook of the Straits Steamship Company used to 'drink out' in the Singapore Captain's Club on the story that he had been shown a bullet-pocked wall and dark stains in the Batavia port area where it was said that one in five of the deserters had been lined up and shot.

12. General Yamashita was to write: 'My attack on Singapore was a bluff – a bluff that worked. I had 30,000 men and was outnumbered more than three to one. I knew if I had to fight for Singapore, I would be beaten. That was why the surrender had to be at once. I was very frightened all the time that the British would discover our numerical weakness and lack of supplies and force me into disastrous street fighting.' John Deane Potter, *A Soldier Must Hang*, London, 1963.

13. Information received from a former senior officer in the Straits Settlements Police who wishes to remain anonymous.

14. Colonel Cyril Wild's papers in the Imperial War Museum.

15. General Gordon Bennett had begun to make his own plans to leave. Despite the order by Percival that all officers should stay with their men, he escaped after the surrender on 15th February, taking with him his ADC, Gordon Walker, who was a member of a well-placed Australian family, and a Major Moses, the head of the Australian Broadcasting Company. Later, in Australia, in what was perhaps the only official inquiry into any aspect of the Malaya campaign, Gordon Bennett's actions were found to be well motivated but improper, and he was never again given an active command. Well motivated or not, Australian PoWs knew he had 'done a runner'. They called their plimsolls 'Gordon Bennetts' after him and the expression 'doing a Gordon Bennett' was born.

16. One of the former policemen who supervised the destruction of the alcohol stocks remembers helping the men assigned to the job. 'At John Littles, the department store, we must have destroyed a fortune, we moved like robots, bend, grab, hurl, bend, grab, hurl. Bottle after bottle, thousands of them, the stuff ran ankle-deep. In a short time, we were all half-stupid with the fumes. Mingled with the sweat running down the manager's face must have been bitter tears.'

14: THE AFTERMATH (*pages 218–228*)

1. Stonor, who retired from the Argylls with the rank of major, says he never heard Percival mention Heenan. Letter from Major Ian Stonor to Peter Elphick, December 1992.

2. (a) The private papers of Colonel A. M. L. Harrison.

   (b) *Syonan Shimbun*, April 1942.

3. Richard Pool, *Course for Disaster*, Leo Cooper, 1987.

4. Correspondence between Squadron Leader (now Doctor) T. C. Carter and Peter Elphick, February 1993.

4a. Interview between Reginald Stride and Peter Elphick, March 1993.

5. Promulgation in this context does not refer to the accepted meaning of to proclaim or to publish abroad, since courts-martial and their proceedings are kept secret.

6. *Great was the Fall*, op. cit.

7. Lawford and Catto, op. cit.

8. Information from Major Peter Adams to Peter Elphick, 1992.

SELECT BIBLIOGRAPHY

Primary Sources

The original documents which have been consulted at the Public Records Office, Kew, have been listed in the chapter notes.

The first-hand accounts of the many people interviewed, both face-to-face and over the telephone, and those who have written in with information, have also been listed in the chapter notes.

In addition the following unpublished sources have been used:

Gotto, Basil. '100 Squadron versus the Imperial Japanese'. Copy kindly supplied by Basil Gotto. The writer is one of the few surviving Vildebeeste pilots. The record of his war was written up on pages of school exercise books in 1942 while a prisoner-of-war at Palembang, Sumatra. In it he names Heenan as a traitor. The books were secreted in the loft of a schoolhouse when Gotto and his fellow prisoners were moved on. They were subsequently discovered and deposited at the local police station. After the war they were recovered by a friend and returned to Gotto.

Rivers, Philip. A manuscript entitled 'Clipped Wings – The Collapse Of British Air Defence, Malaya 1941–1942'.

Wylie, Lieutenant-Colonel C. G. Personal War Diary. The author was an officer of the 2nd/1st Gurkha Rifles. In the diary he describes his battalion's war in some detail.

Lucy, Dorothy 'Tommy'. 'Front-line Daughter'.

Hopkins-Husson, Lieutenant-Colonel C. E. N. War Experiences written up by Peter Elphick. Now in the National Army Museum. London.

Papers of Lieutenant-General A. E. Percival, Imperial War Museum, London.

Papers of Lieutenant-General Sir Lewis Heath, Imperial War Museum, London.

Papers of Colonel Cyril Wild, Imperial War Museum, London.

Papers of Lieutenant-Colonel E. L. Sawyer, Imperial War Museum, London.

Books – a part-annotated bibliography

The 'Official History', often cited in this book, is listed under its author's name, Major-General S. W. Kirby.

Anon. 'Imperial Gazeteer of India', Vol. XX, Oxford, 1908.

Anon. *Then & Now*, Cheltenham, 1991. Official Cheltonian Society history of Cheltenham College.

Anon. *British Vessels Lost At Sea, 1939–45*, London, HMSO, 1947.

'An RAAF Officer'. *Great was the Fall*, Perth, Australia, 1945. This book, which named the Singapore traitor, is epistolary in style, and consists of a series of letters sent home to the author's wife in Australia. Research by Peter Elphick, and now confirmed by Mrs May Elson-Smith, the recipient of the letters, has shown that the book was written by the late Flight Lieutenant A. D. Elson-Smith.

Barber, Noel, *Sinister Twilight: The Fall of Singapore, 1942*, London, 1968.

Bennett, Henry Gordon, *Why Singapore Fell*, Sydney & London, 1944. Written by the Australian general who fled Singapore against orders on 15th February 1942.

Braund, H. E. W., *Calling to Mind – The First 100 Years of Steel Brothers, 1870–1970*, Pergamon Press, 1975. Official history of Steel Brothers.

Brooke, Geoffrey, *Singapore's Dunkirk*, London, 1989.

Bulloch, John, *Akin to Treason*, London, 1966.

Callahan, Raymond, *The Worst Disaster – The Fall of Singapore*, Newark, 1977.

Calvocoressi, Peter, and Wint, Guy, and Pritchard, John, *Total War*, Vol. 2, Penguin edition, London, 1989.

Chapman, F. Spencer, *The Jungle is Neutral*, Cape, 1949.

Chippington, George, *Singapore – The Inexcusable Betrayal*, Hanley Swan, 1992. One of the many books which have been written to coincide with the fiftieth anniversary of the fall of Singapore. Written by an officer of the 1st Leicesters, which eventually combined with the 2nd East Surreys in Malaya to become the 'British Battalion'.

Churchill, Winston S., *The Second World War*, Penguin edition, one volume, London, 1989.

Churchill, Winston S., *Secret Session Speeches*, compiled by Charles Eade, Cassell, 1946.

Day, David, *The Great Betrayal*, London, 1988. A work of particular significance. Gives an Australian viewpoint of Anglo-Australian relations regarding the defence of Malaya.

Dull, P. A., *A Battle History of the Imperial Japanese Navy, 1941–1945*, Annapolis, 1970.

Falk, Stanley L., *Seventy Days To Singapore*, London, 1975. Perceptive account of the entire Malayan Campaign and the events leading up to it. Explains strategy, tactics, logistics, arms and equipment, and comments on the senior people on both sides. Written by an American military historian. It has no built-in bias, unlike many of the earlier British books which covered the same ground.

Gilchrist, Sir Andrew, *Malaya 1941. The Fall of a Fighting Empire*, Robert Hale, 1992. A work of particular significance. Contains an account of the intense diplomatic activity which went on behind the scenes. By a diplomat who was there.

Gillison, Douglas, *Royal Australian Air Force, 1939–1942*, Australian War Memorial, Canberra, 1962.

Gough, Richard, *Escape From Singapore*, London, 1987. Describes many escapes from Singapore. Contains comprehensive list of the ships engaged in Singapore's 'Dunkirk'.

Graham, Brig. C. A. L., *History of Indian Mountain Artillery*, Gale & Polden, 1957.

Hamilton, Nigel, *Monty, The Making of a General, 1887–1942*, Coronet edition, 1981.

Harper, R. W. E. and Miller, Harry, *Singapore Mutiny*, Oxford, 1984. An excellent account of the mutiny of 1915, the events and causes leading up to it, and the aftermath.

Hayes, Vice-Admiral Sir John, *Face the Music*, Edinburgh, 1992.

Hocking, Charles, *Dictionary of Disasters at Sea*, Lloyds, London, 1969.

Howorth, D., *Morning Glory; the story of the Imperial Japanese Navy*, Hamish Hamilton, 1983.

Ike, Nobutka, *Japan's Decision for War*, Stanford UP, 1967.

Iremonger, Edmund, *Amongst Those Present*, Bognor Regis, 1983. Contains a description of the author's life as a new subaltern in the Indian Army in the mid-1930s.

Kennedy, Joseph, *British Civilians and the Japanese War in Malaya and Singapore, 1941–1945*, London, 1987.

Kennedy, Joseph, *When Singapore Fell, Evacuations and Escapes, 1941–1942*, London, 1989.

Kirby, Major-General S. W., *The War Against Japan*, Vol. 1, HMSO, London, 1957. Like many of the early books on the Malayan Campaign this one contains many inaccuracies. That it is the 'official history' should not mislead anyone into accepting all the contents at face value. It now requires to be rewritten in the light of information that has become available since its publication. Many of the people who helped General Kirby on this project, including several generals, had axes to grind and faces to save, and these factors seem to be reflected in some of the 'facts' it contains.

Lawford, J. P. and Catto, W. E., *Solah Punjab*, Aldershot, 1967. The official history of the 16th Punjab Regiment.

Lim Thean So, *The Siege of Singapore*, 2nd ed. Singapore, 1989. An account in novel form by a Chinese citizen of Singapore.

Lovell-Knight, A. V., *The Story of the Royal Military Police*, London, 1977.

Macksey, Kenneth, *Military Errors of World War Two*, Arms and Armour Press, Poole, 1987.

Mason, Philip, *A Matter of Honour*, London, 1974. An account of the Indian Army, its officers, men, traditions, and mores, by a man who was an officer in the Indian Civil Service.

Masters, John, *Bugles and a Tiger*, London, 1956. An excellent autobiography. About the author's early life as a subaltern in the Indian Army in the mid-1930s.

Middlebrook, Martin, and Mahoney, Patrick, *Battleship*, London, 1977. A work of particular significance. The best and fullest account of the loss of HMS *Prince of Wales* and HMS *Repulse*. Uses many personal accounts of participants in the battle.

Montgomery, Brian, *Shenton of Singapore, Governor and Prisoner of War*, London, 1984. Biography of Sir Shenton Thomas. The author was related to Lady Thomas by marriage. The book perpetuates the fiction that the Governor had no foreknowledge of the 'European women and children only' policy regarding the evacuation of Penang.

Orwell, George, *Burmese Days*, Penguin edition, 1989. A novel inspired by the author's life in Burma in the 1920s.

Owen, Frank. *The Fall of Singapore*, London, 1960.

Pool, Richard, *Course for Disaster*, London, 1987. Contains an account of the voyage of *ML310* and the deaths of Rear Admiral E. J. Spooner and Air Vice-Marshal C. W. H. Pulford. By a naval officer who was aboard the launch.

Richards, Denis, and Saunders, Hilary St G., *The Fight Avails – RAF 1939– 1942*, Vol. 2, HMSO, 1975.

Rose, Angus, *Who Dies Fighting*, London, 1944. Written by an officer of the Argyll & Sutherland Highlanders, who became a staff officer and an expert on jungle warfare. He left Singapore on HMS *Durban* on 12th February 1942.

Rusbridger, J. and Nave, E., *Betrayal at Pearl Harbour*, Michael O'Mara Books, 1991. The authors investigate the political and intelligence aspects of the events leading up to the attack.

Shinozaki, Mamoru, *Syonan – My Story*, Singapore, 1975. The personal story of the man behind the 'Shinozaki Affair' of 1940.

Simson, Ivan, *Singapore: Too Little, Too Late*, Leo Cooper, 1970.

Thorne, Christopher, *Allies of a Kind*, London, 1978. Explores the relationship, often strained, between the United States and Britain during the war against Japan.

Tsuji, Col. Masanobu, *Singapore: The Japanese Version*, London, 1962.

Vat, Dan van der, *The Pacific Campaign: World War II – the US/Japanese Naval War 1941–1945*, Hodder & Stoughton, 1992. Describes the emergence of Japan as a world power. Description of Pearl Harbor attack, and other naval battles.

Ward, Ian, and Modder, Ralph, *Battlefield Guide – The Japanese Conquest of Malaya and Singapore*, Singapore, 1989. An illustrated and documented guide map to the campaign.

Wilson, Duncan, *Survival Was For Me*, Wigham, 1991. A view of certain aspects of the Malayan Campaign through the eyes of a soldier in the Royal Corps of Signals.

Wrigglesworth, Dato Michael, *The Japanese Invasion of Kelantan in 1941*, Kuala Lumpur, 1991.

An extensive 'Bibliography of Literature Relating to the Malayan Campaign and the Japanese Period in Malaya, Singapore, and Northern Borneo', compiled and edited by Justin J. Corfield, was published by the University of Hull in 1988. It lists over 1,200 publications.

Articles

Bix, Herbert, 'Emperor Hirohito's War', *History Today*, Vol. 41. December 1991. Reassessment of Hirohito's responsibility for the conflict in the Far East.
Callahan, Raymond, 'The Illusion of Security: Singapore 1919–1942', *Journal of Contemporary History* (*JCH*), Vol. IX, No. 2.
McKale, Donald, 'The Nazi Party in the Far East, 1931–1945', *JCH*, Vol. XII, No. 1.

ABBREVIATIONS USED

ABDA   American, British, Dutch & Australian. General Wavell's Southeast Asia Command from 3rd January 1942

AIF   Australian Imperial Force

AOC   Air Officer Commanding

BOR   British Other Ranks

CIGS   Chief of the Imperial General Staff

DEI   Dutch East Indies

FECB   Far East Combined Bureau (The British Intelligence organisation in the Far East)

FMS   Federated Malay States

GOC   General Officer Commanding

ICO   Indian Commissioned Officer (passed through Dehra Dun)

IIL   Indian Independence League

INA   Indian National Army (Organised by Japanese from captured Indian prisoners-of-war)

KCO   King's Commissioned Officer (British and Indian Armies)

OTC   Officer Training Corps

RAAF   Royal Australian Air Force

RAF   Royal Air Force

RIASC   Royal Indian Army Service Corps

RMA   Royal Military Academy (Woolwich)

RMC   Royal Military College (Sandhurst)

SS   Straits Settlements

TEWTS   Tactical Exercises without Troops

UMS   Unfederated Malay States

VCO   Viceroy's Commissioned Officer (Indian Army)